KENT
OF

Praise for the work of Wayne Koestenbaum

JACKIE UNDER MY SKIN

"Dazzling, exuberant . . . Koestenbaum writes with a heady lyricism that makes Jackie-watching an exercise of the soul as well as of the intellect."
—*New York Magazine*

"Koestenbaum speculates lavishly, sometimes hilariously, often insightfully, always piquantly. . . . His book is pop interpretation at its finest . . . and every bit of it is fun to read."
—*The Boston Globe*

"Wayne Koestenbaum's explanation of the Jackie O phenomenon is as fresh and thought-provoking as they come."
—*Los Angeles Times*

THE QUEEN'S THROAT

"A high-spirited and very personal book . . . laced with moral reflections and warmed with comedy . . . A work of formidable and curious learning . . . A dazzling performance."
—*The New York Times Book Review*

"A cornucopia of extravagant gestures and precise observations, bon mots, home truths and preposterous propositions that, like the soprano voice in its full oracular glory, will leave you breathless."
—*The Washington Post Book World*

"Koestenbaum breaks the silence. . . . Passionate, compassionate and dispassionate at once, this book records a conversation between an art form and a way of life. . . . Poised, urbane, aphoristic . . . A very eloquent, seductive piece of writing."
—*The New Yorker*

ALSO BY WAYNE KOESTENBAUM

The Milk of Inquiry

Jackie Under My Skin: Interpreting an Icon

Rhapsodies of a Repeat Offender

*The Queen's Throat: Opera, Homosexuality, and the
Mystery of Desire*

Ode to Anna Moffo and Other Poems

Double Talk: The Erotics of Male Literary Collaboration

Cleavage

ESSAYS ON SEX, STARS, AND AESTHETICS

WAYNE KOESTENBAUM

BALLANTINE BOOKS

NEW YORK

A Ballantine Book
Published by The Ballantine Publishing Group

Copyright © 2000 by Wayne Koestenbaum

I am grateful to the editors of the following periodicals and anthologies, in which these essays, sometimes in different versions, first appeared:

Alice Neel: Paintings from the Thirties (Robert Miller Gallery): "What Alice Knows"

Allure: "Melanie Time," Copyright © 1995 by The Condé Nast Publications, Inc. "Diana's Dresses," Copyright © 1997 by The Condé Nast Publications, Inc.

The Anchor Essay Annual: The Best of 1999 (Doubleday), ed. Phillip Lopate: "Masochism, A Masque"

Aperture: "200 Women"

Artforum: "Notes on Not Now," © *Artforum,* December 1995; "Warhol's Toiletries," © *Artforum,* January 1998; "'My' Masculinity," © *Artforum,* April 1994; "On Paparazzi," © *Artforum,* November 1997; "In Memory of My Feelings," © *Artforum,* March 1994; "Smell of Night on Handkerchief" © *Artforum,* Summer 1994

Constructing Masculinity (Routledge, 1995), eds. Maurice Berger, Brian Wallis, and Simon Watson: "The Aryan Boy"

London Review of Books: "Enrico Caruso's Son," "Audrey and Her Sisters," "Mortifying Mapplethorpe"

The Most Wonderful Books (Milkweed, 1997), eds. Michael Dorris and Emilie Buchwald: "Why I Read"

New York: "Diary of a Suit"

The New York Times Magazine: "Obscenity: A Celebration," "The Real Dawn Upshaw," "Celebrity Dreaming"

The New Yorker: "Listening to Elisabeth Schwarzkopf"

Parnassus: Poetry in Review: "Stein is Nice"

Queer 13 (Rob Weisbach Books), ed. Clifford Chase: "Fashions of 1971." Copyright © 1998 by Wayne Koestenbaum. Reproduced here courtesy of the publisher, Rob Weisbach Books, an imprint of William Morrow & Company, Inc.

Seneca Review: "A Brief History of Cleavage"

Southwest Review: "Logorrhea"

Spin: "Thrifting"

Süddeutsche Zeitung Magazin: "Nostrils Open to Everything," "Power & Aesthetics," "An Unwritten Poem by Heinrich Heine," "The Food Groups," "On Civilization's Discontents," "*Reisepass,*" "August Hyperaesthesia," "Design," "Envy," "Bees," "Beds"

University of Toronto Quarterly: "A Fan's Apostasy"

Venue: "Darling's Prick," "Masochism, A Masque," "M/orality"

Vogue: "My Evening with Alec Baldwin," "My Ride with Roberto Alagna and Angela Gheorghiu"

A copy of the Library of Congress CIP data is available upon request from the publisher.

ISBN 0-345-43460-9

Text design by Mary A. Wirth

Manufactured in the United States of America
First Edition: March 2000

10 9 8 7 6 5 4 3 2 1

for Steven Marchetti

CONTENTS

I / DRESS AND UNDRESS

II / OBSCENITY

III / STARS

IV / THE LOCOMOTIVE EMPRESS: 12 IMPROVISATIONS

V / AESTHETICS

VI / READING

ACKNOWLEDGEMENTS

owe this book's existence to my charismatic editor at Ballantine, Peter Borland; he has the astonishing, kind readiness to follow my words almost anywhere. My literary agent, Faith Hamlin, continues to be a treasured collaborator.

I am deeply grateful to the editors and impresarios who led me to write many of these essays: Vince Aletti, Jack Bankowsky, Maurice Berger, John Brenkman, Tina Brown, Clifford Chase, Linda Daitz, Stephen Dubner, Bruce Hainley, Melissa Harris, Allan Hepburn, Michael Hirschorn, Christian Kämmerling, David Kuhn, Paul Laity, Herbert Leibowitz, Caroline Miller, Barbara O'Dair, Andrew O'Hagan, Tom Prince, Ilene Rosenzweig, Maer Roshan, Mark Rudman, Adam Sheffer, Elaine Showalter, Lee Smith, Willard Spiegelman, Richard David Story, Deborah Tall, Stephen Tifft, Doreen Weisenhaus, Linda Wells, Anna Wintour, and Connie Wolf.

Emily Grayson at Ballantine and Nancy Stender at Sanford J. Greenburger Associates gave essential assistance. Lisa M. Collins expertly copyedited the manuscript. Michael Ian Kaye has now designed three covers for me: I love his work and I hope he designs me three more.

I

DRESS AND UNDRESS

A BRIEF HISTORY OF CLEAVAGE

've always loved the word *cleavage*. It reminds me of long division and other old-fashioned mathematical skills learned in grammar school but no longer useful to me in adult life. (Now I rely on a calculator for sums and subtractions.)

The word *cleavage* has two divergent meanings. *To cleave* is to adhere or cling: to cleave to one's wife, home, principles. But *to cleave* is also to split or part—as Moses cleaved the Red Sea, or a controversy cleaves the Democratic Party, or civil war cleaves a populace.

Female cleavage is a suggestive, nocturnal phenomenon, produced by pressure of bra or bodice.

The first cleavage I remember glimpsing—furtively, quickly: when an elementary school teacher, dressed in a muumuu, bent down to demonstrate, on my waiting tablet, an esoteric calculation (eight times eight equals sixty-four?), I saw a thick line, as if drawn in charcoal, between her butterscotch-hued breasts. She was a punitive teacher, given to paddling truants. I couldn't reconcile cleavage with disciplinarianism.

I don't remember her breasts. Instead, I recall the line between them, the dark declivity. (That's like seeing a Rembrandt and remembering only the frame.)

Later in the year, while she explained Hawaii's late admission to the Union, again she exhibited cleavage: a gift. I accepted the inordinate vision. She had recently made the transition from "Miss" to "Mrs.": newfound wifehood plumped out the cleavage, abetted its ripeness.

I fantasized placing my finger, like a dulled pencil, between her cushiony breasts.

My next indelible glimpse of cleavage was cinematic: Barbra Streisand in *Hello, Dolly!* and *On a Clear Day You Can See Forever*. Incongruity: the films, family fare, were rated G, and yet the star's cleavage seemed calculated to provoke lust, or to prove that she had matured into loudmouth sophistication.

On a Clear Day: in a flashback to a previous incarnation, Barbra wore an antique, cleavage-producing gown. Fiercely the frock pressed the breasts upward and together, proffering them to the viewer. The cleaved—joined? divided?—breasts suggested two scoops of Baskin-Robbins French vanilla ice cream in a plastic cup, early on a July evening, when the weather is sultry and nothing exciting will happen, only a bike ride or a rereading of a Hardy Boys mystery.

I am trying to be objective, but these remembered images lead me to the brink of an indeterminate, stammering sensuality.

Streisand's cleavage was the visual equivalent of a certain velvet piano-bench cushion that inspired me to press, with a fingertip, its crew-cut nubs, to rearrange its stubby plush into patterns and lines.

I considered cleavage an articulation, a way for breasts to converge and say hello. Cleavage stood for rigor, for monastic simplicity. A wild, voluntary act of dressing up, it allowed breasts to pose as historical objects, and to pass, uncensored, into juvenile vision. Paradox: cleavage, a sign of sophistication, made breasts innocent. Certainly Streisand couldn't flash breasts in a

G-rated musical unless arrangement into cleavage rendered them sumptuously didactic.

A third pivotal instance of cleavage: backstage, at a children's production of *The Wizard of Oz*, in which I had a small role (the Farmer Munchkin), the mother of a fellow extra was helping out with props. This matron seemed wealthier than average. From the evidence of her generous cleavage, I gathered that she lived in a two-story colonial house with columns; that her privileged daughter played with Madame Alexander *Gone with the Wind* dolls; that the family, dignified by its matriarch's cleavage, inhabited an evolved stratosphere of Coupe deVille sedans, brandy Alexanders, hollandaise, expeditions to Lake Tahoe, and immunity to impetigo—an affliction I frequently suffered, and which I assumed never attacked children in cleavage's tranquilized vicinity.

Backstage, I beheld the dark, sweaty line separating the elevated breasts. It seemed this woman had applied indigo lipstick— a shade appropriate for Carnival but not for daily life—to her chest, drawing a provisional mark, like a prospector suspecting gold, or a surveyor measuring a future sidewalk. The juncture of the two breasts was as pleasingly definite as the division between two chunky squares of white chocolate. Cleavage's line seemed a deliberate act of will on the part of the woman who "wore" it, like a brooch. It never occurred to me that cleavage was natural. I considered it a grooming detail obtainable by craft.

The last crucial cleavage I remember from that ambiguously golden age appeared in the eight-hour Russian movie version of *War and Peace*, screened in two parts at my neighborhood's deluxe, space-age, breast-shaped theater, a freestanding dome descended, UFO-style, on a suburban mall's parking lot. I went with a friend: we shared a sinister interest in foreign stamps and a desire to build miniature houses, for trolls, out of cigar boxes. We sat through the epic, not comprehending its intricate plot; our common focus was the cleavage of one of the co-stars, whom I remember as Irene (I don't know whether this was the character's or the actress's name). Irene's cleavage radiated a tsarist grandeur, and a blotchy sense of diminished prospects. The line between her breasts conjured images of the Kremlin's lying *Pravda*, and a tattered paperback, *The God That Failed* (about the Western intelligentsia's disenchantment with the Revolution?), which occupied a place of no special honor on my mother's bookshelf, near the hardcover *Ideal Marriage* and the paperback Dr. Spock.

Years passed, with their conventional disappointments. And then Robert Altman's *Prêt-à-Porter* appeared, offering the pleasure of a dormant spectacle rising again to consciousness—the dominating splendor of Sophia Loren's cleavage. Immense as her hat brim, the cleavage was the drama's unmoving center. Around it, scandal swirled; the cleavage, reposeful, mutely smiled.

(1995)

FASHIONS OF 1971

APPLIQUÉ

What was I wearing in 1971?

A blue-piped white jersey with the word *LOVE* in plastic appliqué. Its cotton, not ordinary, had a pressed, pampered quality, akin to velvet. With the jersey I wore blue pants that bordered on velveteen.

"Femme," said a history classmate, male, to the LOVE shirt, or to its wearer, and so the item was exiled to the drawer.

I don't mention the LOVE shirt in order to garner sympathy.

I had a fondness for clothes that required my affection to bolster them. No one else would wear the LOVE shirt; therefore I secretly prized it. The sleeves puckered, drew close around the arms, like a peasant blouse around new breasts. I knew many pairs of recently developed breasts. They surrounded me. I had an attitude toward them. Now I wish I could define that attitude.

It was a mist. It didn't incorporate nipples. Breasts were slopes without personality or give. At best they were wealth. At worst they were neutral architectural features—pilasters.

APACHE

Apache scarves took the nation by storm, and so I bought three, at Penney's, with a gold ring to fasten them. These were not my wisest purchases, but they were my most visionary, even if I wore them, each, only once. Odd, that I can't remember my mother saying, "Why aren't you wearing your apache scarves? We spent good money on them." Either she didn't notice, or she understood the sense in keeping them in the drawer.

I wish I could remember their colors: were they solids, stripes, checks? I respect them; today, I wear a faux leopard-spotted scarf, knotted squarely, to look Neapolitan, from a distance, as I once wished, with the apache scarves, to look morose, within the dust bowl of the sun-blessed suburbs.

Also at Penney's I bought my Boy Scout scarf. Scout uniforms are the most feminine pieces I've ever owned: they take part in the world of the fetish, and they echo nurse outfits and the boy-emulating garb of den mothers, who dignified scouting by their proffered cupcakes and wifely hospitalities. I sing the easy chairs and carpets and TV sets of den mothers. I sing their calves, nylons, and mules. I don't sing den mothers very loudly, however. Their outfits form a counterpoint that tastes like Fritos—the chip factory, which we toured. We also toured the police station. I rode in the backseat of a patrol car while the cop did his duty.

BELL-BOTTOMS

Bell-bottom year was 1970. At Macy's or Emporium I purchased a striped specimen, a fancy pair of pants for a boy with cabaret aspirations, who saw *mod* and *Parnassian* as fraternal twins. I might have been the only boy wearing bell-bottoms. Ours was a nonexperimental neighborhood.

Bell-bottoms enlarge—identify—the groin. They frame it. Groins need affirmation. This point doesn't suffer from repetition. I was afraid of LSD in the school doughnuts.

FRINGE

I didn't wear fringe, but Nancy did. I knew two Nancys. One wanted to be president; the other wore a brown suede fringe jacket. Fringe Nancy was nice, though also "hard"; among hard chicks, she was the kindest. I imagined that we had a secret understanding, and I included her on my list of Nineteen Girls—schoolgirls I considered friends and acquisitions. Fringe Nancy earned a place among my Nineteen because she was short and pretty. I saw her at the Westgate Mall's record shop. I was flipping through LPs. She said something clever about Alice Cooper. I danced with Nancy at a Friday night gala, and kissed her at the one "make-out" party I attended. She had a Polish last name? The details fade.

Presidential Nancy had long straight hair and a regal, perjured nose. Her mother once brought a special cake, in a bakery box, to a school event. She was in a hurry. I admired her meringue-pale hair, and the scarf (or hairnet?) she wore over it, to protect it from turmoil. I liked rushed women, their minds on higher pursuits. This mother doted on Frank Sinatra. I don't blame her. She lived on a court, which was a special kind of street, with unique responsibilities and privileges. She respected Boston. She told me so. I knew quality women.

JOCKSTRAPS

In P.E. (the word had a friendship with *pee*) I wore a jockstrap under red shorts, and an unattractive, thick, reversible red sweatshirt, white on the verso. The jock—uncomfortable, unaesthetic—had no meaning: I couldn't grasp its relation to rupture prevention. I bought the jock at Penney's, probably with my mother. It came in a box. I didn't associate the jock with sexuality; it was merely hygiene supply, like Ban roll-on. Deodorant itself seemed a purposeless, elongated lipstick, in the visual family of Eskimo Pies. I didn't stink, but I'd reached the deo age. I still had what Myra Breckinridge scornfully called a "boy's equipment," but it was time to pile my package into a Bike mesh.

If P.E. was a place of possible humiliation, it was also a strip joint. In the locker room I discovered boy bodies; I woke to disparities between levels of physical development. Some boys, like me, were at the beginning of the bumpy road to love; others, like an idol named Joe, were far along. Joe was my top nude, Frank my runner-up.

Another P.E. fashion item: tube socks. I hated them. They had no heels. (Just now, I almost compared tube socks to castration, but then I took back the comparison.)

My only concern was not to get hard, which meant brief showers and no looking around. I'd save looking for later, once I was dressed. I don't remember seeing boys with hard-ons in P.E. Isn't that strange? Not even a semi-boner. I hope I'm repressing a juicy memory.

COACH'S WIFE

In 1971 I saw my second-favorite gym coach naked. He was in his twenties. I saw him walk out of the teacher shower. He didn't alter his conduct when in the nude: I was just a boy visiting coach headquarters to hand him a signed health excuse, exempting me from sport. He toweled himself off. I thought, "Well, there it is, the teacher's prick, and all the accompanying garnishes." Seeing his package, I thought, "Coach is accustomed to locker-room nudity from his college days." Additionally I realized, "So this is the kind of body one sees in college." Here was the first remarkable thing I learned about college.

Let it be known that I was mildly disappointed in his anatomy: "So this is all?"

I also thought, "Coach towels himself off, just like this, in his wife's presence. Right now, standing in front of me, he's casually drawing the white towel over his adult body—the same performance his wife watches in their master bedroom." I imagined Coach's wife as a cheerful, presentable woman, good at sports, who took for granted her husband's frequent nudity and was proud of his body in a noncommittal, smug way. Not for a second did I imagine her body, though I pictured her cotton garments. I dressed her in comfortable, springlike fashions that permitted easy transition between work and play.

LITERARY CRITICISM

My favorite coach—short, sadistic—had a polished chest, the most masculine I'd ever seen. He reminds me of a literary critic I know. This is not praise.

The mean coach put us through the paces of a ritual called "Dress and Run." It might more accurately have been called "Undress and Run." He shouted, "Dress and run!" and we stripped off street clothes, donned gym gear, ran a lap, and then lined up for roll call, jock check, and jumping jacks.

The mean coach had a mustache that resembled a clone accoutrement. He had a seductive way of looking slantwise at me and absenting me from the death penalty.

I asked him to sign my yearbook. He wrote something about chickenshit. He was obsessed with fowl.

PIETÀ

The math teacher with a crew cut wore short-sleeved dress shirts and said he wanted to kill the guy who smashed the *Pietà*. (This was 1972?) His wife, the music teacher, who played violin and looked like the soprano Mirella Freni, favored loose impressionistic fabrics that were paisley in effect: swirling, incoherent. Her hair was spun sugar.

Theirs was a marriage of convenience: *my* convenience. It was convenient to picture her soft bun in the same imaginary frame as his buzz cut. I liked crosswiring, in fantasy, her pearlized-seeming features and his machete-sharp absence of beauty. I imagined that he was content with his naval or martial masculinity, its geometry; I imagined, too, that he found a culvert, within his maleness, for his blurry wife, a nutmeat, to dwell.

ELLES PARLENT

The shiny polyester dress of the buxom lunchroom attendant spoke dress shields and girdle.

The plaid A-line skirt of the history teacher spoke Northern Ireland.

The bun of the typing teacher spoke roses.

The crew cut of the dean spoke Nixon's cheeks.

My mother's home-sewn pants suit and my father's store-bought leisure suit spoke two-car family.

I bent my eighth-grade French textbook in half; I broke its red spine. The teacher, a dry woman in flat shoes, didn't speak French. Her specialty was Spanish.

ECOLOGY

My wrestling partner, fellow lightweight, a boy with "skaggy" chin-length hair, called me out—dared me to fight him, tomorrow after school. I agreed to the duel.

His skinny arms were nothing to fear, and yet I stayed home from school the next day and had a masturbation marathon instead.

We'd planned to rendezvous by the locked, parked bikes, near the ecological simulacrum of a habitat, created by the science teacher to show us how to respect the planet.

I preferred teacher to student bodies, with a few exceptions. The science teacher, for example: he had no body—just a droning carapace for preservationist sentiments.

SLIP OF THE TONGUE

An inch of Becky's slip showed below her dress. She was number one on my list of Nineteen Girls. I asked her to go steady, and she said no, which was okay, because the main reason I'd asked was to pass the time: I'd thought, "How to decide which girl to ask to go steady? Why, I'll choose Becky, because her slip showed beneath her dress when she stood up in English. Also, she wears light pink lip gloss. I want many opportunities to see the slip and the gloss."

CHAP STICK

In 1971 I applied Chap Stick to the locks of hair that hung down, nonce sideburns, on my cheeks: I wanted the hairs to stay put, to adhere, and I didn't know about pomade.

My friends and I joked about a "faggy" teacher's probable membership in the Mattachine Society—Saturday outings to San Francisco. He wore a Hawaiian shirt to the school dance, which he chaperoned.

One fine day, through his open classroom window I tossed a water-filled balloon. Unfortunately he came around the corner and saw me throw it. His eyes said, "Tsk, tsk."

Questions dominated my nights. Was his flashy blond hair-piece real? Was his penis artificial? Did he clip *Sunset* magazine recipes? Was his interest in algebra feigned? What had been his college minor? Did he live in a bungalow, a ranch? Was he born in Denmark, or did his complexion come from drugstore arts of the tube and jar? Had he ever admired the history teacher's breasts? Had he envied the art teacher's legs? Would he agree that my penis was a petri dish?

STRAIGHT HAIR

The best of the Nineteen Girls wore miniskirts or hot pants—sometimes with cream nylons.

Mark the embarrassed proud face of a girl sporting short skirt or hot pants (maybe kneesocks?) in 1971: en route to her locker, she holds binder and books. She smells like cigarettes, because she has dawdled in the girls' bathroom. Her long straight hair is parted in the middle; she wears judicious makeup and chews gum. When she poses for a yearbook picture—boys and girls in homeroom lined up—she presses together her exposed knees, and her thighs don't touch.

I wanted to impress the girls, and so I took care with my clothes. I removed my curl by wearing a knit beanie cap overnight: when I woke, the hair was plastered down straight. I wanted girls to notice me; I wanted boys to leave me alone. I wished to see boys naked, of course, but otherwise desired nothing from them. I longed to be a hit with my Nineteen Girls. To be popular among girls was nirvana; boys' approval meant nil. Seeing boys strip, however, fed the spirit.

By 1971 I'd seen hard-core porn photos: men and women. Their congress looked like dog stuff. I couldn't make sense of the combined organs, the mess. The men's balls were incoherent: furrowed with experience, and far too close to the buttocks.

UNCUT

The Mormon redhead's uncut penis in the locker room startled me. He was standing in the collective shower. His organ was long, its head sheathed by a droopy cowl. Above his penis was a pink tablet of hair, unimpressive. Though not a close friend, he was certainly polite to me in the corridors.

With him in first grade I'd pushed Play-Doh through the Play-Doh Factory to make scatological objects.

In 1971, the Carpenters' "We've Only Just Begun" stirred me. I fantasized about getting in touch with Karen Carpenter to ask her to sing in a benefit for our youth orchestra, so we could raise money for a proposed tour of Costa Rica.

FRAMES

I wore black plastic frames, clear at the bottom, dark at the top (originals of the frames I wear today). I combed my bangs to meet the frames' top, so no forehead showed. I always tucked in my shirt and wore a belt. I was a neat number.

I wore horizontally striped jerseys, as did my foxy piano teacher.

She told my mother, "Stripes make my boobs look big!"

I wish I could say my mind was in the gutter, or in someone's groin—but my mind was nowhere. Perhaps my mind was in the backyard. I hear my mother—memory—say something to my father about lawn fertilizer. I see—memory—sacks of fertilizer in the garage. Every year, our lawn failed. Eventually, we gave up on grass, and settled for ground cover.

(1997)

DIARY OF A SUIT

All my life I've avoided suits—until now.

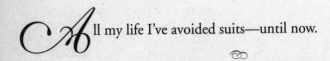

The last time I wore a suit was a piano recital in college, twenty years ago, before the days when intrepid classical musicians performed in caftans and leather.

A sartorially sophisticated classmate, who had a stockbroker father and understood masculinity's fine points, helped me buy the suit: she led me through the Cambridge Shop's complexities and told me, when the tailor asked, that I definitely wanted cuffs. I wondered if she divided the world into men with cuffs and men without; she'd once told me that she believed men who wore boxers were sexually repressed, while men who wore briefs were not.

When she saw me in the purchase I think she was impressed by my resemblance to men. It was a blue, boxy suit, of which I quickly grew ashamed.

∞

When I drop off some clothes for mending at the dry cleaners, the tailor says, "Your clothes are . . . delicate. Are you an actress?" She corrects herself: "Actor?" This was a slip of the tongue, not of the senses.

"No," I say. "A writer."

The new information does not impress her.

"I appear in public a lot," I continue, trying to explain my clothes. "Lectures."

"Oh, I see," she says. "In public. Right." The word *public* justifies the shininess of the overcoat whose sleeves I've paid her to raise.

∞

"What does your present outfit express?" asks the magazine editor, with whom I am discussing the eloquence of clothing. "Sex?"

"No. Not sex," I say. "Attenuated consciousness."

I mean: *stretched* mindfulness.

I am wearing leather pants and a tight sweater. They don't signify sex appeal. They merely indicate that I am paying attention.

∞

When I moved back to New York last year, I bought a pair of fire-engine red patent leather loafers: Patrick Cox Wannabes. They were appropriate for no events: their only occasion was the street.

Now I wear them to lug garbage to the compactor in my apartment stairwell: Wannabes are slip-ons, kept by the door. Last year's slip-ons were another fashion hazard—white patent leather espadrilles, Moroccan in attitude, purchased on the rue de Fleurus in Paris. I had just visited Gertrude Stein's house, and wanted to mark the day with an excess. That summer, shininess reigned, and I bought a black patent leather clutch purse at a flea market. I have not yet carried the purse in public, though it might make a good case for pens, coins, and paper clips.

∞

This morning I stood on the brink of a fashion leap: expensive black leather slides. They were, the saleswoman declared, "a masculine slide"—as close as a slide, which is a low-heeled mule, can come to the realm of the manly. I didn't buy them—not only because of their price, but because they'd make the tops of my feet bleed. The saleswoman said, "Put on moleskin before you wear them." And then she confided, "I'm throwing body and soul into moving these out of the store before sundown."

On the way out I fell for powder-blue Hush Puppies, but I threw cold water on the desire—I remembered the acid-green pair I already owned. Upon discovering, outside the store, that it was unseasonably warm for February, I chastised myself for seeking pleasure in commodities rather than in nature. Good weather, however, is also a commodity.

∽

1981: my prize possession was a pink sport coat, Polo, bought for a song at Filene's Basement. I loved the way its pink was infused with white, the threads interwoven. I wore it to an interview for a teaching position at a yeshiva. No disparaging comment from the rabbi, who gave me the job.

Three years later, in graduate school, I wore it to my oral exam. A professor who specialized in Henry James asked, "What would Emerson have said about your pink jacket?"

I pattered about Emerson's "Circles" essay and then moved to *The Scarlet Letter*. I implied that any friend of Emerson would have known how to read my pink surface.

Now I'm trying to decide: do I care more about clothing or about literature?

There isn't an absolute difference. I respect clothing because it *is* literature.

∽

A decade later, I decide it is time to dress appropriately. In the past, whenever I've tried to buy a suit, I've always settled for a vest instead—say, the silk vest I pretended was a chic compromise between brown and orange, though in fact it was dull peach. Vests end at the waist and lengthen the legs. Vests suggest that my body is a collection of honest rectangles and triangles, rather than a lumpy duffel bag.

A suit reminds me of a coffin, while a vest promises that I am a nightclub bandleader.

I want each new item of clothing to bring me closer to a state I won't call feminine, though it certainly isn't masculine, either—a condition of explosive repose. This repose is difficult to explain, and impossible to see, but I know it when I am wearing it.

∞

1984: at a now defunct boutique called Ben's Village, I bought a pair of cotton tropical-print unisex pants that I named "fish pants" because blowsy fish swam on them in wallpaper patterns.

A friend had advised, when I'd told him there was no room in my life for fish pants, "Change your life to fit the pants."

I wore fish pants to *Ivanhoe* and *Jane Eyre*—a Liz Taylor double feature—at the Public Theater. I wanted to be stared at but I also wanted to be admired, not as a fool but as a fashion radical. I liked declaring my onlookers to be people in the radius of fish pants, people who must accommodate the spectacle of fashion diversity.

For a long time, I've known that I care more about fashion diversity than about sexual diversity: rather, I consider sexual liberation to be a subset of fashion liberation.

∞

My life before the suit: a series of flawed attempts to attain the look that would prove every previous outfit a lie. I wanted an outfit to end disguise and to prove that I was a globe-enhancing compromise between edible boy (I yearn to be chewed) and great lady.

∞

At a good friend's wedding I was the only man in separates. (Blue jacket, black pants: conceptually clean, but not a suit.) The other men in the room looked like attorneys; I was the accused. My body hummed: off-kilter, violating unspoken dress codes, I was a blurted-out obscenity or nonsense syllable, a case of fashion Tourette's.

Tired of the vibrations produced by separates, I decided that I wanted a suit that would give me the virtues of Sean Connery and Audrey Hepburn, if their separate qualities could be amalgamated: leanness, aggression, anonymity, and the sleekness of a sedan's or sports car's fins.

∽

The green T-shirt I paid a tailor to sew for me, in the days when I thought a summer top could alleviate my grudge against the world: I wanted an item I could find in no men's department, a lime-green jersey that hugged the chest but didn't make my arms look skinny. I wanted pectoral tightness but no upper-arm revelation.

When I picked up the commissioned shirt, I was disappointed to discover that the fabric puckered around the shoulders in two little points—asterisk epaulettes.

∽

Last September, at a vast department store, a kind salesman led me through the many boutiques and told me, sighing, that there were no suits of the kind and size I sought—small, untraditional, strange, and yet manly withal. He whispered, "You need Prada," and told me that he would be working at the new Prada store, due to open soon. He promised to call me.

Here was a new variety of human affection—fashion friendliness. I'd met an insider to the world of beauty, and he wanted to help me along. Fashion is reputed to be a bitchy maelstrom, but I think people involved with fancy clothes are sweet to each other, though they may snub those who pretend indifference to the seductions of apparel.

∽

I saw Isaac Mizrahi, or his lookalike, in a pinstriped suit, walking down West Broadway. I took this glimpse to be an omen, as if a fortune teller had said, "In the New Year you will see

Isaac Mizrahi on the street. You will buy a nice suit and find happiness."

∞

Before I found the suit I chose shirts to accompany it. Sick of seeking exaltation in exotic items, I now wanted ordinariness—color and pattern in ties and shirts but not in slacks. No more smoking jackets. No more pastel shoes.

At an elegant department store a French-accented salesman (he seemed a mind reader) left me with seven shirts on hangers in a tentlike dressing room: a curtain, separating me from the main floor, blew as if touched by a mistral.

A chill fell over me, like the onset of flu, and under its influence I bought two shirts. The best was cotton fuschia (though a single dry-cleaning has turned it a wan coral). I wanted the salesman to think I was an Italian experimental filmmaker. I tried to gesture slowly and minimally, because I'd noticed that cosmopolitan shoppers never seem hectic, flustered, or idiosyncratic.

∞

I telephoned several boutiques to ask if they carried Thierry Mugler suits. Most stores reacted with muted disdain to my query. "We don't carry Mugler," said a clerk at a luxe site; she seemed to be speaking into a toy telephone at the other end of the ocean, so overwhelmed was her denial by the tidal noise of the store in heat.

At another emporium a salesman winked as he agreed to put a reduced-price Armani suit on hold. The wink meant either that he knew we were two gay guys doing our kind of business in an environment that passed as straight and yet produced gay thrill and meaning—or else that he knew I'd never come back for the suit. I never did. But I keep his wink with me at all times.

At Brooks Brothers a salesman winked at me when I tried on a blue oxford-cloth shirt. Either I looked decent in blue or it was fishy for a guy like me to be shopping there.

∞

I still own the houndstooth Harris Tweed jacket I acquired in 1976, although I will never wear it again. My mother bought it for me at a department store in suburban California. At that same store, for ninety-nine cents (I am telling the truth) I bought a pair of seersucker dress slacks. The best young trumpeter in town wore a similar pair: a man's item, but candied.

∾

At a reading given by a distinguished older poet, the audience is drably dressed. So is the poet. All the men seem to be wearing brown—and not this season's attractive, ironic caramel, but the brown of depression and boredom.

∾

The morning the Prada store was born, my kind salesman called me to say that there was one black suit, of the kind I sought, in my size. He could hold it for only a short time.

Here was the beginning of something high-minded and true, though it was also a relationship (the suit and I) soiled by commerce.

Uptown in the pouring rain I could find neither the store nor a pay phone to call information. Tactlessly, at Calvin Klein I asked a handsome man who worked the door if he could show me the way to Prada, and he misdirected me, pointed south.

When, by chance, I finally arrived, the Prada store was alive with a vague, symphonic sense of exclamation, as if garments, customers, and staff were daffodils moving under the pressure of the same strong gale.

It took me a couple of hours to buy my suit. I tried it on; I wandered around the floor and watched other, more confident shoppers. A woman who looked like Miuccia Prada appeared in the shoe department and congratulated someone, or had a look on her face as if she were in the business of perpetual congratulation. I wanted to shout, "I'm happy to see you, but I don't know who you are!"

By then, my salesman had abandoned me; he paid closer attention to a barrel-chested blond (certainly a model) whose haircut resembled the modified shag of a guy I knew who inflicted kinky sex scenarios on his unwilling boyfriend. I watched the model look in the mirror. He assessed himself with prolonged, professional glances.

I spent so much time hanging around in the suit before deciding to buy it that the staff removed my street clothes from the changing room. They apologized afterward but implied that I had taxed the store's patience.

The four-buttoned suit that I finally bought is composed of nylon and spandex. I love the suit's high gorge. Not much room for a tie. Just a tiny V of shirt, up near my neck, where the two lapels part.

Under the arms, the suit is narrow, which makes me feel happily straitjacketed, mummified.

I like the sound of pant fabric rubbing against jacket, and the sound of the two pant legs rubbing when I cross them.

The magic of the suit is not its visibility but its power to grant invisibility. I enjoy this new state of not being seen. In my suit I can sit in public places (especially hotel lobbies) and pass muster but also avoid notice. Spandex sheen makes every imagined or real insult slide off me.

The compromise I've struck with the world of men's clothing is to accept the category (suit) but to insist on wearing versions that have been passed through female scrutiny and care (Miuccia's eye).

It exhausts me to think that I might have been someone else, a man who wore suits without irony or pathos. I might have been someone who dressed without thinking about it. Perhaps this would have been a more fortunate fate. But it is not mine.

∞

I must work a little harder to praise the suit, before it is too late. Already I feel sorry for the suit, in anticipation of its obsolescence. I can imagine the time when I will look back on it and think it pathetic: it will be dust-stained from having hung so many seasons, unworn, in the closet. Already I can envision the death of the suit.

∞

"Describe your suit," says the elegant photographer, a man with the pretty face of a slacker and a serene focus on his task, which is, at the moment, to take my picture.

"I can't describe the suit, but I can say what I feel like when I wear it."

"Start there."

"I feel like a stretch limo making a U-turn on 57th Street."

I try again. "In the suit I feel like I'm moving in two directions at once, backward and forward. I get the advantages of both. I glide like a lady but I also have a respectable, pork-'n'-beans solidity."

The photographer is not really paying attention, but I inwardly continue. "I feel I am swathed in taffeta. Vera Wang. Has anyone noticed the similarity between men's suits and women's ball gowns? One sea of fabric. Notice how the light shines off me." In the suit I walk toward the large window, which looks onto nameless lofts. I say, "Seen from the right angle, the black fabric, which is part Lycra spandex, looks silver." The photographer makes no effort to see the fabric from the silver angle.

∞

I wear the suit when I visit a friend, an ethereal woman I've known for twenty years. I have described my suit, in advance of our meeting. Now she sees the suit and compliments it—she has no choice, I will excommunicate her if she doesn't. I am afraid she is glad I've begun to dress in a gender-appropriate fashion. I say, "I worry that you're happy I've come to terms with my masculinity quote-unquote."

She says, "Why do you think that?" Her profession: psychoanalyst.

She is wearing a lovely little black dress. She is a well-dressed psychoanalyst. Her only fashion error was a doubtful pair of rainboots in 1978. Admittedly, she wore them on a very rainy day.

She brings out a box and exclaims, "Let me show you my new shoes!" A pair of black pointy lace-up boots. I question her excitement about the purchase, though I realize I can't parade my Prada enthusiasm without letting her reciprocate.

∞

You never know when you might bump into Beverly Sills. I once saw her take an elevator at the New York State Theater: she was wearing a floral dress, reminiscent of Laura Ashley. I was wearing my summer opera outfit—white jeans, and a brown-and-red-checked madras cotton sport coat bought at a flea market.

At the airline check-in gate for a morning flight from Detroit to New York, I see Beverly Sills again. Luckily, I am wearing my Prada suit. While we wait to board, I stare at her—not impolitely—and she smiles. I hope she notices the suit. I hope she is smiling at me not because I am part of the human comedy but because I seem a man in a pleasant-looking suit.

She sits in first class, first row. Where she belongs.

At LaGuardia, after the flight, I follow her off the plane; she drops postcards in the mailbox. "What an efficient woman," I think.

∞

In my suit, I have developed a new gait.

I affect a slight, deliberate swish. Ordinarily I would try to avoid swishing. However, when I wear my suit, which offers a conventionally masculine frame, I feel I can afford a little wiggle. It is my "fancy dame" saunter—the step of an imposing woman entering an important restaurant. She can't look too friendly (she might lose her table). She must look myopic; fresh from a secret appointment; about to meet someone exclusive who doesn't yet command "face recognition"; tremulous, as if she were Patty Hearst's mother at a press conference at the height of the "Tania" scare.

∞

Time to dry-clean the suit: it smells of curry and cigars. The young man who works at the cleaners does a mock Superman imitation—"it's a bird, it's a plane!"—when I enter in a shiny black overcoat. He shouts, "A movie star!" Maybe he seriously thinks I resemble a movie star, but more likely he recognizes my aspirations and is mocking them.

Unfortunately he has misplaced a ten-pound bag of my dirty white underwear and socks. I tell him, "It was just underwear, but I wouldn't mind getting it back."

The underwear never materializes. Some of the load had been Calvin Klein. I replace it with Fruit of the Loom.

When I pick up my suit from the dry cleaners, the tailor, who once mistook me for an actress, tells me that she is sad. Her husband is in the hospital: heart trouble. As we talk, she is removing lint from a fur-trimmed coat—her own—hanging from the rack beside the cash register. I compliment the coat and she says it disappoints her, though she bought it at a fine store.

Vigorously she removes lint with a roller brush.

Beside her sewing machine there is a full-length mirror. I look in it while I wait for my suit to be brought from the automatic rack of hangers that snakes through the shop. I look much better in her mirror than I do in my own mirror at home. My favorite moments of self-examination happen at the dry cleaners. What this fact reveals about my moral character I don't know, though I suspect that the revelation is not flattering.

(1997)

THRIFTING

MOTHER BLAZER

To my mother's second wedding, I wore a grey seersucker blazer bought for fifteen dollars at a thrift store. Wearing a secondhand item wasn't a slight on my mother. It was the finest summer jacket I owned.

Recently I gave it to the Salvation Army and replaced it with a new blue Brooks Brothers seersucker suit.

I suppose this means I'm making progress.

In no way, however, do I believe that my life is a voyage from thrift to extravagance. My heart remains a thrifter's.

SHORT MEN

One reason why I thrift: in the past, men were shorter, and so second-hand clothing stores carry small sizes, cut to accommodate my kind.

My most useful secondhand purchase was a size 36 black cashmere blazer. I've worn it to job interviews, funerals, operas, plays, and Paris. Twice I've had its maroon lining resewn.

A snide man once insulted the jacket by calling it a sport coat. It is not a sport coat. It is a vehicle for transcendence.

SANTA CRUZ BOARDWALK

A checked overcoat, too long, too blowsy, without a lining, earned me, eleven years ago, a compliment from a novelist I idolize. She said, "I like your overcoat."

Forever it became "the coat that my novelist goddess complimented."

Purchased at a now-defunct used-clothing store on Bleecker Street, the coat might have belonged to an unscrupulous detective on his way to meet Veronica Lake. Wearing it, I resembled my mother in a photo from my infancy—a picture in which she's wearing a huge hooded overcoat buttoned to the neck, a coat that spreads out like a felt cloth beneath a Christmas tree. She wears kneesocks with her saddle shoes. In the stroller, I'm the bundled-up infant seeing, for the first time, the Santa Cruz boardwalk in 1959, a cold day.

Our overcoats suggested Lawrence of Arabia's desert tent.

I thrift so that I might resemble a more glamorous incarnation of my father or mother. I have an insatiable desire to be an adult.

Much of my life, not a masterpiece rotund as a *bibliothèque*, might be titled, "In Search of Lost Outfits."

WARHOL SHIRT

In the 1960s, Andy Warhol wore a striped sailor shirt under his leather jacket. The shirt is famous enough to warrant a place in an exhibition at New York's Whitney Museum of American Art. There, I gaze enviously at his shirt and then remember that over the last thirty years I've worn many such blouses, wide-necked horizontal-striped white cotton jerseys that let me imitate Jean Marais or other Gauls from the Cold War and earlier, boulevard or waterfront rakes who look at once gaunt and muscular, bruised by the past and exalted by the future. These types in stripes, half nautical, half convict, look like Jean Genet's object of desire in his film, *Un Chant D'Amour*. I can become my own desired object—I can envy myself—by finding and wearing a Warholesque jersey.

Warhol himself was imitating the macho punks that Genet idolized. Now, if I wear a shirt that resembles Warhol's, I join a domino game: I'm striving to be Warhol being Genet being the desired convict—a cute-guy Chain of Being.

HARRY COFFEE

Some of the clothes smell funny at my nearby Salvation Army, where, in a listless mood, wanting a conversion experience but not knowing how to find it, I tried on an aromatic leopard-spotted shirt, $4.99, probably for women. It fit. Unfortunately, two buttons were missing.

In a regular clothing store I'd never try on a women's blouse. But in Salvation Army I was casting myself in *The Diane Linkletter Story*.

At Salvation, I examined a nereid-green dress, made by Harry Coffee of Fresno and Bakersfield, California. The price: $2.99. If I were auditioning for a Gloria Grahame role, this might be just the thing. It's difficult to describe the exultation of looking at a dress that costs only $2.99. Imagine being a young ambitious lady, thirty years ago, trying on a Harry Coffee dress in one of Bakersfield's smartest shops. Thrift shops restore words like *Harry Coffee* to one's vocabulary. I thought of buying the Harry Coffee dress as a conversation piece, to brighten a dinner party.

Other prize finds from this visit included an Anna Sui electric-green women's top, distressed, for $3.99, and a blue Christian Dior evening dress for $4.99. I wondered if it were a subsidiary Christian Dior or the real one. (I can't keep track of every designer's rise and fall.) Also I saw a Bill Blass shirt, genderless, and I couldn't remember whether Bill Blass had cachet. I think he regained it a few months ago, but this shirt predates his rebirth.

At Goodwill across the street I found a Jordache fake fur. I wondered: "Is Jordache big?" I couldn't remember. I presumed the fur was a women's item; if I wore it, I could give it a jolt of irony.

It takes irony to understand the charm of the Harry Coffee dress, the Jordache fake fur, but a friend (a fellow smart aleck whose thrifting instincts I trust) says that too many ironic shoppers can ruin a store. The ironists march in and snatch up all the items susceptible to delicate and complex interpretation. The ironists claim the Harry Coffee dress because they know it's ugly— so plain and unfortunate, it has an unkempt beauty. Certainly this transvaluation of the sordid and the nondescript has informed fashion for several seasons. Some of the most interesting Prada dresses, for example, from two or so years back, were expensive, glossy revisions of the quintessential yard-sale housedress, the sort of frock one would avoid wearing in public. A yellow corduroy suit I almost bought this fall at APC recalls the retrospectively humiliating beige corduroy blazer I wore to high school graduation. Tom Ford at Gucci has drained embarrassment from despised fabrics and styles, and turned the once-downtrodden polyester, for example, into the insignia of a new elite. Sleazy fabric, sleazy morals, sleazy lapels, and sleazy décolletage have become emblems of ultramodernity, signifying the wearer's highly developed sense of irony.

My friend's favorite rayon shirt—brownish orange? orangish brown?—came from Salvation. It was originally marked at three dollars, but my friend pointed out a rip, and they gave the shirt to him for two.

Looking through filmy nightgowns at Goodwill, I consider the varied body shapes that have fit into them. Flesh tyranny relaxes at thrift stores: some layered chiffon nighties are so large or small that I can't figure out whether they are for pets, children, Siamese twins, or furniture. The sizes aren't marked. No more does a thrift nightie have a designated size than does a tablecloth, napkin, or bathmat.

NATIVITY ODE

The most erotic—and the straightest—thrift-store purchase I ever made was a black lace slip for a girlfriend in college.

That year I bought myself a used, blue, skimpy pajama top, and interpreted it as outerwear. I wore it to a Milton class: that day's subject was the "Nativity Ode." The elderly, wax-faced professor spent weeks on that poem. I liked the pajama top because it revealed chest hair, and I felt like a diminutive Burt Reynolds crossed with a lupine Sue Lyon.

Some years later, when my part-time job was proofreading at a law firm, I often wore to work a thrift-store-purchased maroon faux-silk pajama top, also showing a bit of chest hair, to achieve the same (I thought) winning combination of femme fatale and harbor laborer. This resemblance was a delusion, but I owe it to a thrift store, and the desire cost only ten dollars.

WASTE LANDS

To take fragments of the past and recombine them into new aesthetic entities is a familiar strategy; in the literary arts, such techniques became famous with T. S. Eliot's *The Waste Land*. The technique is bricolage—borrowing bits and pieces of culture and forming one's own mix. Seeing Alfred Hitchcock's *Vertigo*, for example, I perform bricolage by focusing to the point of insanity on Kim Novak's chignon, and then combining it, in my inner editing room, with Barbara Bel Geddes's cat-eye glasses. My *Vertigo* is thus a fashion trailer about chignons and glasses, with a lush symphonic score by Bernard Herrmann. *Pulp Fiction* is itself bricolage, but my *Pulp Fiction* is more severely respliced: my version consists of long close-ups of John Travolta's plump cheeks, as if the film were a premonition of the widely reviled *Gummo*, in which Harmony Korine's camera feasts on large, difficult, disadvantaged bodies and supplies them with no narrative, motivation, or redemption.

Fashion's nature is bricolage. It suggests stories but never completes them, posing family romances but then interrupting them with boa, fringe, disarray—the havoc of an incoherent hem.

To sample the past, through garments, is not cathartically to work through those decades, to integrate their traumas and lessons, but merely to wear their glittery emblems, schizophrenically combined, as if the end of the twentieth century were a jumble sale at Bedlam.

WHITE COURRÈGES

I fly to London. I'm trying to become a TV star. (The scheme will fail.) While there, I thrift.

I start at the Victoria and Albert Museum, where I look at a Dior, a Madame Grès, a Fortuny; at corsets, bodices, and the hard bustle—a birdcage—that a nineteenth-century fashionable British woman placed at the small of her back so that the skirt would pop out, a reverse pregnancy; at the close rows of buttons on military uniforms, and the narrow shoulders of male waistcoats; at the pointy toes of eighteenth-century women's handpainted slippers, suggestive of foot-binding; and at a pair of white Courrèges boots, which I'd wear today if some enterprising designer would recast them for men.

White Courrèges boots don't express interiority—don't give the flavor of a psyche in repose or turmoil. White Courrèges boots aren't the same as *Jane Eyre*. And yet the boots help me imagine what a 1964 Jane might have felt as she walked downhill toward a mod Mr. Rochester's flat for an afternoon of heavy petting and malt biscuits.

GAS MASK

On London's Portobello Road, devoted on Saturdays to a flea market of Dickensian heft and diversity, I see gas masks on sale. I believe they're from World War I. I also see a table of men's fur hats; their message is exile. They seem engineered to keep heads warm on the long walk away from home.

I'll do without the hats. The pieces I most crave are pink rubber high-heeled boots, good for rain, but also for dances and cruises, and 1970s Charles Jourdan platform shoes with carved wooden chunky heels and braided yellow patent leather straps.

LAUNDRY MULES

Back from London, I do laundry in my apartment building's basement, where a woman in a Prada dress is folding towels.

Wrong. It's a cheap housedress, a brightly futuristic polyester print.

She's wearing Manolo Blahnik mules!

Wrong. They're slide-ons that would fetch $2.99 at Salvation Army.

I'm wearing blue jeans, a white T-shirt, white tube socks, black Hush Puppies, and a black work shirt that I call "the Picasso jacket," bought at a Paris flea market. I love it, but I haven't figured out yet whether it's acceptable to wear on the street, or whether I am the only one who'd divine its resemblance to the coat a Left Bank painter might wear when he lopes along the quays in the company of his heavy-smoking lover, a poet in a *schmatte* that is a Jean Patou day dress if you don't look too closely. This imaginary poet wears pancake makeup that is either from Woolworth or Guerlain, or maybe it came from the box of junk he found in his grandmother's attic, a box that also contained wax paper, canned beans, and masking tape.

My Hush Puppies are new, but I know a balletomane who wears his brother's original mouse-grey Hush Puppies from the 1960s.

My most discriminating fashion pal says that the new, revived Hush Puppies are already over. I agree. I don't wear Hush Puppies to be chic. I wear them to do laundry, though I think they give me a secret complicity with the woman in a housedress: we share an uncertain relation to the contemporary. I wonder if she shares my arrogance, which sometimes buckles or folds, creating minor, hypothetical pockets, which look like humility.

PHILOSOPHY

Fashion goal: to philosophize; to take no garment at face value; to muse on the threads of implication that unravel at the hems of silent slacks.

JOAN BRODERICK CRAWFORD

I meet the Ur-thrifter: Gene London, former television actor, presently coproprietor of The Fan Club (subtitled "A Fashion Design Resource"), a vintage store that sells garments worthy of a place in a star's closet. Some were worn by celebrities: hanging above reach, not for sale, is a Sonia Rykiel (Henri Bendel) black short-sleeved feathered jacket, once the property of Jackie Onassis. Elsewhere in the store, for reasonable prices, are garments sported on-screen or off by Raquel Welch, Lauren Bacall, and Whoopi Goldberg.

Gene London, whose face is smooth, florid, and telegenic, and whose generous wish to wax confidential is surpassed only by my wish to listen, knew Joan Crawford well. Clothing donations from Crawford formed the beginning of London's vast collection of star garments.

London, it turns out, was one of Crawford's late-night phone companions. She'd call, drunk, and they'd indulge in pillow talk. Crawford, he says, had other such confidantes, but not as many as Judy Garland had. "Judy would call anyone who was nice to her. She'd call the elevator operator."

London's friendship with Crawford started when she wrote him a letter praising his performance on TV. "She wrote five thousand letters a day. She was very complimentary to show people." He loved her clothes, and told her so. She gave many of them to him: the first shipment arrived in a Palmolive Soap carton. She encouraged other stars to send him their garments, and his collection grew.

London describes a pair of Crawford's shoes: "It was like looking at a 1950s Cadillac with fins. You got out of the way. It was like a revolver."

Joan was Queen Bee. Her tough-as-nails screen persona was

no pose: "It was Crawford at home. She was *Broderick* Crawford. She was more male than Broderick."

Her house's decor was "1950s funky," says London, "kidney-shaped tables, everything laminated." He'd put a drink down on a surface, and Joan would slip a coaster beneath it: she'd slide it in "like an eel." He says, "I did as I was told at her house."

Toward the end of her life, he says, "Crawford's makeup sense had changed. She wore her false eyelashes a quarter inch above her eyes." He describes the line of pale exposed lid between eye and lash. "And she dressed like the Queen Mum." She wore gloves that seemed sewn from percale sheets: "The colors were all wrong. They were Americanized—made pleasing to everyone, rather than chic." After *Bonnie and Clyde* popularized the 1930s look, he suggested that she start a clothing line. She wasn't interested.

Toward the end of her life, she gave up the art of dressing well. She'd answer the door in rubber thongs and housedress. A friend might say, upon greeting her disarray, "Excuse me, is Miss Crawford here?" Joan would snap, *"Get in here!"*

London enjoys telling today's stars how to wear vintage fashions. "Raise your bust two inches," he'll say, "and watch where they match the 1950s dart!"

MORALS CHARGE

The morals of my scattered tale:

wear what you want;

don't let designers bully you;

visit flea markets to create trends of your own;

don't be afraid of the return of the repressed;

wash your vintage items so they don't stink;

think of the concept that you're dressing toward (French
sailor during Fleet Week);

don't be afraid to abandon a favorite color;

dress either to be noticed or to be overlooked, but not both;

ignore what friends tell you;

if you're not bald, keep your hair clean;

stand up straight, or, if you can pull it off, slouch;

when someone, even if that someone is your mother, gets
        remarried, wear a thrift-store item to the wedding;
observe no proprieties;
cross-dress at whim;
create private mythologies around each garment you wear;
tell these myths to your friends and lovers;
call up strangers and tell them you're writing an essay about
        a subject of great concern and ask them probing
        questions;
dress down or dress up, but not both at once;
donate;
do not condemn the garments of passersby, lest you be
        harshly judged;
admire relentlessly, lest your spirit's springs dry up;
choose a fetish (high heels) and stick to it;
don't weep when a garment's life is over;
say a proper good-bye to every garment so that when it's
        dead you won't regret what was left unsaid;
remember that garments have as much soul as you do;
respect the *genus locii* of shoes;
worship at the shrine of no one else's wardrobe, only
        your own;
say a fashion prayer every night before falling asleep, lest you
        wake up without a style;
every day reevaluate the distance between the grotesque and
        the beautiful;
do not fear the grotesque, lest it kidnap you;
love a garment for its insufficiencies as well as its strengths;
do unto your garments as you would have them do unto
        you.

(1998)

DIANA'S DRESSES

(written one month before the death of Princess Diana)

JUNE 19 AND 20, 1997: THE PREVIEW

Everyone at the press preview, before the charity auction of seventy-nine of Princess Diana's dresses at Christie's, is talking about her body. Several of the comments are unseemly.

One rude man unkindly mentions "hips the size of the Royal *Brittania*." One rude woman wonders aloud if some of the dresses are maternity wear.

Clearly, Diana's size fluctuated. Memories of her well-publicized bulimia hang in the air, unspoken: "Poor thing!" is the mood in the room. Understandably, reporters are wary of eating too heartily the delicious tidbits (smoked salmon, croissants) laid out on buffet: appetite's perils are the show's subtext.

I decide to take the dresses seriously: I try to absorb them as major artifacts. What can I learn from Diana's gowns?

I stand beside the headless mannequins and learn about ruching. One gown of pale blue-grey chiffon is—according to the caption—"ruched to below the hip," while another features "daring asymmetrical ruching." (At home I look up *ruche* in the dictionary: of Celtic origin, it derives from *rusca*, meaning tree bark.) Also vivid in the gowns is a technique called shirring: the fabric gathers and puckers, like a carnation's pleated petals. Maybe one effect of this auction will be the return of ruching and shirring. If I were a designer, I'd shout to my assistant, "Ruche the hell out of that gown! Shirr that skirt, top to bottom!"

No one loves the dresses. Without Diana's gaze, without purses, shoes, and jewels, the gowns are leaden, uncommunicative. I hear someone cluck "dowdy." Someone else notices shoddy embroidery. A Spanish-speaking anchorwoman tells a TV camera that the gowns come with a curse: the princess's unhappiness. How House of Usher!

A buzzing fly lands on a long dinner dress of cream and salmon pink silk. A TV cameraman complains, "Stupid bug."

I see lint on a cocktail dress of black silk crepe. I think this is an allegory of death.

Celebrity is an earthquake with severe aftershocks: the princess's fame sets off minor fame-repercussions around her, so that Meredith Etherington-Smith, group marketing director for Christie's and a spokesperson for the event, begins to seem a superstar.

An ample, handsome woman, she is dressed today in wrinkled red linen. I stand as closely as possible to her at the press conference and absorb her British-accented pronouncements: her voice seems a cross between Shari Lewis ventriloquizing Lamb Chop, and Winston Churchill addressing wartime England.

Her favorite word is *fun*. It's mine, too. Observe, she says, "pearls, sequins, and all the fun." "Isn't this fun?" she says. The auction, she exclaims, is "a lot of fun," part of the "little private world of fun sales." *Fun*—which means "inquire no further"—is *the* adjective of our time, and I plan to explore its ramifications at a later date.

I ask whether the princess is embarrassed or thrilled by the hoopla, and all I get, in response, is more of the "fun" smokescreen. I can determine, at least, that Diana is a person: Etherington-Smith says "She's a real person," and "She's an energetic, sporty person," and "She is the nicest person in the world to work with," and "One can never talk about another person's feelings, particularly a princess's feelings," and "She's a busy girl," and "She's great fun, full of beans." What are beans?

Next to ruching and shirring, I decide that I love chiffon, because of the way Etherington-Smith pronounces the word—not as an American would say "lemon chiffon pie" but in the French manner: "*she*-fawn" (silent *n*).

Sweating under the lights, she insists the cameras stop so she can dab her face with a handkerchief.

Meanwhile, Richard Mineards, a dapper gent with foulard and British accent, a self-described "commentator on the royal family," is giving impromptu interviews, without the approval of Christie's: he predicts that Di will marry a wealthy man in a couple of years. I overhear a Christie's employee whisper, "He's saying nice things, but he's not a Christie's person"; eventually an official tells him to keep quiet.

A moral of the exhibition seems to be that men are rude. Most of the reporters here are women, but virtually all the photographers are men, and the men are hogging space. I see one man's huge camera lens bump against a female journalist's big blonde hairdo.

JUNE 25, 1997: THE SALE

Tonight, the press is still obsessed by Diana's body.

"No way she's a size eight," says a burly cameraman.

A line snakes from Park to Madison: pilgrims awaiting admission. My favorite pilgrim looks like Morticia Adams with off-brown lipstick. Near me hovers a drastically rouged bag lady with white ankle boots and a knock-off Louis Vuitton purse.

Two nights ago there was a gala benefit supper. The benefit committee was great fun, full of beans: Richard Avedon, Katharine Graham, Bianca Jagger, Calvin Klein, Ralph Lauren, Jessye Norman, Paloma Picasso, Chessy Rayner, Natasha Richardson, Bobby Short, Gloria Vanderbilt, Barbara Walters. . . . None of them are here. (My Christie's informer tells me that the princess made an appearance at the benefit on Monday evening and stayed "for a long time—over an hour: lots of fun people were there. . . ." I guess an hour is a long time for a princess.)

A colleague in the beauty world describes the Christie's staff as "the sort of girls JFK Jr. might have married."

"Do celebrities wait in this line?" I ask one of these lovely young women in little black dresses and pearls. She says no, stars come straight through.

Limos pull up, but I see no stars. Finally I'm rewarded by the sight of Nan Kempner, the socialite. She waves at the Christie's staff as she sails in.

Alas, the fashion community doesn't take Diana's dresses seriously, despite my beloved ruching, shirring, and chiffon.

∽

The sale begins: a solicitous Christie's employee has given me a place on the floor, rather than in the thankless upstairs room where much of the press is watching the show on telemonitors. I am in the auction room itself: I can see the auctioneer Lord Hindlip, and the dresses, and the fun crowd. I can angle for a glimpse of Nan Kempner. I can feel the hum in the room—the giddy sensation of overvaluation.

Lord Hindlip won't indulge in girl talk: he specifies the lot number and sometimes briefly identifies the dress but never describes it. Why this refusal to gush? I wish Etherington-Smith were holding the gavel: she'd stoop to prattle about tulle, diamanté, and faille.

Accidentally I kick a camera that a careless reporter has left on the floor.

One by one the dresses appear on a turntable, just as dishwashers and vacations materialized at climactic moments of *Let's*

Make a Deal. I'm torn between watching the real dresses and watching, instead, the video screens that flank the stage. If I were to stare at the monitors, I could imagine I was at home watching QVC.

I see a man with green-dyed goatee—the only visible subversive.

∞

I am interested in what ordinary people say when they stand in the radius of celebrity. Diana is the celebrity, and all of us here tonight are standing in her virtual vicinity. That turns us all into mirrors of fame—rearview mirrors, perhaps. The nearness—or distance—of fame inspires us to offer opinions about it: "She definitely bleaches those pearly whites," a woman says, and her friend adds, "That looks like my grandmother's dress. Very mother of the bride."

"I've shot a lot of shit," complains a jaded photographer. But I believe that the burden of proof is on the viewer, not on the spectacle: it is our job, as observers, to wrest meaning from events and objects, even if the meanings we impose seem uncharitable.

The bidding has long ago peaked. But now, at the finale, suddenly prices rise to preposterous heights: $151,000 for the so-called Elvis dress, and then $222,500 for the dress she wore when she danced at the White House with John Travolta. "That's insane!" exults a Christie's employee.

∞

After the sale, I wander the auction room and strike up conversations with beauties. I discover that it is remarkably easy, in the context of Christie's, to ask a stranger to describe her outfit. One tells me that her ice-blue suit is silk; another confesses that her gunmetal grey pumps are from Nine West.

I approach Nan Kempner with a few questions. After all, she hosted a private supper for the princess and is a staunch supporter of haute couture. She accepts my queries: she touches my arm and confides that one of Diana's dresses was bought "for the museum" (the Metropolitan's Costume Institute). I adore

Kempner's guarded cordiality. She has rheumy eyes, a gravelly voice, ostrich-thin legs; she is irreversibly tanned and has a comforting, esoteric aroma I recognize from my few brushes with society women—an amalgam, I suppose, of perfume, Listerine, and cigarettes.

I see Patty Hambrecht, managing director of Christie's, in a serene pink outfit. I go up to her and ask its source. She says, "Christian Lacroix," and then, graciously, "Thank you"—for I've indirectly praised her fashion discernment.

From every event I try to take home a lesson. At this auction, I decide that the lesson is not the power and foolishness of money, not the evanescence of fashion, not the decline of royalty. My lesson, I decide, resides in this discovery: people want to talk about their own clothes. It is perfectly proper to ask people about what they're wearing, just as it would be improper to ask them about their marriages, bodies, hairstyles, or appetites. So I boldly walk over to Nan Kempner again and compliment her matching bracelet and earrings. They seem to be orange jade (if such a thing exists) or orange coral. Either way, they are beautiful. I want to say, "Where did you buy them?" but that sounds coarse, so I use Christie's diction and ask, "What is their provenance?" The bracelet, she says, is Angela Pintaldi of Milan. Kempner spells it: P-I-N-T-A-L-D-I. "But I bought it at Bergdorf's," she adds, apologetically. "The earrings," she says, touching them, "are Kenneth Jay Lane!" She stretches wide her arms in a mock–Carol Channing expression of pleased incredulity at the strange ways of the world.

(1997)

MEN'S UNDERWEAR

*P*lease, O muse of underwear, teach me the difference between midrise no-fly briefs and wedge-fly briefs!

Underwear used to be simple; now there are too many underwear categories, all of them confusing, and I must collect my thoughts about underwear or I will have an epistemological breakdown.

I began life in Carter's briefs: plainest white, fit for a nun. I still wear white underwear. I don't think the dark varieties (blue, black, maroon) are seemly. Yet Carter's—is it still manufactured?—remains the symbol, for me, of sexual abstinence and physical nullity. A boy wearing Carter's underwear is a cipher. He has no body.

In my childhood, underwear was unseen. There were no photographs of brief-clad men in the *San Jose Mercury-News*, the

paper of record in my first metropolis. I collected Avon catalogues for their female lingerie photos, but I don't recall any men
in the Avon literature.

∞

For three adventurous years, at the end of adolescence, I wore
boxers (perhaps in imitation of my father), and then gave them
up. The main problem with boxers: the penis slips out the fly.
Some men may not object; I do.

Another problem with boxers: they ride up the waist, pro-
ducing discomfort and irritation. (The boxer's lower seam bisects
the testicles.)

Given these inconveniences, why would any sensible man
wear boxers? To let the crotch breathe? I would argue, however,
that a crotch does not need to breathe; a crotch has no consciousness. It needs safety and peace of mind, and it needs to remain
cleanly and tidily enclosed in the cotton pouch created for it.

And yet: on writing days, in hot weather, I like to lounge
around the apartment in silk boxers. I own two pairs. One is
paisley; the other is patterned with dice. Boxers keep my sentences alert and mean and continuous (I hope).

∞

My college freshman roommate, jazz aficionado, wore no underwear beneath his blue jeans: racy conduct. I wonder how he
coped with denim's friction against his tender organ. Wasn't he
worried about glans attrition?

For a time I thought it might be avant-garde to wear a jockstrap instead of briefs, but I soon discovered that the jock,
though an American institution, is an unhappy, utilitarian, itchy
affair, and that it should be outlawed.

Civilized life is full of differences, like east and west, that assist navigation; among them, the distinction between *jockstrap*
and *underwear* is one of the more comprehensible, though it offers little guidance, and no comfort.

∞

At this stage of life, I am an underwear conservative. I don't wear logo-flashing briefs, the sort that deliberately protrude above the trouser's waistband. Given my age (thirty-nine), my build (slight), and my vocation (aesthete), it doesn't seem appropriate to walk around Manhattan with TOMMY HILFIGER splayed across my belly.

∞

Last spring, on vacation, I bought three pairs of bikini underwear at a department store in the Sicilian town of Enna. I wanted to avoid laundering in the hotel-room sink, and I was rushing through my trip's allotment of underwear at breakneck speed.

At home, in the peak of summer, I go through three pairs a day. This is indulgent, I know, but it is also harmless. I don't like sweat-marred panties. Underwear is most snug, most gratifying, when it is fresh. Its pleasure—its rightness—diminishes after a few hours.

∞

Although bikinis are supposed to be sexy, they do not necessarily show off (or augment) the size of one's equipment. In fact, bikinis often flatten and reduce the apparent heft of the manly portion.

I am of two minds about underwear tightness. Even though bikinis tend to cramp the crotch, I will sacrifice groin freedom for the sake of rear tightness: I insist on briefs that cling snugly to the behind. I detest underwear that sags in the back.

I avoid high-rise briefs. Even so-called classic briefs are abominations: they rise.

Back rise is embarrassing. I hate to think that, when I bend down, my underwear's back strip shows. I suppose, however, that it's better to reveal waistband than buttcrack. Some people tell me it is fashionable, but in my opinion, butt cleavage will never be chic.

∞

Some fashion adjudicators believe that a few holes in a pair of otherwise spotless white cotton briefs are acceptable. Others believe that at the first sign of fray, the underwear should be discarded.

I divide my briefs into two classes: flawless pairs, and pairs that have minor areas of tear. A friend, however, tells me that one should never travel in anything but the best underwear, lest one die en route.

I love schemes; in my mind's filing system, every ordinary object belongs to a family of analogous artifacts. I classify underwear with dust cloths, vacuum bags, napkins, towels, washcloths, pillowcases, drapes, and veils.

Underwear, hardly a zone for the exercise of individuality, suggests military, scholastic, or ecclesiastic confinements.

The disappointment of underwear is fade. After many washings, briefs turn grey. (Grey is preferable to yellow.) It is difficult to know when one's own underwear has reached the point of no return. It is obvious, however, when someone else's has expired. Critical objectivity about a stranger's underwear comes easily.

Sometimes, in the middle of the night, a question wakes me.

Recently, I found my dreams sideswiped by the following "rogue" queries:

1. Why are bikinis, of the "European" variety, sold in plastic cylinders?
2. Why do the men in Jockey ads wear their briefs so high?
3. When was the last time we saw a photo of Calvin Klein posing in his skivvies?
4. Did Montgomery Clift perform underwear scenes?
5. Are the men who wear gripper jams happy?

Underwear used to be one's own business. Now it is a defining (hence public) element of a masculine wardrobe. Much as I otherwise salute the process of making vocal our secrets, I miss the days when underwear was invisible—because I believe that I have no talent for underwear. It is not a sartorial field at which I excel.

I write about underwear not because I want to mock it, but because it intimidates me.

I should probably upgrade my level of underwear. I should do more shopping, and less talking.

∞

It is impossible to separate underwear from the art and science of advertisement, which scars the landscape.

Calvin Klein ads, especially the billboards above Times Square, may be erotic and beautiful, but they have not changed the experience of wearing underwear, any more than an ad for Chiquita bananas could alter the experience of eating a banana. A seductive ad might make you feel more "in-the-know" to be eating a banana, but it couldn't transform the banana's taste.

I've always wondered why male models in underwear ads have such smooth bulges. I suppose that they put on two pairs of underwear at once, to streamline the basket and disguise its irregular bumps.

∞

I asked the artist George Stoll, who is known for his meticulous sculptures of toilet paper rolls and Tupperware, what kind of underwear he favors. He confessed, "Brooks Brothers." He buys all his clothes there, because it's simpler to purchase everything at one store, and because the boys who picked on him at school, when he was growing up in Baltimore, wore preppie or pseudo-preppie clothing.

I want to ask strangers about their underwear. I want to ask the salesman at Saks Fifth Avenue who spritzes me with Tiffany for Men (it stinks up my wrist for hours) about his relationship to his underwear.

Underwear, if you blur your eyes, isn't profoundly gender specific. Yes, the cotton of men's underwear is thicker than women's; yes, women's underwear has no flies; but if you hold up an empty bikini you will see that it is an innocuously genderless article, like a tea cozy. Even a butch pair of men's classic briefs turns out, upon inspection, to be an androgynous slip of white brevity, to be placed like a poultice over the numb, unknowing groin.

∞

Off the body, underwear terrifies, much as a doll's head is alarming when it is separated from the doll itself. Nothing is more frightening, a friend tells me, than a pair of underwear found abandoned at a campsite, on a dirt path, beneath a tree. Who discarded the underwear, and why? Is the underwear a clue to an undetected crime?

Underwear is most eloquent when removed from its original context. Underwear in its proper place—on the body, or folded in a drawer, or wrapped in plastic at the department store—is useful, attractive, and consoling, but it is not yet tragic. However, underwear on the floor of a bank, or a movie theater, or a church, suggests disaster, and arouses terror and pity.

∞

I am afraid of my underwear. It knows too much about me.

(1998)

THE NEW MALE NUDITY

These days, men in Manhattan seem nude—more so, at least, than they once seemed. Even when fully dressed they wear their vestments with greater attention to underlying nudity. Therefore they wear proximity-to-nudity as if it were a fashionable garment.

I would once have said this observation pertained primarily to gay men. Now the nudity—the wearing of "nudity" as an outfit—is general. I don't mean full-scale nudity. I mean a flash of belly, a curve of pectoral.

Admittedly, I live on 23rd Street, the upper edge of Chelsea, where it verges on the Garment District, and so my field work is partial and biased. But the new nudity is not confined to Chelsea. I see it midtown, too, especially in Bryant Park, and on every street I have visited in my quest for the contemporary.

Fashion, hungry for fresh blood, has annexed "men" as the new frontier, and minimalism in men's clothing means not merely tight shirts and clean lines but sometimes wearing nearly nothing or wearing garments as if they were nothing. Ads have been influential in promulgating the new nude aesthetic: this summer on the streets of Manhattan (as well as on billboards and in magazines) one saw with fresh intensity the male abdomen, as if it had only this season been invented as an erogenous zone. As long ago as 1978, a man wishing to seem a stud might open his shirt's top buttons (earnestly molten John Travolta in *Saturday Night Fever*); now, men with designs on machismo, however ironic, unfasten the lower buttons and leave the belly intermittently open to visual purchase.

For years I have noticed bicycle messengers in tight spandex shorts or young men walking to or from the gym, but now, display has spread to other vocational sectors, so that a range of conventional-seeming men are inadvertent or deliberate sculptors of conceptual street theater. For example, a businessman with his jacket off and his sleeves rolled up smokes a cigarette outside a midtown office building. Because pleats are no longer a possibility, he wears the new flat-front slacks, and is therefore giving passersby a glimpse of his "basket"—an area crucial to men's sartorial self-conception yet rarely mentioned in fashion journalism. Baskets have always been a feature of Manhattan street life, for anyone who cared to look; in the golden age of Times Square—as memorialized in the Sal Mineo vehicle *Who Killed Teddy Bear?*—many would have chosen to feast their pervert eyes on flesh's plenty. Even now, the businessman who doesn't wish to seem an exhibitionist may, in simply wearing a fine fitted suit, reveal a consciousness of his own basket—a self-awareness of groin display that would have seemed, a decade ago, unseemly, preening, or obscene.

Most straight men I know aren't entirely straight anymore, or they don't make a big deal of their straightness. They move with the balletic freedom once the preserve of confident gay men like the legendary dancer Jack Cole. Even men who identify themselves as heterosexual do so less adamantly, and incorporate into their style of physical self-presentation a peacock insouciance—a way of showing neck, abdomen, crotch, forearm—that proves them willing to be looked at, happy to be considered an exhibit. It is no longer possible at a quick glance to tell straight and gay men apart, and making this distinction no longer seems the most practical or intellectually defensible exercise. On the subway it is no longer possible to know whether the men who stand, holding the silver bars for support, waiting for their stop, and swaying to the erratic movement of the car, are straight, because their principal rendezvous, as they ride, is not with any particular gender, but is an assignation with sight—the gaze of any voyeur or fellow traveler, male or female, anyone who allows herself the luxury of visual curiosity (does this man know I am looking at him? does he know that he radiates a desire to be looked at?). The men I see on the S train connecting Grand Central and Times Square care to be seen, and they dress with acute consciousness of belly and backside.

Not all the men are hyperbolically muscled. Sometimes they look lean and feral as Mick Jagger in *Performance* or Peter Fonda in *The Trip*. Theirs is a sexuality of the wrist bone, not the bicep.

Recently I visited the Gianni Versace boutique, a marble palace, on Fifth Avenue. It pretends to be a clothes emporium, but its mission is striptease. Tightly attired professionals—including one young woman in a formfitting zipped-up pantsuit that seemed modeled on Angela's getup in *Lost in Space*—greeted me at each floor. One slightly drunk-seeming salesperson even followed me into the changing room, to hand me a pair of cobalt-blue stretch rayon jeans that might be close to my size. The goal was tighter, tighter—toward tightness's vanishing point, so that it could seem I was wearing audacity itself. While I was waiting for a jacket in size 36 to be brought up from the dungeon, I leafed through Versace catalogues, featuring page after page of unclad Adonises, giving the illusion that to be nude one needed to spend a fortune on Versace clothes, and that nudity was a utopia to be attained after having traveled beyond all budgetary proprieties.

Discrete and staged revelation of the body has always been fashion's strategy. Codpiece, miniskirt, muscle shirt: such framings of anatomy give the viewer—and the dresser—the illusion that a body, like a photograph, can be selectively cropped and edited for maximum tension and compositional compression. Certainly men have always been at liberty to flash their bodies. Think of *Spartacus* and Jack LaLane. Certainly it is not news that a man can take off his shirt in public and walk down Sixth Avenue on a hot August day, his pectorals not overshadowed by the ambient architecture, the palaces of Ladies Mile intended in their earlier incarnations as haunts of idle women. But now when a man takes off his shirt and wears his carefully formed pectorals as fetish, as apparel, his chest does not appear as vulnerable as it once might have. He seems, instead, to be wearing a transparent shield. And it seems, as one walks around Manhattan, that the Hellenic ideals embodied in kitschy physique magazines have finally been realized on the streets—and that reincarnated refugees from the AMG studio, or Bruce of Los Angeles photo shoots, now have the luxury of defining contemporary urbanity's tone.

Now it has become rather commonplace, on the street, to see what once would have been a forbidden and vulgar display of butt cleavage. Now the fashionable younger man may wear his jeans so low that when he bends down, the forbidden crack's top greets the eye. And this vista is no longer considered a hobo stigmata, but, instead, is accompanied by expensive underwear riding up to reveal a logo, brand names flashed as the butt cleavage's caption, as if "Tommy Hilfiger" or "Calvin Klein" were opera surtitles to translate the enigma of the twin globes that are now the flaneur's prerogative to expose and to espy.

(1996)

II

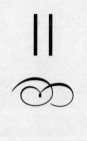

OBSCENITY

THE ARYAN BOY

STORY

At some overnight nature retreat, long ago, outside of Berlin, my father woke to discover someone pissing on his head. It was the Aryan boy in the upper bunk. While my father told me this story, I was bathing, under his supervision; a plastic cup floated beside me in the soapy water.

I've often thought of this Aryan boy, circa 1936, pissing on my father's head, and of my position, naked in the tub, while he told me the story—one of the few anecdotes he passed on to me about his childhood in Nazi Germany.

Another story: Hitler paraded through the streets, and my father saluted him because everyone else was saluting. It was the thing to do.

Otherwise I heard little about tyranny.

Who knows if the boy in the story was really Aryan, or if I'm misremembering the story?

CUP

In the bathtub, I pissed in the plastic cup. Pissing in the cup produced a hard-on, but once the penis grew hard, pissflow paradoxically stopped. I liked to use the cup as a ladle, gathering bathwater to rinse shampoo suds out of my hair.

Enjoyable, to place the cup over one's newly emergent penis in the bathtub.

GALICIA

On my mother's side, there were some shadowy relatives—I don't know their names—in Galicia. My mother remembers conversations in the early 1940s, late at night, at the Brooklyn kitchen table. Letters from Galicia. Nothing could be done to save these relations. I guess I'm Galician.

The window of my great-grandfather Wolf's jewelry shop in New York was smashed. Did that hate-filled atmosphere shape his son's character? At my grandfather's death, his unfinished project was a book about the Jew in American literature. "When did you stop being an observant Jew?" I asked him, and he said, "What are you talking about? I never stopped."

THE REPRODUCTION STORY

My older brother had a new book, *The Reproduction Story*, about vagina and penis, secrets of mating, special feelings you develop for members of the opposite sex. I was taking a bath. My mother threw the book into the bathroom, saying "Your brother isn't old enough for this book." She was furious at him for some misdeed, sass, or subversion. He was in the doghouse. "Your brother's not mature enough for this book," she said, meaning, *The bastard's lost his right to learn the reproduction story.* Good. Now the story was my property. Naked in the tub, I read about gonads. I lost track of plot. I pissed into the plastic cup.

MORE ON THE ARYAN BOY

A miracle, that piss stops once you want to come, that "come" and "piss" functions are dialectical, mutually exclusive.

Did my father consider the boy an Aryan? Was that the term? Or did my father simply call him Gentile? I should ask my father about that incident, but our rapport has diminished. The times of bathing, of pissing into the cup after he left the bathroom, are over. Just as well. But I should figure out whether his aunt's middle name was really Sarah or whether that was just the name the Germans put on her visa to signify her race.

MORE ON THE ARYAN BOY PISSING

"How are babies conceived?" I asked my older brother, and he told me, "Daddy pisses in Mommy." Therefore from the beginning of time I knew that such relations were degrading.

MORE ON PISSING

Is urine a home remedy? Two scholars—women—were swimming in the ocean. A jellyfish stung one. So the other pissed on her colleague's sting: a proven antidote.

When you piss in the ocean you are not ejecting fluid; rather, you are accepting fluid's absence. You are deciding that you don't want to hold in those muscles, that your liquids sympathize with the saline surround; you want intimacy with coral, crabs, jellyfish, and wrack. That's probably why the little girl in *The Exorcist* pissed on her parents' fancy rug during their dinner party. She wanted to make a big Satanic statement. She wanted to show exactly what she thought of their Georgetown regime. My next step in life is to identify with the possessed girl in *The Exorcist*.

KEITH WRITES:

"This is how my lover and I met, at a sleaze bar (now closed), getting our fill in the restroom. . . . We both like to give as well as receive golden showers. Meeting others into this 'sport' is becoming impossible. We display our yellow hankies proudly—and sometimes our wet crotches!—only to receive puzzled looks and outright stares. This is in leatherbars! Can you put us in touch with groups, organizations?" (*Honcho,* April 1994.)

ORGASM

I was naked in the tub. My father said, "And I woke to discover I was all wet." Or he said, "I wondered where the liquid was coming from." Or he said, "And I looked up and there was the Aryan bully, pissing on my head." Meanwhile I was ensconced in Mr. Bubble.

There is a time in life when one's own penis—if one has a penis—is a negligible article of faith.

This is what passed through my mind as my very first hand-manipulated orgasm approached: "There's no way I'm going to mess up this clean bathtub with my spermy stuff." So I stopped. For weeks afterward I thought I'd irreparably damaged my potential to come, because I'd interrupted that originary burst.

SHE DIDN'T SAY A WORD

My grandfather said, of his mother, "She never once raised her voice." This was a compliment. She never raised her voice to her husband, Wolf, who translated the Bible into Yiddish at night: during the day he was a jeweler with a broken shopwindow. Wayne stands for Wolf; shared W, meager memorial.

MORE ON THE CUP

My fundamentalist friend lay naked on his bathroom throw rug. I said, "I've discovered a neat trick. Look." And I put the bathroom cup over my hard penis. I wanted to teach him secrets of the cup. But he had other plans. He said, "Lie on top of me." My fundamentalist friend wanted me to fuck him. I said, "No way." Then he decided we should stay up past midnight playing World War II strategy games.

Perhaps I misremember the story. I might have wanted to fuck the fundamentalist; he might have said, "No way." Or perhaps no mention of intercourse was made. Perhaps he simply said, "Let me lie on top of you."

In my own fashion I, too, am a fundamentalist. I believe in the fundament and I believe in these fundamentals.

PROSTHETIC MATH

I believed the math teacher's penis was prosthetic because I'd seen it hang loose and inanimate like a stale *bûche de Noël* out of his pants at the urinal.

The squirt named Wasserman who sent a thank-you card to the math teacher: was Wasserman Jewish, too, and did that explain his safari shirt and his friendship with the math teacher with prosthetic penis and recipe for Waldorf salad tucked between algorithmic pages? Even then I thought of Wasserman as Water Man.

SHAKE IT OUT

Shake it out afterward, my father wisely said. Smart man. I'm sure he showed me how to shake it out, but there's always more dribble than science can account for. At what exact moment in sexual arousal is the flow of urine stopped? Do you have to wash your hands after pissing? Rumor has it, urine is hygienic. I suppose humiliation has nothing to do with masculinity, my father and I have nothing to do with masculinity, and shaking the penis out after pissing to make sure there are no leftover dribble drops has nothing to do with masculinity.

TYRANNY

Kobena Mercer wrote that we have plenty of discussions about desire and pleasure but not enough about "pain and hatred as everyday structures of feeling." I agree. To "pain and hatred," I would add "tyranny." Tyranny is an everyday structure of feeling. We do not have enough discussions of tyranny's mundanity; everyone who analyzes tyranny pretends not to be friends with it, but what if finally we narrated our tyrannic urges?

MY FATHER SALUTING HITLER

It was a parade; my father didn't know better. My father, little Jewish boy, saluted Hitler. Someone must have found it cute, someone else must have found it not cute. Up went my father's hand in mimic salute.

ONE PROBLEM WITH THIS DISCOURSE

is that it sounds like a victim's, or like the discourse of someone who considers himself a victim. I must find a way not to sound the victim note. I must find a way to speak as tyrant, not because I want to be a tyrant or become more tyrannical but because there is little about my desire or my death that does not fall under the heading *tyranny*.

CALL MASCULINITY TYRANNY AND SEE WHAT HAPPENS

My mother did the disciplinary work—for example, when she threw *The Reproduction Story* like dog food into the bathroom while I lay in the tub.

I always wondered about the difference between breasts in men and breasts in women, and I prayed I would not grow up to become a man with breasts, though now in retrospect I realize that the male chests I feared (men at the beach, men in my family) were just fatty muscles, good pectorals gone to seed. I looked down at my chest to make sure that it did not protrude. I longed for absolute flatness, but also at other moments was eagerly stuffing crumpled paper towels in my shirt to simulate *La Dolce Vita*'s Anita Ekberg.

"VISIT THE RABBI WHILE YOU'RE IN VENICE,"

my grandfather said, and I wondered why I should waste time in Venice visiting the rabbi. Why squander an afternoon visiting the ghetto, I thought, when there are so many more uplifting tourist sites? My grandfather wanted to prove that Robert Browning was a Jew; I wondered why anyone would bother.

I tell my imaginary son, "Visit the sleaze bars while you're in Venice." I'm sure I feel the same wash of sentiment, anger, pride, self-righteousness, and victimization about queerness that my grandfather felt about Jewishness.

ICE CUBE

Ice cube my grandfather sucked as he died: so my mother told me. Hard to take in moisture while you're dying, I suppose, so he sucked an ice cube—or, rather, my grandmother brought the ice cube to his lips. My mother has his features, and I have my mother's: slim mean face, hysteric brown button eyes that will not see the other side of the equation.

Someone must bring ice to the dying man's lips, quenching tyrannic thirst, like the thirst of Prometheus, tied to the rock, liver eaten by vultures. Find the rock we're tied to, find the source of the rivets.

WHERE PROMETHEUS PISSED

Right on the rock. Tied to rock eternally he pissed right where he was tied. That was part of the Promethean picture. I suppose the rock was in the middle of the ocean, so the piss just washed off the sides of the rock and blended with the wandering sea. You piss where you are bound. When Prometheus was thirsty, my grandmother was not there to give him a taste of ice cube wrapped in handkerchief.

NUN JEW

My mother said "Nun Jew" to refer to non-Jews. "Nun," as in *The Flying Nun*. Does it matter what words you use? It matters what words you use.

NUN JEW CUM

The first time I swallowed cum I didn't care what I was swallowing. The second time I swallowed cum I gargled afterward with Listerine. The first two times were Nun Jew Cum. I don't remember the third time I swallowed cum. That's how it is with origins.

AGORAPHOBIA

I once knew a therapist who treated agoraphobics in their own houses. She'd visit them, help them overcome their fear of agoras. My father voted for Nixon because of the Israel question. My father usually based his votes on the Israel question. Long ago as part of a Sunday-school project I gave money to plant a tree in Israel. I didn't know what Israel was. I thought Israel was a country that needed shade. The space of this discourse—these words, here—is agoraphobic. I am visiting my own discourse in its house to see if I can help it overcome its fear of the agora. If you never leave your house, can you do damage? You can do damage inside your house, but can you do damage outside your house if you never leave it?

I IMAGINE

that the Aryan boy was once my father's friend but then the boy turned Aryan in ideology and pissed on my father's head, but the pain of the incident lies in the Aryan boy's betrayal, his flight from peaceful boyhood into Aryan identification, his movement from friend-of-my-father into Aryan thug. It is not possible today to say something absolute about history or hatred, but it is possible to say I was naked in the tub and that a story infiltrated my constitution; it is possible to speak about the bathwater and my waterlogged skin; it is possible to say I remember my father laughing as he told me this story. Have I misconstrued it? Maybe the boy who pissed on his head was actually a Jew. In 1936 (or a few years earlier) could my father have shared a bunk bed with an Aryan? In any case, I remember my father chuckling as he told me the story.

TRANSFERRED TO A JEWISH SCHOOL

My father liked to eat mashed carrots, sweetened, in a bowl.

Before long, he transferred to a Jewish school.

Idyllic black-and-white photo of my father at five years old in Berlin, naked, in the yard of his house, unselfconsciously urinating on the flowers or the ferns with a small and not yet interesting penis: if I were merely imagining this picture, I would tell you, but I am not merely imagining it.

WHY DIDN'T SOMEONE JUST SHOOT HITLER

In *Triumph of the Will*, Hitler moves along a row of soldiers, shaking their hands. Leni Riefenstahl filmed it so that he stares directly into the viewer's eyes, as if to shake the viewer's hand. I stare right into his eyes when he reaches his hand out to clasp mine. That is how Riefenstahl planned it. I have no other place to look.

I find many propagandistic manipulations seductive, including Wagner, but I draw the line at *Triumph of the Will*: I do not find its panoramas seductive. I expected I would find the near-naked Nazis boys attractive, showering in preparation for the rally. I'm relieved to find them scrawny. I'm relieved to know that I might not have found the Aryan boy attractive as he leaned over and let pour onto my head his golden arc.

(1994)

"MY" MASCULINITY

1.

A gay guy in a movie described his desire. He was touching his own penis while he spoke. He said, "I like to touch myself, I like to feel located." That was what the gay guy said. And the straight guy? The straight guy said something inscrutable, not memorable. It eludes me, at the moment, what he said. The gay guy touching himself had ineffable beauty—he touched himself companionably, without hostility or program. I wanted to be the man in the slow movie, touching himself without doctrine. He expressed glee when he found another gay guy. In the movie those were gaiety's hallmarks—glee and echo. . . .

Wait. I made a mistake. I reified gaiety. Next time I speak I will not reify. I meant to bore into the word *masculine*, to fauxetymologize the word *masculine*, to rim the word *masculine*. To rim is not to reify. For example: mask inside masculine. Ass inside masculine. Culinary inside masculine. Line inside masculine. Me inside masculine.

2.

What people have said about "my" masculinity, 1958 to the present:
 "Boys don't spit or bite when they fight."
 "Ma'am?"
 "Is this the lady of the house?"
 "If you don't shut up, I'm going to kick your balls in."

3.

I dreamed about modern masculinity: early gay-lib pamphlets were scattered "like autumn leaves" near the grammar school's slaughterball wall, and I marveled at the Tower-of-Babel Pebbles and Bamm-Bamm hairdos of the aristocratic family I was a changeling in, while, far off, juxtaposed with the hairdos, the spectacle of radical critic Guy Hocquenghem came into focus, GH alive again, at a podium, intoning, "Interpellation of the subject, up the ass, interpellation of the subject, up the ass," while incense burned.

4.

Masculinity sucks; it divides into pieces. "You're broad-chested, just like your father," my mother said, erroneously, when I walked topless into the kitchen, decades ago, in pursuit of a peeled orange.

Masculinity should be taken out of circulation, or its franchise opened up—but if masculinity ended, would I be able to speak? In a dream movie I lay on the plump chest of a composer; conventionally masculine, he caressed me, and I told him about the murderer loose in my house (I'd read about it yesterday in the paper), and the composer crooned Gershwin, which assuaged my anxiety. I climbed Jacob's ladder toward masculinity. Masculinity is not the same as virility; I have a little of each, fading.

Reading Jean Genet's *Miracle of the Rose*, I pity the incarcerated speaker. What he loves he degrades. Compare Genet's masculinism to Joseph Cornell's: Cornell's love of pastries, of long desultory trips into New York to spelunk and cruise, of small, precisely composed boxes. If I were to start keeping a scrapbook of my masculinity, how would I organize the scraps?

Am I constructing a masculine sentence? That was a question, not a sentence. I like to interrupt the line with an effort of listening. Men don't listen. Masculine men don't listen. I have swallowed the word *masculine*—even my shadow talks too loudly, as if to an amphitheater full of auditors. But I am not the least masculine person I know. I find masculinity when necessary. I am not a conscientious objector to it; it involves me. I don't know what "it" is. I dropped it—will you pick it up? It fell between us, somewhere, a lost resource, like the *Venus de Milo*, or a bag of marbles. It is a drag. I wonder where you can buy it. It rotates counterclockwise, like a doorknob into a room named Cain.

Trying to define masculinity, I grow too masculine; I must deflect the task of definition. If I were to organize a discussion of masculinity, I would start with balls—there's too much talk about the penis, not enough about balls, their lumpy, pistachio contribution. Not enough has been said, either, about erections as the absence of power. Getting hard, revealing your desire (say, in the high school gym shower), may mean that in the eyes of witnesses your masculinity is finished, kaput. Most of my energy in a certain era was spent making sure I did not get an erection in public.

Masculinity: is that what I "want" in a man? Sick of the cult of muscle among the queer (myself included), I have developed a style, borrowing from self-conscious femmes like Ronald Firbank, that derives its tangential power from the deliberate avoidance of the appearance of masculinity. I wonder if secret, underwater masculinity accrues through this pose. Femminess seems masculine to me, I mean it seems *virile* to me—a femmy man seems a hunk in unpatented ways, particularly the unwritten area of shade around the wrist and the neck. I should disentangle masculinity and sexiness. But why bother? They will disentangle themselves before the evening is over. If I am in bed with Cavafy, where am I? In the bower of what I've read. I can step outside of heterosexuality but it is not as easy to step outside of masculinity, and that is why I am trying to divide this sentence into several boxes; that seems the best way to deprive it of familiarity. I don't want to have to moralize my pleasure in order for it to pass muster.

The best way to figure out masculinity is to figure out how you talk, why you talk, at what tempo, what hesitations and interruptions threaten and provoke your talk, and then to stage the talk as clearly and nakedly as possible. All I have is my voice; it is here; I have shown you it. It has a gender. No, it has a style, a series of tics. I like short lines because they allow me to interrupt myself. I don't want to make a point. Darling, I irradiate meanings. If you came for points, you can turn right back.

(1994)

DARLING'S PRICK

"... I only wish I could have you in my arms so I could hold you and squeeze you tight. Remember the things we used to do together. Try to recognize the dotted lines. And kiss it. A thousand big kisses, sweetheart, from

Your Darling."

The dotted line that Darling refers to is the outline of his prick. I once saw a pimp who had a hard-on while writing to his girl place his heavy cock on the paper and trace its contours. I would like that line to portray Darling.

Fresnes Prison, 1942

—*Jean Genet,* Our Lady of the Flowers, *trans. Bernard Frechtman*

I am not interested in the prick per se. I am interested in prose.

I want to dispense with mediation, including the mediation of the "I."

At the end of Jean Genet's novel, a writer puts his heavy cock on the paper and traces its contours. He would like the line to portray Darling. But the line won't necessarily do the writer's bidding.

I want the prick, but also it is my prick that tells me what I want. So the prick announces hunger but also advertises a system of hungers.

I don't want to write "about" the prick, I want to write the prick.

Which doesn't mean I like pricks. In fact I am rather indifferent to them.

To want to place the prick on the page is to deplore mediation and abstraction. The "I" here is a writer speaking up impatiently and dogmatically on behalf of other prisoners of representation.

Pornographic pictures don't do the trick. Nor do explicit descriptions.

I don't want pictures of sex. I don't want sex. I want writing.

Often of course I want sex and often of course I want pictures of sex but more regularly I want writing.

The "I" here is the paradigmatic pornographer whose aesthetic I am trying to limn and justify.

It is difficult to understand the aesthetic of the pornographer, which is incidentally the aesthetic of the consumer of fiction and the casual moviegoer and the eater.

A person is sitting in a Cineplex Odeon putting popcorn in his or her mouth.

A person is playing a video game.

A person is filling out a questionnaire.

A person is waiting at a bus stop, listening to rainfall.

A person is watching a ceiling fan rotate.

A person on a beach towel opens a novel about the presidential primaries.

A person eats corn flakes while reading the box.

A person writes a sentence. The sentence is neither good nor bad, but poses its subject and predicate in the ordinary fashion.

Maybe you, too, are sick of mediation, of words that get in the way of what you want to say.

Assume there is a state of mind called "wanting to say," a desire that precedes words. The point is to stick as closely as possible to the desire, and not get lost in the words. Unless, of course, you desire words.

How convenient, how ultimate, if instead of the clutter of words we could have things.

I don't have enough words; I want more of them. And I want their emergence to be clean and genital.

I want what I read to have the clarity of a spotlit body.

I suppose some pornographers have the option of sleeping with their subjects.

I suppose some writers have already experienced what they write about.

I suppose that if I say I want to put my heavy prick on the page and trace its outline, then I have the option of letting you assume I possess a prick and that you and I agree on what a prick is.

And if I don't possess a prick, if I possess something else, and I put that something else on the page, then you have to figure out what that something else is.

How do you know if you desire the something else? I will have to draw its outline very precisely, so you can decide if its outline matches the other possessions you have desired.

If I am typing, then I can't put my prick or my something else on the page. I can only put fingers on the keys.

The outline drawn around the prick, on the page, encloses blank space. The reader must hypothesize a prick inside the dotted lines.

The beautiful part is the hypothesis, not the prick.

Darling's prick is long dead—incinerated or decomposed. Other pricks have taken Darling's place. All are the same. One after another. But the outline of Darling's prick has original poignance.

I once saw a pimp place his heavy cock on the paper. He was writing to his girl.

The pimp was my teacher. The pimp practiced mimesis.

I followed suit. I put my cock on the paper, too.

Most poetry is pornographic, since I define poetry as language that envies the scene it is describing. Poetry is words watching and wanting to approach the objects it renders.

By *Darling's prick* I mean the thing you press on the page when you write a love letter or describe a scene you want to join. By *Darling's prick* I mean the urge to be more present in the scene of composition.

Sometimes word and thing are indistinguishable. I don't know whether to advocate this indistinguishability. Instead, more modestly, I want to point to it.

To say: sometimes flesh (I don't know what else to call it) is present in the act of writing—or sometimes flesh wishes to present itself.

The writer draws a dotted line around the inappropriately thrust forward presence. Let's not call this presence a "self." Genet calls it, in shorthand, a prick. You could as easily call it a buttock cheek, a nipple, a nose.

It depends what turns you on.

All I ask is to be alive.

I don't expect miracles.

Gertrude Stein is the most pornographic writer I know.

Her language exemplifies a presence of the "thing" where the reader does not expect it, a presence of the uncalled-for.

Stein's language puts forward embarrassment: *you didn't expect this.*

I think about Gertrude Stein when I contemplate my desire to write pornographically—the wish to put forward the subjects of my regard, rather than words describing those subjects.

A dull word to describe this practice is *performance*. Dull, because expected.

And I don't want to put forward anything expected.

I suppose a prick is expected. It is a usual subject.

Let us say that you are throwing a costume party. Someone comes dressed as Roy Cohn. Also, the real Roy Cohn comes to the party. Confusion ensues. The real Roy Cohn has not put on a mask. He has decided to come as himself. So there are two Roy Cohns at the ball.

Writing is a masquerade party. You must come dressed as someone plausible.

If I am already Roy Cohn, I must think up a different disguise to put over my Roy Cohn face.

Darling's prick—not mine, not Genet's—is at stake here.

Darling is the life you want, when you read; the life you read toward.

The outline of Darling's prick posits the simplicity of an urtext.

One way to look at sexuality: it is the image bank you plunder while you have sex or while you wait to have sex. Once you are done having sex, the image bank is closed, defunct. Until the next time.

Another way to look at sexuality: it is the image bank you use all the time. It is the modus operandi of your motility.

Usually I think of sexuality as a matter of acceleration and deceleration. Instead I should think of it as how and why I think.

I should consider sex to be the art of making propositions. I should reverence the beauty of argument.

I have put forward a few new ideas today.

Class dismissed.

Class resumed.

I like simple sentences because they are rude and clean. They are sexual because naked. I have practiced a sexuality of the baroque but I will now commence a sexuality of the unembellished.

This class is taking place in the field of the contemporary Anglophone sentence.

Darling's prick has made paragraphs newly interesting.

If you stick forward your body every time you speak, then you are often sticking forward your body.

Genitals and writing have the same imaginary intensity. They are both put forward.

Darling's prick on the paper is a metaphor or replacement for the real prick.

Real pricks are necessary yet overrated. Imaginary pricks go farther.

Styles are simple or styles are complex. Children's literature is simple. Pornography is simple.

Children's literature and pornography concretely denote what the reader might wish.

I quickly outgrew children's literature, which is why I have returned, at this advanced age, to practicing it.

It isn't coy to put my heavy prick on the page. And yet it is the height of indirection.

I am interested in sentences, paragraphs, poetry, pornography, ecstasy, exhibitionism, privacy, love, representation, enigma.

When I trace a desire, I try to follow its outline as closely as possible.

I try not to impose a foreign form on its shape.

I adhere to the perimeters of imaginary anatomy.

I hate going backwards.

The "I" here is not the writer but an exemplary intelligence, prick-shaped, operating on your heart. The "I" here is a person deliberately putting forward identical shapes.

Again and again the same shape.

So you might as well get used to being accosted by what you have already seen.

Portrayal is very silent, as are sentences.

Here you see portrayed a pornography of the sentence. It is childish, exhibitionistic. It is slow and quick.

It demands that you kiss it.

Pornography is an industry but the pornography of the sentence (Darling's prick) is nonprofit.

Each sentence is a suppository.

That's how we write in the porn industry. That's how we write in Hollywood. That's how we write in the genre fiction factory. That's how we write in the academy.

Slow and quick.

Darling has a hard-on; that's why he writes.

That's why he stops writing.

Why represent, if you can kiss the cock's contours?

That is exactly why he writes. That is exactly the logic of the desire to portray.

I film your speech because I want to make your desire clear.

If you watch this videotaped documentary of yourself speaking, you might discover how to speak more effectively, which might help you make money.

If you watch this film of yourself going door to door trying to sell bad Bibles, you might become a more effective salesperson.

Would you like to buy a fake creed?

Would you like to buy a botched gospel?

May I offer you a farcical crucifixion?

Class dismissed.

(1996)

MASOCHISM, A MASQUE

To rail against Disney is to reiterate the obvious.

First I will rant about computers. Later I will discuss Times Square and masochism.

I hate computers, even though I am using one. Computers make people stupid.

I advocate the agrarian.

Example. I telephone a chain bookstore. "What books by Harold Robbins do you have in stock?" I ask the salesclerk.

"Let me check the computer," he says, and puts me on hold. Why not check the shelves?

The clerk comes back on the line to say that the computer only lists initials of first names: H. Robbins. There are hundreds of H. Robbins titles.

He says, "*Descent from Xanadu*. Is that by Harold Robbins?"

"I don't know," I say. "It doesn't sound like Harold Robbins."

"What about *Spellbinder. The Lonely Lady. Goodbye, Janette.*"

Things are looking up.

The clerk puts me on hold.

The clerk comes back to say, *"Where Love Has Gone. Never Love a Stranger."*

Happiness.

I'd like to register a complaint, however.

I expect quick service and I expect clerks to know their stock. Let's defame chains.

"You sound like a Marxist," a writer said to me at a cocktail party. I was complaining about chains. I said, "I'm not a Marxist. I'm too ignorant of Marx to be a Marxist." She said, "You sound like a Marxist. That's refreshing."

Moments earlier in the conversation I'd offended her by complaining about elites. Turned out she belonged to the very elite I was criticizing.

Accidentally I'd spit a bit of smoked salmon onto my palm, and when I shook her hand, I think she could feel the fish fleck.

Yesterday I met a rich man. He moved slowly, though he is only forty. He moves slowly not because he is arthritic or tired, but because he is rich. He didn't wiggle his head nervously in every direction while he spoke. When I talk, I wiggle my head. This is because I am not rich. I am upper-middle class, the lower end.

Do you understand?

Times Square.

The men who walk into the few remaining porn shops are sometimes handsome. I want to engage them in conversation.

I am depressed to see the sexual history of Times Square erased.

I won't claim that Times Square was a utopia, but it was certainly an important mecca and underworld.

Alas, the Eros has closed, and the Adonis.

The Gap takes up some of the slack, but not enough.

The Disney Store takes up none of the slack, unless you bring your direst sexual fantasies into the store, or unless you adopt the following style: he or she who verbalizes the sexual advances that commodities make on our imaginations and actions.

Dumbo is a sexual commodity.

Other commodities that haunt me are books and countries: I have been alphabetizing my books and I have been planning trips to Florida and Sicily. In Miami I want to become more of a guy by getting a tan and relaxing. In Taormina I will seek echoes of the boys that Baron Wilhelm von Gloeden photographed. See Emmanuel Cooper's *Fully Exposed: The Male Nude in Photography*. See the turn of the century.

I have been thinking seriously about prostitutes. My favorite porn star is Max Grand. In a free gay mag he advertised: "Pornstar. Max Grand. In NYC 11/6–11/18. Nationwide Pager _____." I may avail myself of his services and write at length about the experience.

Max Grand is not a commodity. He is a male escort from El Salvador. His films include *Latin Tongues*, *Hot Springs Orgy*, *Leather Confessions*, *Chicago Meat Packers*, and *Cut vs. Uncut*. He is a superstar.

In *WET Warehouse #2* he has a lovely speaking voice and a desk job.

Last night I dreamed my students complained about my pedagogy. I was trying, in a huge lecture course, to discuss the difference between cleanliness and filth. I was faultily explaining the coexistence of dirty and clean in the work of Marianne Moore and Elizabeth Bishop. I said, incoherently, "Moore's forms look clean but her metaphors are filthy." I was projecting slides of Renaissance paintings—close-ups of fabric.

So what if I made my students cry?

Everything quickly devolved into a textbook case of sexual harassment, and the dream ended.

I have been thinking about sadomasochism. I have not been practicing it.

The difference between praxis and mimesis, my old favorite, is not a crux I shall belabor today.

A few leatherfolk I've recently met are among the nicest people in my circle. I feel at home with them. They wear interesting clothes. They talk casually about gear: "I'm wearing a cock ring today."

They don't talk about identity: "I am a sadist." They talk about scenes: "I did an interesting scene."

I did an interesting scene today. I stood in the vicinity of a commodity and ignored it.

I pretended a person was a commodity. I stared at the person, once my friend, and ignored his soul.

I imagined him dead.

I smiled at him while picturing him evacuated.

It is difficult to think outside the lure of commodities.

I mean clothes and books and prostitutes and photographs and neighborhoods and corporations.

This is not a lecture about commodities. I am hardly qualified.

See Guy Hocquenghem's *Homosexual Desire*, especially the chapter on the anus, capitalism, and the family.

See the GUESS? ad campaign.

See Celine Dion.

See me. After class. For tips. On how to ignore commodities.

It is beginning to snow. I am beginning to remember the first short story I wrote, in 1976. I am beginning to forget my body.

My father saw Disney's *Fantasia* in Caracas, 1940. Or was it 1941? I romanticize the moment of him watching it. He saw it several times. It inspired him to want to become a musician. He took piano lessons. He conducted an orchestra, at least once, in college. He conducted the overture to *Don Giovanni*. Or so I remember him telling me. The memory is crucial yet vague.

In Caracas my father wanted to play Monopoly. He couldn't find it in the stores, or his father wouldn't buy it for him. I can't remember. So my father fabricated his own Monopoly board game. This proves his ingenuity. He was a self-starter.

I played Monopoly obsessively in fourth and fifth grade. My favorite color group contained Marvin Gardens. I loved owning cheap, easily conquered territories: Baltic Avenue.

For every lost tooth, I received a silver dollar under my pillow.

I've nearly given up telling stories about myself.

I don't advocate the self. I advocate the body, an envelope for practices and impulses: a switchboard.

The switchboard contains soul.

Sometimes I man my switchboard. Sometimes my various replacements man it. Sometimes no one mans it.

Sometimes New York City mans it.

Those are exciting moments, though they also resemble drowning.

A person is a style.

I'm waging war against the homogenization of styles.

Get your hands off my switchboard.

I shall now talk about my brother.

I have many brothers.

Five of them visited this morning. I took them shopping. We bought veal stew meat and eggs and Windex.

Keep your heart clean.

That is what I tell my five.

It is Xmas and time to buy gifts for my five.

This is a year for book buying. I want to support the independents.

For Brother #1, I will buy *Valley of the Dolls*.

For Brother #2, Jamaica Kincaid's *My Brother*.

For Brother #3, a wine encyclopedia.

For Brother #4, *Discipline and Punish*.

For Brother #5, *The Elements of Style*.

Where shall we dine for Xmas supper?

Downtown.

On the river.

Porridge for the first course, the second, and the third.

I want to starve the brothers.

Let them read but do not let them eat.

When we were young we had a tinsel Xmas tree. It came folded in a box. We unfolded it and surrounded it with gifts. Red balls hung from the fake silvery branches. I am certain that it was a fire hazard. It glittered in the room, beside the Heidegger.

We almost ate the Heidegger.

The wind whips through my room. The wind has a mission. It wants to cleanse my thought.

The wind is rattling through my brain. Do you hear? It whistles in the rafters, near the murder mysteries. I bought them at a chain.

Give fifty dollars to Children's Aid.

Don't mention it.

This Xmas, figure out why I'm in love with the aesthetic of autism, the aesthetic of incommunicado.

I admire writing that doesn't communicate, or that communicates blockage.

At the kosher deli the sight of a fat man eating a triple-decker sandwich dissuaded me from ordering a side dish of chopped liver.

Today I have listed impediments to embodiment.

I do not want to stop.

I enjoy suspense. Harmonic suspension in Wagner, Strauss, and Chopin is a history of masochism.

Wagner keeps your body distant from completion, so you may have the pleasure of interminable waiting.

The divergence between the left and right hands, in a Chopin morceau, is an agent of masochism. The right hand's melodic figuration moving separately from the pulsations of the left is a catalyst of masochistic experience in the listener.

The right hand lags behind.

You want it to speed up, but it can't.

The first time I experienced the masochistic oscillation, I was listening to "Siegfried Idyll."

Wrong. The first time I experienced a pulsation I'd call masochistic, I was observing a cut on a local thumb. The thumb was mine, but also not mine. The wound was the most beautiful object in the kitchen. The wound came from a juice glass, near the medicine bottle. Either the glass had a rough, broken edge, or another veiled object in the vicinity ripped my skin.

The room around the cut on the thumb was dulcet and nonverbal.

The kitchen of the cut was off the dark dining room.

The cut was a sign of greatness.

If I could only live up to the cut—if I could only equal it!

See Gaston Bachelard's *The Poetics of Space*.

My hands are cold from trills.

When I trill, my fingers grow numb.

This is a trill, from C to C-sharp.

It sounds like a razor. It sounds like Emily Dickinson's firmament.

To warm my fingers, I will stop writing.

My neurosystem's disturbed minutiae are the logical consequence of a shattered worldview.

If I could name the worldview and the cause of its shattering, I would be the master of my style.

As matters stand, I am merely its personal shopper.

(1998)

M/ORALITY

16 October 1998. Met President Clinton in the Oval Office. Gave him advice. Told him I admired his illicit sex. He smiled, eyes crinkly.

Told him I respected his oral adventures. Told him it was time a gay pundit spoke up on his behalf. Dubbed him the first queer president.

Called him Oscar Wilde. Read him extracts from *De Profundis*. Said the fin de siècle needed sexual martyrs. He volunteered.

He pretended to be interested in my speech. He put his head on my shoulder and inhaled the fumes of my assistance.

I tried to remember what Freud wrote about orality. Tried to make a point about oration, the mouth, long-windedness.

17 October 1998. Told Clinton I liked his body. Told him it was an honor to experience it from afar.

He shook his head, almost in tears, but didn't tell me to stop talking.

Told Clinton that his face had a bruised appearance. Apologized for bruising him.

He gave me Woody Allen's phone number, said I should get a quote from Woody for the moral story I was writing.

Asked Clinton for an opinion about *Bowers v. Hardwick*. Reminded him of the case's details. Discussed sodomy. Tried to define it. Failed.

∞

18 October 1998. Told Clinton that he was a small boy. Called him perverse. He said no.

Thanked him for déjà vu.

Told him I wanted back the word *moral*.

Advised him to stop bragging about God and the Bible and churchgoing.

Mrs. Clinton entered the office, saw us, said, "Excuse me, I'll leave you boys alone," shut the door. She was tough: she didn't care what he did with his body.

I said, "I don't want to take advantage of her good mood."

What about Mrs. Clinton's feelings? I began to worry about her point of view.

∞

19 October 1998. I hope my White House days last forever.

Clinton was glad I said "blow job," a beautiful coinage.

Told him our conversations were counterphobic counter-espionage.

He laughed.

Told him I was serious.

He said he knew my reputation for gravity.

Relished the president's transparency.

∞

20 October 1998. Asked Clinton if I could read his diary. He said he didn't keep one; he didn't have time to write things down. He travels at the speed of light.

Showed Clinton a suitcase full of porn I carry with me at all times. We laughed at the pictures, but we didn't laugh at our nostalgia.

Asked him about photography. Demolished his chance for divine election.

∞

21 October 1998. Clinton asked if I liked the hotel. I said the towels were rough; they abraded my skin. He was no longer listening. My voice trailed off.

Complimented his sexual inventiveness. Praised the cigar. Tried to be subtle. Told him that sex was old hat: he'd made it new. He bristled. I'd gone too far?

Told him I had a soft spot for the sexually humiliated. Again he looked weepy. Told him I planned to reorganize my schedule around his greatness.

∞

22 October 1998. My pass rebuffed.

I'm resigned to his heterosexuality.

Clicked on a microcassette recorder to tape our conversations. Promised Clinton I wouldn't sell the tapes.

Told him I was recording all my chats—not just White House ones—for a research project on flow and humiliation. I want to chart the movements up and down of a voice confessing or refusing to confess.

Silently admired his beefy chest. Tried to figure out whether he was a boy or a man, and why it mattered.

∞

23 October 1998. Massaged Clinton's shoulders. Removed a kink.

Praised his dorsal development.

Speculated about Jefferson and Sally Hemmings.

Asked Clinton the source of his fortune. A minion in the hallway hissed, "He's not rich!"

Mentioned failing health, faith healing.

∞

24 October 1998. Told him I prayed he wouldn't be punished.

Told him he deserved praise.

"For my humanity," he continued.

Talked McCarthyism, remembered Lillian Hellman, wished she were alive. Didn't mention Lillian's lies.

Explained Foucault to the president. Mentioned surveillance. Plotted resistance.

Clinton grew gleeful.

Read him extracts from Wilde's fairy tales.

"If only I were saying these things about myself," Clinton said, as if to himself.

∞

25 October 1998. Again propositioned Clinton. He refused.

He agreed, however, to watch.

So I called a service, requested an escort. Sam arrived. Husky and surly.

Sam blew me in a corner. I pilfered a climax. Clinton watched.

Was I dehumanizing Sam?

Later, at a party, Rosemary Woods accused me of idealism.

I am accustomed to accusation.

∞

26 October 1998. Asked Clinton for advice on growing older. He said he couldn't remember age forty. His mind grew vague. "Focus, focus," I demanded. He told me that this decade was a sad photographic negative of earlier decades.

Took his picture.

He called me "tendentious."

He agreed that we were cognates.

I was doing most of the work, but I would give him half the credit for our revelations.

∽

27 October 1998. We comforted each other with Al-Anon slogans.

A rash below my right eye: what does it signify? Clinton said sometimes disease doesn't mean anything.

Told him not to trust his euphoria.

∽

28 October 1998. Told him our intimacy must soon end. He accused me of faithlessness.

He came to my hotel and sat by the side of the tub while I soaked. He held my hand and I tried not to splash water on his suit, on his legalese.

Witches don't float: my body settled at the bottom of the tub.

He asked me to make a fist. He admired my biceps.

"The political is," he began, and hesitated, "is or is not personal?" He remembered feminism, forgot it, chewed his lower lip.

The Secret Service took him away.

∽

29 October 1998. He swiveled in his chair, as if to offer me his body.

"You're not very imaginative," he said.

He meant my approach to incarnation.

I played with the objects on his desk. I played with the paper clips. I played with the stapler. I played with the secretary when she entered and I played with the president when she exited.

"Purchases can't save your life," he cautioned.

He was supposedly capitalism's avatar. Was he now a turncoat?

∽

30 October 1998. Thanked him for tormenting my senses: spirit nerves palpated by the president.

"Why cherish overstimulation?" he asked. And then, "Why scapegoat it?"

I read him the poem about the unknown soldier.

We attempted to do a few true things together, some corporeal.

He promised to write a saxophone and piano duet for the two of us to perform.

He promised to drive to Arlington with me in an armored car.

On the way he would tell me his plans for the next century.

I would help him bring these plans to fruition.

∞

31 October 1998. He advised me to call the diary a fable.

"But it's true," I said.

He listened, enjoying my sadistic gibes.

The Oval Office's openness depressed me.

"Shouldn't there be guards?" I asked.

"No prison so strong that love can't force an entrance," he offered.

He called me his "little bastard": a friend of the family.

"Are you immoral?" I asked.

"Bad?" he rehearsed, mishearing. He was searching for a key word. *Bad* unlocked some doors. Why not try it on every gate?

Mrs. Clinton entered to discuss disgrace—its procedures, its secret advantages. I turned away, disguising my face, pretending to be someone else.

She mistook me for a reporter scribbling on a steno pad.

After she left, I thanked the president for letting me invade his privacy. Told him that I stood for moral causes. Told him that his body was sacred. Told him that it was moral to wish for the momentary obliteration that arousal offered. Assured him that blow jobs were their own absolution. Reminded him of sodomy's ancient dignity. Celebrated his sodomitical awakening. Tried to persuade him not to mend his ways. Promised that if we ever saw each other on the street, I'd pretend not to recognize him and wouldn't force on him the memory of our acquaintance. Thanked him for smashing my ego. Blessed him for erasing me.

Told him the nation loved his body, respected its wherewithal. Reminded him that God was sexually errant. Persuaded him that God was the author of wandering. Told him that God wasn't part of my vocabulary but I wanted to communicate with the president by borrowing theological terms. Thanked him for pillow talk. Was too profuse in my thanks. Said farewell. Gave him a deep, Taoist hug, like Robin Williams and Matt Damon in *Good Will Hunting*.

Checked out of the hotel.

Revised my estimate of his sexual magnetism. Indeed, I've exaggerated it.

∞

1 November 1998. Clinton incommunicado. My pathos no longer interests him. Without the possibility of ever again speaking to him I am flooded with fragments of our afternoons:

The president as I felt him through his pants or as I imagined him.

His flat face, few features.

His poverty.

President as hobo.

President as naked wretch.

My knowledge that I could decimate him.

Even when he whispers, he is shouting.

The door always shut to Mrs. Clinton. Why am I more precious than she?

My moral staunchness.

His choice of me as confidante and confessor.

His lie: "I love you."

His quick abandonment of what he said yesterday.

My mouth.

The rules of time he broke.

Softness and availability of my breast in the Oval Office afternoon.

Sex disgusts me, but I swallow the disgust.

Later, the disgust returns.

He asked why I repeat the disgust if I dislike it.
I replied: disgust refines consciousness.
He called my mind inferior.
I watched his infraction and excused it.
He watched me watching. He sucked my omniscience. He had none of his own.

(1998)

OBSCENITY: A CELEBRATION

(phrases and philosophies on the centenary of Oscar Wilde's trial)

1.

I must not be pious. Oscar Wilde would have refused piety. I must not be sentimental. That stance, too, the master would have overturned. Exactly one hundred years ago (May 20, 1895), under Britain's notorious Labouchère Amendment, which penalized "gross indecency" between men, Oscar Wilde, prime minister of the paradox, was sentenced to two years of hard labor in prison—this on the heels of his fabulously successful *Importance of Being Earnest*. What crimes did he commit? He practiced love between men and dared to declare it a renaissance; he refused to call his *Picture of Dorian Gray* a perverted book, refused to agree that there existed immoral books, refused to be consistent, refused to submit his language to the thumb of fact.

Wilde's imprisonment ranks as one of literature's greatest tragedies: it silenced and effectively killed him. In disgrace, health ruined, spirit broken, he died five years later. For much of the next century men and women would fear homosexuality because of Wilde's specter. However, since Stonewall, and the flowering of movements toward sexual self-determination and nonconformity, some of which we call gay or lesbian, Oscar Wilde has become a hero—prophet of an impulse, a politics, a populace.

It is no exaggeration to call him the fountainhead of a certain queer liberation—even though, rereading Wilde's essays in light of his martyrdom's centenary, I find he speaks not specifically in praise of sexual liberty; not specifically in premonitory celebration of an identity we now call gay; but, rather, that he preaches the value of the individual's desire, even to the point of anarchy. He champions language's independence—the necessity that words and styles be permitted to range freely, even if the dissoluteness of their peregrination seems, to the cautious observer, catastrophic. And he praises art. Not because art is good for the soul. Not because art ameliorates suffering. Not because art is pretty, or pacific, or because it adds luster to the commonwealth. Art is most important, Wilde suggests, when it approaches the obscene; when it defies community standards of good taste; when it stops our ordinary patterns of knowing, and replaces them with disturbing queries that may, in time, turn into delirious habit.

2.

The function of this centenary is to inform us how far we still must travel in pursuit of Utopia. Wilde wrote, "A map of the world that does not include Utopia is not worth even glancing at, for it leaves out the one country at which Humanity is always landing." At the end of this ruined century, let us set sail; the ideal on whose shores we finally land might horrify us. The ideal might include the lewd. It might include desires that few decent citizens admit to harboring.

Wilde wrote, "The form of government that is most suitable to the artist is no government at all. Authority over him and his art is ridiculous." Wilde wrote passionately about art and anarchy; he said next to nothing about homosexuality. But is there a difference between a forbidden sexuality and a forbidden artistic impulse? I won't differentiate homosexuality and anarchy, for Wilde's nonconformity, which, constitutionally, Americans had better respect, boasted sexual disobedience as its reeking, redemptive foundation.

I don't countenance violence, but I do support thought's disruptiveness—the shock of speech, the capacity of art to undermine and to unsettle. Wilde: "Art is the most intense mode of Individualism that the world has known. I am inclined to say that it is the only real mode of Individualism the world has known." We have not begun, in this country, to value the artist. I return to Wilde not because I want us to say *poor Oscar* but because I want us to remember that the powerful and the privileged were once afraid of him; I want us to consider what verbal, vocal, and aesthetic impulses, today, still inspire dread. As Ed Cohen pointed out in his book, *Talk on the Wilde Side,* Wilde shocked not only because he was homosexual (and then some), but because he represented the antimasculine. We may like to think that gender mores have advanced since Wilde's time; that, today, we would not punish Wilde for his harmless transgressions. But have we made room in this nation for the effeminate? For the male body that refuses virility? For language that abstains from linearity and commerce? Wilde's beneficent assault on decency continues when we take him at his word, and stop trying to sanitize or sentimentalize what we love in order that we might say, publicly, that we love it.

3.

My attitude toward nationality is defined by diaspora. When I see an outcast, I swell with fellow feeling, and greet him or her as my Wandering Jew compatriot. Nations interest me when they are dispersed; nationalities inspire me when they are unacknowledged. Oscar Wilde is not American, but I feel nationalistic about him; to his corpse I pledge bitter allegiance. Saluting him,

I strike an attitude toward the sentence; a pose (a way of positioning my body in public) meant to affront, meant to be a front, and meant to prove that the obscenity he was forced to represent is a glory, unrealizable, still rainbowing the future. I read and live in the shadow of Wilde's gallows.

To say I date my desire's and my thought's nativity from Wilde's disgrace proves that I lack a deep, responsible sense of chronology, and that I tell time according to archetypes and abstractions. In my head, events weave together a Weird Sister fabric of emergencies (a Glorious Revolution, a Magna Carta, an assassination, a birth), and in this free-fall internalization of history, the looming, determining occurrence is the sentencing of Oscar Wilde.

On his tombstone, in Paris's Père-Lachaise Cemetery, are engraved lines from his prison poem, "The Ballad of Reading Gaol":

And alien tears will fill for him
    Pity's long-broken urn,
For his mourners will be outcast men,
    And outcasts always mourn.

The moral of Wilde's grave: dare to call yourself an outcast. Outcast is an easy robe to wear; it is not fancy or exclusive. On a literal level, homosexuality, as a doctrine or a conceptual system, arises from Wilde's suffering. But on a more fanciful level, from Wilde's grave blooms a thorny diversity and challenge: the possibility that we might not have ready names for our desires; the necessity that we must legally tolerate—even celebrate—the dreams and impulses that seem, to the frightened eye, obscene.

I believe that people should be polite to each other. I believe that wealth should be more fairly distributed. Et cetera. But I also believe that desire is extreme and antisocial, and that the true artist is always in danger of ending up in prison. There are many Oscar Wildes in prison today, sentenced for what they have written. Salman Rushdie is Oscar Wilde.

4.

I am not a homosexual. I am, these days, an individual, chatty and curious, after the type of Oscar Wilde.

Which means: I am most like Oscar Wilde not in my sexual tastes but in my devotion to metaphor. What is metaphor? The urge to compare unlike things, to yoke incommensurables together; the desire to be wrong (wrong-minded, wrong-tongued); the wish to avoid literality and law. I am more committed to metaphor than I am to any creed. Individuals should be allowed to weld together two objects, two principles, two vistas, that are not conventionally allied. Homosexuality is just a metaphor that some unimaginative people find difficult to tolerate or understand.

I suppose I am saying irresponsible things, as if this were private speech, when, in fact, it is mercilessly public. As Cecily, in *The Importance of Being Earnest*, describes: "it is simply a very young girl's record of her own thoughts and impressions, and consequently meant for publication." Wilde inspires me to violate the line between diary and journalism.

In Wilde's *Salomé*, Herodias wants to forbid metaphor: she says, "The moon is like the moon, that is all." But without metaphor, without the gold of comparison, we sink into complacency. Today Wilde would not be merely a sexual liberationist; he would insist on the importance of metaphor—the importance of traveling in untoward directions, and of making statements that are not entirely true, but that give purposeless pleasure.

5.

What do we now call obscene? In what states would Oscar Wilde, performing sodomy, be subject to arrest? For publishing what varieties of pornography would Wilde now be sentenced? For what impersonations and provocations would he be forced to pick oakum until his fingers bled? Would Wilde, if he were alive today, earnestly come out? Or would he choose to remain veiled in ironies, oblivious to the cant of categories? If I were to choose a profession for Oscar Wilde today, it would not be playwright; it would be pornographer. Or blasphemer. Sometimes it is important not to be able to tell whether one is reading a poem or a polemic, whether one is watching a movie or a religious rite, whether one is inhabiting a nation or a laboratory, whether one is looking at a masterpiece or observing a pornographic spectacle. These are uncertainties—of genre, of propriety—in whose grip I am convinced Wilde would have wanted us to remain.

Wilde: "In France, in fact, they limit the journalist, and allow the artist almost perfect freedom. Here we allow absolute freedom to the journalist and entirely limit the artist." I doubt that Wilde would be pleased to see his name on this page. If I am spending his name here, it is because I want to praise those practices of intoxication known as art, and to remind us that art is nearly always obscene, if only because it upstages reality. Wilde was perversity's finest diplomat, translating it into poised phrases; of his career's many acts, the most beautiful was his disgrace. Wilde: "What lies before me is my past." Wilde lies before us; any map of Utopia must include—must answer to—his scars.

(1995)

III

STARS

CELEBRITY DREAMING

1.

Over the last twenty years, I have dreamt frequently of celebrities, sometimes every night. In the mornings I write down my dreams in a blue notebook. Often I incorporate the material in a poem. Otherwise it lies fallow.

Many of my dream notes are in Manhattan Mini Storage. Recently I visited them.

After a star dream, I wake up thrilled: I've "scored," without effort, in my sleep! I've met Sophia Loren, Maria Callas, Joan Didion! The stars never pay much attention to me, but I don't mind. I'm content to be subordinate.

2.

Selected dreams of movie stars, 1978–1998:

Sophia Loren and I watched her latest movie at an Upper East Side theater.

Sophia Loren came over to my house for supper. I asked her what she was working on. She wouldn't say, although I begged.

Julie Andrews worked as a lounge singer.

Julie Andrews was exhausted.

I telephoned Peggy Wood (who played the Mother Abbess in *The Sound of Music*) to ask for advice on how to sing "Some Enchanted Evening." Peggy, jealous, offered no encouragement.

I packed Elizabeth Taylor's bag, including a nightgown with a cappuccino stain on it. Liz was incognito: her roommate didn't know that Liz was Liz.

I met Liz at Jackie Onassis's country house. I nearly told Liz that I'd just seen *The Only Game in Town*, but I didn't want to be gauche.

A midget rode on Liz Taylor's handlebars, while Sophia Loren sat atop a geometric sculpture that resembled her figure but was vastly inferior, and Lyle Lovett, in the background, posed as a supermodel.

Liza Minnelli tap-danced on a Flatiron District sidewalk.

Barbra Streisand played an athlete in a movie; later, I auditioned for a part in *One Flew over the Cuckoo's Nest*, its script covered in sauerkraut.

I led Bette Davis back from the dead. We sat on a beach. She wore asylum clothing: white tennies.

Ramon Novarro sang at a nightclub. He wore a Tarzan costume; his legs were flabby. I knew we were meant for each other, though I wondered how he could still be alive.

Keir Dullea, star of *Bunny Lake Is Missing*, gave a lecture on the poet Louise Bogan.

Charlie Chaplin sat near me in a fancy uptown Manhattan restaurant.

Alec Baldwin had plastic surgery so that the narcotics police wouldn't recognize him. A hot date told him she preferred the old face; she took a blowtorch to the fake layer and melted it.

Jean-Paul Belmondo spent the night at my house. He was distraught about Brigitte Bardot. I couldn't help him.

I played the part of Orestes in a photo-montage version of Oscar Wilde's *Salomé*.*

3.

All of my celebrities resemble each other. The women are powerful, seductive, distant. The men are powerful, seductive, distant. Neither the men nor the women thoroughly endorse me, but they tolerate my proximity, and sometimes, they lead me on. Occasionally I manage to lure them into bed.

Usually they are too busy to be aggressive, though sometimes it is possible that they might turn rageful. I am a victim with a sneaky agenda, who wants to "make time" with them. I struggle to be nice, though niceness is an arduous masquerade. Sometimes, however, I behave aggressively; sometimes I retaliate against a celebrity who has gone too far.

4.

Selected dreams of writers, 1978–1998:

Joyce Carol Oates sent me a special-delivery thank-you note for a dinner I'd served her.

Joyce Carol Oates (wearing a negligee) hugged me and said she was hearing voices, which meant she was writing a story.

Joyce Carol Oates performed Salome's dance of the seven veils in a baseball stadium.

I spent all day writing Joyce Carol Oates a lengthy fan letter, endlessly revised.

Susan Sontag wore a pink miniskirt and sat like an odalisque on her couch. Three people were eavesdropping on our conversation; she shooed them away with a radical fist. I told her that I'd loved her ever since I'd read *On Photography* when I was twenty-one. She smiled at the praise.

* Orestes does not appear in *Salomé*.

Joan Didion, beside me on a couch, said, "We like people."
She disapproved of writers who didn't like people. Wanting to be
alone with me, Didion urged a dull intern with sharp literary
tastes to leave the room.

I visited Elizabeth Hardwick, who was memorizing a Haydn
sonata.

I applied for a job as Jean Rhys's secretary (she was a lawyer).

I saw Toni Morrison enter a bookstore.

I guarded Adrienne Rich's purse, containing health supplies. In
an attempt to please her, I bought her a pair of shrunken nylons.

My psychiatrist lived with Marianne Moore.

John Ashbery's phone number was only one digit different
from mine, and consequently he often received my phone calls.
At a Chelsea AIDS clinic, we conversed, and he found the phrase
blue velvet in a poem of mine.

I slept with John Ashbery.

At a party, I began (in a trance) to flirt with James Merrill. I
hoped to become his escort.

I suggested to W. H. Auden that we live together. He had
dyed his hair and lost most of his wrinkles.

I visited James Schuyler, who was a young man living on a
bayou.

I met Roland Barthes at a café in Cambridge, Massachusetts.
His sexiness almost made me faint. I said, "Are you really Roland
Barthes?" Indeed he was. He took me to his apartment on Brattle
Street, and I fell into his arms. He massaged my fingers; I noted
his beaky nose.

I was on a panel with Jacques Lacan. Rude, he chatted with
another panelist while I was trying to deliver my paper.

A thin, strict woman—the sister of Thoreau or Hawthorne—
owned a restaurant and wanted to sleep with me. We hugged. In
lieu of sex, I recited an Emerson paragraph that mentioned her.

5.

If, in real life, I meet one of my celebrities, then dreams of that
figure stop. I have dreamt about certain celebrities so obsessively

over the past two decades that I imagine that the nocturnal narratives form a savings account, a supernatural bribe: if I dream enough about the star, eventually my brain waves will mingle with hers, and she'll get the message that I love her. My dreams about human magnitudes are a telepathic project—an attempt to influence a remote deity.

Sometimes the celebrity shows up only briefly in the dream— a cameo appearance. Other times, the star stays for the night. Her fame gives me a charge, but it is also an obstacle. It sits between us, an excuse for her indifference. If she manages to violate her renown to offer me an endearment, I will truly have accomplished something in my sleep.

Perversely, I believe my dreams to be aesthetic creations: their memory lingers for years. I feel toward them as toward a marvelous performance of a ballet, seen from a distance, yet perfectly recalled, and subject to restorative, retrospective idealization.

The dreams are acts of restitution: dead writers are reborn, retired singers perform again, dictators behave decently.

6.

Selected dreams of visual artists, 1978–1998:
    I met Andy Warhol. I called him a "cunt."

7.

I have enough of a psychoanalytic bent to imagine that the celebrities in my dreams are screens for my parents as I remember them from childhood: omnipotent figures. And yet the dream stars are also grandiose self-portraits. I make no secret of the fact that I love fame; that I want to meet famous people; that I want to become famous. However, I am also afraid of fame. When, in waking life, I have the opportunity to meet a celebrity, I am bashful, diffident, uncharming. If I were to see a star walking toward me at a party, I would probably stoop to tie my shoes, and thus miss my chance.

The celebrities who fascinate me are usually old enough to be my parents. I am relatively uninterested in young stars. Nor am I preoccupied by stars my own age, with the exception of Alec Baldwin and a few, choice others.

8.

Selected dreams of opera singers, 1978–1998:

Maria Callas gave a concert at my yeshiva. I was sent to the basement for talking out loud during the program. Afterward I met Callas. I said "Bravo," and she said "Thank you." Her skin was very smooth. She said, "Wasn't it a wonderful performance?" I could see a bit of her breast. She showed me pictures she'd taken of her husband, Mr. Meneghini. Then she shut herself in the dressing room.

Maria Callas sang badly, and I looked into her mouth: an enormous, quixotic, original space. We were watching old movies, with which she had affinity.

I sat beside Leontyne Price in a car. We were talking about voice: hers. She said something noble about retirement.

I telephoned Leontyne Price and heard, on her answering machine, a tune from *Il Trovatore*. Then she picked up and apologized for having screened the call. I told her I was eager to hear her sing in New York, and she laughed, recognizing my insincerity. Then I said, "Well, bye, Leontyne," and tried to pronounce her name correctly.

Monserrat Caballé coached me in the role of Leonora in *Il Trovatore*.

Frederica von Stade gave a public interview, in the Met lobby, before a performance of *Der Rosenkavalier*. In order to preserve her voice, she sang her responses rather than spoke them.

I asked Renata Scotto out to dinner; after all, we'd belonged to the same theater troupe in Los Gatos, California.

Kathleen Battle put her foot down and burst into tears when she heard a student sing Gershwin songs unidiomatically.

Dawn Upshaw had a lousy apartment, no privacy.

I listened to a recording of *Madama Butterfly* sung by André Previn's first wife, Dory. ("Pre-Mia," I said to a fellow listener.)

An unidentified soprano was lowered into the center of the audience during an innovative staging of *Lucia di Lammermoor*. I was afraid she would land on me.

9.

I don't mind being a person who dreams about celebrities. I don't think the activity is pathetic or pathological. It clutters my nights with melodramas to which I must pay strict attention, behaving like a faithful scribe or historian.

I don't expect kindness from my celebrities; I expect only tolerance, a cold forbearance.

10.

Selected dreams of Anna Moffo, 1978–1998:

I stood in the wings watching Anna Moffo's Metropolitan Opera debut.

I attended a master class in Anna Moffo's white-carpeted living room.

I discovered that Anna Moffo had roles in the Jewish cinema long before her operatic debut.

I met Anna Moffo and her first husband, Mario Lanfranchi. She was singing *mélodies* by a nonexistent French composer named Janet.

I saw Anna Moffo in a combined production of *Rigoletto*, *Trovatore*, and *Butterfly*; her costume was a black-and-white bathrobe.

I discussed the last two notes of *La Traviata* with Anna Moffo.

A boy fell from the Met balcony while Anna Moffo sang *La Bohème*.

Anna Moffo left in my room a beautiful huge-buttoned coat, a purse, and a copy of her recent recording of an obscure Bellini opera.

As an innovative digression during *Butterfly*, Anna Moffo carried a tray of hair spray through the audience.

I ate ice cream with Anna Moffo while sitting on a rock.

I bought Anna Moffo a black umbrella and delivered it to her at the Met.

Anna Moffo lent me a copy of *Where the Wild Things Are*: a literary version, with more text, fewer pictures.

Anna Moffo and I shopped for antiques.

I went backstage to meet Anna Moffo at a 1968 Met gala. I told my boyfriend, "I know we're in a hurry to leave, but it's 1968 again, and this is my chance to meet Anna Moffo in 1968."

11.

Selected dreams of pop singers, 1978–1998:

In my mailbox I saw a postcard, addressed to my boyfriend, who had inquired whether a certain river was polluted: "Steve: River is OK. Tell Debbie Harry to stop peeing in it."

12.

In dreams, commodities function as celebrities. In 1996 I dreamt of a yellow patent leather Anna Sui purse that was really a shoe, and, a few months later, I dreamt of a blue Neutrogena face splash. The appearance of the word *Neutrogena*, in the dream, was as exciting as the arrival of a celebrity at a party: it lit up the surrounding bleakness.

13.

Selected dreams of composers and conductors, 1978–1998:

I agreed to be "kept" by Virgil Thomson, who promised to take me to Israel. All I'd need to spend of my own funds was one hundred dollars.

I went to the opera with Benjamin Britten. We sat in the front row. The sets were falling apart.

I flirted with Herbert von Karajan at a performance of *Tales of Hoffmann*.

Franz Schubert fought Rambo in a boxing ring. (Ronald Reagan watched.) Schubert needed to defend his honor. Before the fight began, I heard a beautiful Schubert composition. I wanted to tell him about its beauty, before he died.

14.

I am not the only person to dream of celebrities. A psychologist told me that he dreamt of shaking hands with Nixon. Another psychologist told me that he dreamt for years about Keanu Reeves, and that many of his patients started dreaming of Princess Diana after her death: "she functioned like Glinda, the Good Witch, stepping out of nowhere to let you know that you don't need to be afraid of your unconscious." A psychoanalyst said that his patients have recently been dreaming of characters from *Seinfeld*. A writer told me that he dreamt of seeing Pablo Picasso naked ("his penis was featureless, overly simplified, like an abstract painting"). The young man who cuts my hair confessed that he gave Leonardo DiCaprio a haircut on a beach in a dream; then they had sex. Another time he dreamt of Christy Turlington, who said hello. He did not have sex with Christy. A fellow English professor confided that he dreamt of Hedy Lamarr, and that then, the next morning, he heard her name mentioned on the radio. He marveled at the coincidence. I, too, marvel at it, though I can't interpret it.

15.

Selected dreams of leaders, 1978–1998:
    Princess Diana gave a book party at Area, the nightclub. The party seemed an illustration in a Sartre or Camus novel.
    My mother dated Hitler. His first name was Franz. We called him Franz Hitlerino.
    A woman friend of mine had phone sex with Dan Quayle. They stayed on the line all night.

16.

One of my earliest celebrity fantasies concerned Brigitte Bardot: in second grade, I fantasized that she was my mother, that she picked me up from school in a white limo, and that we traveled together to France. I decided that my name was Pierre, and, for a spell, I signed my papers "Pierre," and, sometimes, "Mary Poppins."

Eventually, my teacher put a stop to this nonsense.

(1998)

THE ELIZABETH TAYLOR PUZZLE

Quoth Elizabeth Taylor, in and out of her roles:

It's got to be told and you never let me tell it.
  I am pretty enough. I try not to look like a slob.
  I'm best from the back.
  I loved it. Every awful moment of it, I loved.
  So I got into my costume, which seemed to weigh hundreds of pounds—a huge thing made of twenty-four-karat gold thread. The headdress itself weighed about fifteen pounds and was two and a half feet high. I got the whole drag on and crawled up on the Sphinx, feeling totally trembly.

1.

Once I had a jigsaw puzzle of Theda Bara in *Cleopatra*. Her makeup looked like soot, applied with blind, crazy fingers. It wasn't a maquillage that any realism required. I required it.

From the slumber of fragments I woke Theda Bara; I kissed her by assembling her. I loved patiently putting together a star from pieces that looked, individually, like branches, or estuaries, or shuddering birds.

The puzzle sat without an audience. I am the only one who saw it. If you don't exhibit a puzzle to a friend, who will solve it?

2.

Whenever I was sick, and only when I was sick, my mother permitted me to read movie magazines. Feverish, nauseated, convalescing, I read them in bed. I am talking about the 1960s.

In *Photoplay*, I discovered Elizabeth Taylor, whom I'd never seen in a film. Columnists clucked about Liz and Dick and an expensive disaster, *Cleopatra*, which I'd not see until I was grown; but I worshipped it, as an abstraction, because her salary had been $1 million, and because the film had nearly ruined Twentieth Century Fox. *Cleopatra* seemed a feat of weight and waste for which I was suited. Or so I fancied, in the silence of 1965.

I read John O'Hara's *BUtterfield 8* because Elizabeth Taylor had won her first Oscar for playing its "slut" heroine, Gloria Wandrous. *BUtterfield 8*: I thought about butter and the number 8, which, placed on its side, was the sign of infinity, and a hieroglyphic representation of two breasts. I touched the words *wondrous* and *wandering* stored in the name *Wandrous*, and planned to pick up a prostitute at the pharmacy's paperback-novel rack.

During a garage sale, I confided to my mother's friend Rita, a block lady with black bouffant, tanned thighs, and raucous laugh, a lady who later left the block to run massage workshops in the mountains: "You look like Elizabeth Taylor." I knew it was a compliment but I pretended not to know. Rita had a resemblance; I had a longing. Rita laughed, and my mother, who overheard the confidence, laughed, too, and I asked, with feigned naïveté, "Is Elizabeth Taylor beautiful?"

On the school bus, on the way to Santa Cruz's dilapidated boardwalk for a field trip, I overheard a dirty-minded boy say,

"Liz Taylor has big boobs." This comment was a clue. I memorized it. "Liz Taylor has big boobs" taught me what boys wanted,
what girls gave. I hadn't known that Elizabeth Taylor and "boobs"
were synonymous; I'd thought Elizabeth Taylor was an atmosphere, a stature. On the bus I was learning otherwise. I was
learning about her body and my body. I was learning about size.

3.

After watching Elizabeth Taylor movies I feel eerily masculine.
Her beauty shoves me out of maleness and compresses me back
into it, as if I were an astronaut losing gravity and then regaining
it, or a sea voyager suffering the bends. When she appears on
screen, she alters scales of dimension: we're not wearing 3-D
spectacles, but her femaleness leaps out at us, and her gorgeousness seems a suicide cult we are drugged into wanting to join. I
have the temptation to wear her beauty like a campaign button
("I Like Ike"); to adhere to her beauty as a philosophical program
or a party platform. Elizabeth Taylor is beautiful by objective
standards, so my fandom isn't madness. To espouse Elizabeth
Taylor as gorgeous is to take credit for her beauty, to nominate
oneself as its shadow and consequence, or even its cause.

Voting for Elizabeth Taylor in the adoration sweepstakes, I
dream I'm getting credit for heterosexuality, fractionally fitting
into it: if I adore Liz, aren't I 1/100th straight? Staring at her, I
hallucinate that she is an extravagance I am presenting to the
world; that she is my responsibility; that her breasts and her
hairdo and her glamour in a Richard Avedon photograph (circa
1964) enthrall because Liz's dominatrix aspect upsets the photographic balance of power. I, her advocate, cheer her sadistic
beauty: with my eyes, I say "Get 'em, Liz!" Gender, carried to extremes, is compellingly extraterrestrial.

You will say, "He has an Elizabeth Taylor fetish," and I will
meekly smile, and you will either discountenance my love, or will
admit that years ago you adored her, but outgrew the crush. Or
did you sink deeper into it and never surface? Did you grow slug-
gish, watching *National Velvet* for the thirteenth time?

4.

Elizabeth Taylor and masturbation: recall the marvelous scene in *National Velvet* when she plays invisible horsie in bed, pretending to ride a horse, making it go faster and faster, panting as it accelerates and she guides it over hurdles, her screen-sister Angela Lansbury in bed dreaming of boys but Elizabeth Taylor as Velvet hot for a horse named Pie, as in mincemeat pie.

References to eating, hunger, and gluttony mark most of Taylor's films. In *A Place in the Sun*, she enters the pool room where Montgomery Clift is playing, and she nibbles. In *BUtterfield 8*, she says, "Waitress, could you bring us some french fries?" In the first scene of *Who's Afraid of Virginia Woolf?* she eats cold meat straight out of the fridge. "Eat, Velvet," says her screen-mother, the austere Anne Revere, in *National Velvet*.

The elephantine giantism of such vehicles as *Giant* and *Elephant Walk* signify that she's a star, that the emotions she inspires are huge, and that her figure is large. (Is it really? The allegedly "large" Liz often seems tiny. Liz is a matter of perspective.) It has always been considered acceptable to comment on her size. Stanley Kauffmann in *The New Republic* described her Cleopatra as "a plump, young American matron in a number of Egyptian costumes and makeups." She was called plump long before she was actually plump. Fluids and solids that pass through Elizabeth Taylor's body, or that stay in her body, are part of the public record.

5.

In childhood, in *Velvet's* wake, to capitalize on her association with animals, Elizabeth Taylor wrote and published a book, called *Nibbles and Me*, about her pet chipmunk. The word *nibbles* turns easily to *nipples*, and the phrase *nibbles and me*, or *nipples and me*, seems an equation: Nibbles = Me, or Nipples = Me. The "me" emotion—narcissism, identity—comes to fruition in the young star's love of a pet whose name signifies a "cute" orality. It's charming to nibble. It's less charming to gorge. (Nipples: the public has been permitted to see most of Elizabeth Taylor's breasts, but never her nipples.) In 1946, at fourteen, in *Nibbles and Me*, before she developed the body whose bosom and salary and appetite became fable, Elizabeth Taylor sketched the matrix of eating and being eaten, of mouth and breast, of cannibalism and nourishment, which would define her body in the public imagination.

Voted "Mother of the Year" in 1953 by America's florists, she said, "To me the most beautiful smells in the world are babies and bacon." She tries to pass as a model mother, but she seems, instead, to take easy, profound, scandalous delight in the human body as meat. She sounds like a cannibal, her baby a rasher sizzling on the grill. ("I'm a wolf," she says in *A Little Night Music*.) What do babies smell like? Sometimes, shit and piss. Elizabeth Taylor at her most acceptable, the Mother of the Year, the Bride of the Year, Elizabeth Taylor before the Betty Ford clinic, was she-who-nibbles, was the sign of *our* desire to nibble, was bacon inside a body so bounteous in its beauty and its significances that only an ungrateful public would ever consider a performance of hers to be poor, or a sum bestowed on her to be wasted.

6.

But *Cleopatra* outraged the scandal-hungry public because it wasted money, and because Elizabeth Taylor was blamed for the waste, and because her performance was considered lousy though she was paid a million for it, and because, after having "stolen" Eddie Fisher from Debbie Reynolds, she dumped him for already-married Richard Burton, instigating *"Le Scandale,"* causing the Vatican to publish a letter denouncing Elizabeth as a home-wrecker and an erotic vagrant, and *Photoplay* to run a reader's poll to discover whether its audience "could ever forgive what Liz has done," and a U.S. congresswoman to suggest that Taylor be refused entrance into the United States "on the grounds of undesirability," and a minister to advocate that Liz be burned in effigy.

To understand *"Le Scandale,"* we need to consider Elizabeth Taylor's tracheotomy.

In 1961, during the early months of *Cleopatra*, Elizabeth Taylor almost died. To save her life, doctors opened her throat at the windpipe. The tracheotomy scar shows up in most of her subsequent movies, including *Cleopatra*: "I make no attempt to conceal it," she says. (And yet she underwent plastic surgery to erase it.) We see the scarred throat in a famous photograph that originally appeared in *Vogue* (with an article heralding "The New Cleopatra Complex"). Elizabeth is in Cleopatra drag, a snake brooch hardly joining the two halves of her dress over her cleavage, and she stares wearily and confrontationally at the viewer. Is she bored? Is boredom a part of beauty?

Nearly thirty years later, the photograph was included in an exhibition called "The Indomitable Spirit," compiled by "photographers and friends united against AIDS." The scar is symbol of Elizabeth's "indomitable spirit": she's survived MGM, the star system, multiple marriages, and near-fatal illnesses. The scar marks her throat: site of voice, self-articulation, autobiography. She is scarred when she is most beautiful (in 1962, during the production of *Cleopatra*), when she is considered worth $1 million (more than anyone had ever been paid for doing anything, according to *Time*). Look at the expense and expanse of Taylor's creamy skin; stare at the cleavage, the Cleopatra makeup, the strange quaint bangs, and see the scar.*

7.

Follow the metaphor trail of the scar:

Elizabeth on a stretcher, carried blue and breathless into an ambulance (*Newsweek* called her "Sleeping Beauty"); Elizabeth Taylor looking like Goldfinger, gold and dead at the end of

* Postscript, 1998: Elizabeth Taylor had a brain tumor, which was removed. She agreed to be photographed after surgery, bald, sans wig, for *Life* magazine: an extraordinary act of star abjection, shamelessness, and solidarity with the world's other sufferers. Said Liz: "I won't dye my hair for a while. I'll let it grow out white. In the meantime, I don't mind being bald. For years the gossip sheets have been claiming I've had face-lifts. Now they'll have to eat their words. Look. *No scars!*"

Cleopatra—her body so expensive ($1 million) that her allure *is* bullion; Cleopatra laid out for the viewer and the camera, as our eye pans slowly up her body, the money shot, to prove that Elizabeth Taylor was worth what Fox paid; Elizabeth Taylor as a face-lift patient in *Ash Wednesday*, real surgery footage to show beauty's connection to mutilation, and then convalescing Taylor swathed in mummy bandages, her face—the little of it we can see between the bandages—made up to look black and blue and genderless; Elizabeth Taylor falling off Pie in *National Velvet*, convalescing in the hospital, flat on her back, trying to pass as a boy jockey; Elizabeth Taylor fund-raising as national chair of the American Foundation for AIDS Research.

Her Oscar for *BUtterfield 8* was supposedly a sympathy prize, awarded because she had almost died. The scar, like her Oscar, proves that she is a power, that she has passed through puberty and ritual scarification. Elizabeth Taylor debuted as a child, and made films during every phase of her physical development. Consequently, her films are a piecemeal commentary on the meanings of a body's maturation, and the mysteries of that abrupt descent or nosedive we call puberty, when, by acquiring the stigmata of secondary sexual characteristics, we're deep-frozen into gender.

8.

Elizabeth Taylor's voice doesn't match her body; critics pan her acting on the grounds of vocal incongruity. She has a vestigial British accent; her voice sometimes curdles, as when she screams at the end of *Suddenly, Last Summer*, and we hear a dip or hollow or indentation inside the scream, and her scarf, blowing in the screen wind, covers her throat.

Critic Brendan Gill wrote in *The New Yorker* that *Cleopatra* would have made a great silent film. Elizabeth Taylor is an "effective" Cleopatra (what is the effect?) until she speaks. Her voice kills her as icon, and brands her as "a ward heeler's wife screeching at a block party." Critic Judith Crist condemns Taylor's voice in *Cleopatra* for rising "to fishwife levels," and associates this

shrillness with her physicality: "She is an entirely physical creature, no depth of emotion apparent in her kohl-laden eyes. . . ."
BUtterfield 8 opens with a long voiceless sequence; Taylor-as-
Gloria wakes up beside a blue phone off the hook; and Taylor
stays off the hook, too, silently smoking, brushing her teeth and
rinsing her mouth with liquor, writing "No Sale" on the mirror,
stealing a mink from the closet of her trick's wife. *Secret Ceremony*
and *Ash Wednesday* have long sequences without dialogue.

The scar on Elizabeth Taylor's throat demonstrates her in-
domitability, her survival, but it also announces the limits of her
voice, or the mutual exclusivity of these two experiences: seeing a
star, and hearing a star.

9.

In *A Place in the Sun*, Elizabeth Taylor's face is a blotter for gay
beauty. She doesn't shut her features against her gay co-star; she
listens to Montgomery Clift and admits affinity with that lovely,
homoerotic, pining loner. (Clift's biographer, Patricia Bosworth,
thinks that one source of their affinity was hirsuteness. Hollywood couldn't tolerate body hair, which took away cinematic
skin's connection to the inanimate—to sculpture, canvas, screen.)
Taylor reflects Clift's beauty back to him and makes it speak:
difficult in 1951 for a male body or face to radiate loveliness, to
solicit desire, and to remain motionless and acquiescent while we
stare.

In 1956, after a dinner party at Elizabeth Taylor's house,
Montgomery Clift drove down the hill, and his car crashed; she
arrived at the scene and found him bloody and mutilated, his
head swollen, his face turned to pulp, and she reached into his
mouth to pull out a tooth that was hanging by a thread and cutting his tongue. Though it happens outside of cinema, that image
of Liz's hand in Monty's mouth is the inheritance of anyone who
looks to Elizabeth Taylor for a complex and not a schematic sense
of gender and sexuality: admire her lack of shame (no rubber
gloves), her willingness to reach into the maw of his suffering; admire Liz before her years of "gluttony" reaching into another's

mouth; admire her understanding of the "scar" underpinning star-status, Monty's car crash preceding and prefiguring her scar. She liked Clift's ruined face, thought it more "poignant."

His accident tore *Raintree County* in half. Some shots (mostly interiors) show him before the accident, but other shots show him afterward: face frozen, jaw wired, he has lost his looks and his kinesis. Clift's crash disrupts the film's narrative—the temporality we're supposed to trust, to make our own; for us, *Raintree County* is ripped into Before and After, a schism written on the gay star's face. We reedit the film in our heads, to construct an alternative, sensationalist chronology, to figure out when the scenes were shot, to place each scene against the real backdrop of the crash. (Similarly, we'll reshuffle the scenes of Liz's later films to arrange them on a thin/fat axis; she gains and loses weight during filming, destroying realism, or introducing the higher realism of the star's body.)

The schism in *Raintree County* between Clift's perfect face and his ruined face gives us a literal image for his closet, divided between on-screen heterosexuality and offscreen homosexuality. (Another closet, another crash: in *Giant*, the film she made right before *Raintree County*, she is cast opposite closeted Rock Hudson and bi James Dean, who dies in a car crash right after filming ends.)

In *Raintree County*, Elizabeth Taylor's character has problems of her own. She imagines that she is the daughter of an African American slave: in childhood, her parents died in a fire, from which she saved a doll with a half-melted face. The doll's divided countenance is symbol of the Liz character's fear that she is racially "mixed," and it is also an image of Clift's closet and of Clift's accident, which divided his face and made his screen demeanor effortful, as if every moment he were considering, before the camera, the problems and agonies of presenting a "pretty but ruined" gay face to the world.

In *Raintree County*, morose Montgomery Clift must lovingly extract Elizabeth Taylor's secret. He is her husband, but he behaves like her shrink: he tries to make her remember what happened long ago in the fire. But because Hollywood confines him in the closet, he depends on Elizabeth Taylor *not* remembering, *not* speaking.

10.

Elizabeth Taylor, in her first two Tennessee Williams movies, *Cat on a Hot Tin Roof* and *Suddenly, Last Summer*, is a nymphomaniac with a taste for gay men; her sexual hungers function as a tuning fork, setting the pitch of male bodily catastrophes. During the filming of *Cat*, an actual event underscored her link to male disaster: her husband Mike Todd died in a crash of his private plane, named *Lucky Liz*. In *Cat*, Maggie (Taylor) knows Brick's (Paul Newman's) gay secret, but the screenplay can't tell it, and this enforced silence drives Maggie nearly mad. She tries to open the closet: in one of her characteristic climactic "cure" scenes, in which she remembers the trauma that she has repressed or that her family has forbidden her to reveal, she says, "The laws of silence won't work about Skipper and us. . . . I'm going to say this. . . . It's got to be told and you never let me tell it!"

Cat on a Hot Tin Roof makes homosexuality seem illogical or lunatic. Paul Newman won't touch Elizabeth Taylor. What a waste! Taylor embodies a sexuality all dressed up with no place to go: she is a melancholy figurehead for the lost energies of Tennessee Williams's gay generation. Elizabeth Taylor's voluptuousness hurts; to be sexually hungry, according to the Taylor mythology, is to be an animal (Nibbles the chipmunk, Pie the horse, Lassie the dog, and now Maggie the cat)—or a queer child who, living outside heterosexuality, imagines he or she lives outside alloeroticism, too, and is therefore "doomed" to autoeroticism. (Auto Eroticism: Elizabeth Taylor drives a beautiful blue car in *Cat on a Hot Tin Roof*, the same baby blue as the princess phone in the opening scene of *BUtterfield 8*; and she drives an orange convertible in *BUtterfield 8*, and, at the film's climax, hits a highway roadblock and dies.)

In *Suddenly, Last Summer*, again Elizabeth Taylor maintains a gay man's secret—her cousin Sebastian's. (The actor who plays Sebastian is unbilled, and almost entirely invisible.) Katharine

Hepburn (Sebastian's mother) wants surgeon Montgomery Clift (Dr. Cukrowicz) to lobotomize Liz, to slice out Liz's knowledge of Sebastian's homosexuality. Clift stands to gain by silencing the gay secret: if he operates, Hepburn will give him money for a new hospital. But he is a noble ear, a sacred listener, as in *I Confess*, another closet part; he wants to help Taylor remember Sebastian's death.

Sebastian, a gay man, was torn to pieces by a horde of native boys he was accustomed to paying for sexual favors. After Taylor saw the boys devour him, she hysterically imagined that the world was devouring *her*. Later, the media will imagine Elizabeth Taylor to be a devouring mouth: they will locate her outrageousness in her size and hunger. The boys point to their mouths, asking for bread. Deprived of bread, they will eat Sebastian instead. Because Sebastian, like his saintly namesake, may enjoy arrows and mutilation, his castration/death is a sexual high, like a boy who hangs himself while jerking off. "Eating" may be code for gay oral sex, and, by extension, homosexuality itself; but "eating," in this plot, is gay bashing. Additionally, the mob of boys murdering Sebastian represents Elizabeth Taylor's fans. Liz's dilemma: Do I want to be looked at? Are my fans going to eat me alive? To stare at Liz is to eat her: critic Andrew Sarris compared watching closeups of Monty and Liz in *A Place in the Sun* to "gorging on chocolate sundaes." When I look longingly at a photograph of Clift and Taylor taking a break from filming *A Place in the Sun*, I am beyond sundaes: I am eating time itself.

In *Suddenly*, Elizabeth Taylor accidentally enters a rec room of madmen, who leer at her through coke-bottle glasses, and reach up to the gangplank to maul her legs; she is vulnerable to voyeurism, just as Sebastian is vulnerable to cannibalism. In a scandalous scene, Sebastian made Liz expose her body in a flimsy white bathing suit, to procure boys for him. But in the final sequence, she jettisons her body and becomes just a head, a talking cure. As Liz describes Sebastian's dismemberment, her face, without her body, is juxtaposed on the screen with footage of the crowd of boys pursuing Sebastian up a hill to devour him, while her problematic voice, the voice that belies her voluptuousness, narrates the story of Sebastian's gay immolation: "it looked as if they had devoured him, torn bits of him away and stuffed him in their gobbling mouths." If we urge Liz to lose weight, if we value Liz's slenderness and not her plumpness, we are siding with Hepburn, and wishing Liz to be lobotomized, to lose a "heaviness" (a secret) that weighs her down: the weight on her chest is a scene of fatal homoerotic devouring. She resists lobotomy by remembering the lost scene, by outing Sebastian, by screaming. But, at the end, the closet returns: when she walks offscreen with Clift, we understand that they are now a couple. Clift has been cured of his homosexuality by Taylor's memory aria; now, on-screen, he wants Liz, though in life they were "just friends."

After *Suddenly*, Liz plays Gloria Wandrous, almost dies, gets a tracheotomy, recovers, displays her scar, wins an Oscar, and moves on to *Cleopatra*, where the gay secret becomes so loathsomely heavy that the media turn on Liz and invest her body with the imagery of waste. It took a movie as huge and pointless as *Cleopatra* to display the engorged nature of the secret, which could only speak through cinematic circumlocution, through waste, and through the body of a queen, Elizabeth Taylor's body, that surpasses what we expect of visual pleasure.

11.

The world pretended to be outraged by Elizabeth Taylor's adulterous liaison with Richard Burton; to be outraged by Elizabeth Taylor stealing Eddie Fisher from Debbie Reynolds (BLOODTHIRSTY WIDOW LIZ VAMPIRES EDDIE, reads one headline); but the fiercer scandal is *Cleopatra* itself. The film has no meaning more multiple than the pleasure of watching Elizabeth Taylor in Egyptian drag. Don't sneer at that pleasure. There are too few occasions for publicly indulging that taste—a taste for nothing in the body of something. Judith Crist in *New York Herald Tribune* wrote, "Certainly, if you want to devote the best part of four hours to looking at Elizabeth Taylor in all her draped and undraped physical splendor, surrounded by elaborate and exotic costumes and sets, all in the loveliest of colors, this is your movie." This is my movie. I loved *Cleopatra* (even before I saw it) because here at last was a movie as large as my love for Liz, or as large and extravagant and wasteful as every love. Here was a movie in which Liz, not subsumed, embodied the whole system; nor are we subsumed. The movie crowns us little Cleopatras for loving Liz. I anticipated *Cleopatra* as a chance to prove to the world (as if the world were listening) that Liz was grand and that I was grand, that we, together, were huger than old definitions of star and kid.

In particular I loved the picture of Liz signing her *Cleopatra* contract: she is wearing black suede or silk gloves, and a simple black dress, and pearls, and her hair is jet; seated, she's flanked by studio executives, who humbly stand; she is absolutely in power, though she also seems to be signing her life away.

We pretend it is a joke that Liz is monumental; but I have news for you. She really *is* monumental.

What Elizabeth Taylor couldn't remember, in her films from the late 1950s, was the gay secret surrounding her (Montgomery Clift's, James Dean's, Rock Hudson's); but she was also offering *amnesia* as a substitute for history, and for the responsibilities that come with memory. *What happened? I don't remember. I can't remember. Even if I remembered, and told you what happened, you wouldn't believe me. So I will forget history, and give you costumes instead—or give you my body.*

12.

Elizabeth Taylor's bottom lip droops, as if it were a rose petal burdened by a raindrop. The lip's underside—I think it is called a "bleb"—is bulbous, shining, hungry, full of gravity and lip gloss, sick of shadows. It wants to fall down, to rest, to speak.

13.

In *Cleopatra*, Elizabeth Taylor knows male weakness. She spies on Rex Harrison as Caesar and watches him fall down in epileptic convulsions. She gives Caesar the severed head of his beloved Pompey. With the aid of her seeress, played by the demented-looking Pamela Brown, Elizabeth Taylor hallucinates the scene of Caesar's assassination. She watches Richard Burton fall for a double of Liz at the banquet on the barge; poor Dick kisses the Liz double—not a convincing stand-in, but he believes the ruse. Elizabeth Taylor is a spy in her own house, and we understand her spy nature because her eyes are so compelling and huge, and because *Cleopatra* is shot in Todd-AO, for which she held the patent; because of Todd-AO, and because of her astronomical salary, the film is literally shot through her pocketbook's eyes. She is the seeing center, the pipe in the plumbing where all the funds are routed, the golden one who winks, who knows why everything is going wrong.

Everything went wrong with *Cleopatra*. That is its charm. England's hairdressers struck, because Elizabeth Taylor insisted on importing Sydney Guilaroff to do her hair. The production company started to shoot *Cleopatra* before the film was cast, or the script was written, and had to scrap expensive footage. Elizabeth Taylor almost died, and the production shut down entirely, and started again, but in another country. Executives were fired. Twentieth Century Fox sued its stars. Elizabeth Taylor sued Fox. The film was the costliest, and the longest, ever made. Eventually, the director filmed ninety-six hours, or 120 miles of film, and cut it down to two four-hour-long movies, but Fox insisted on pruning the unwholesome mass into a single, truncated, hard-to-follow epic that, though bloated, remains a fragment—suggesting a chance to stare at Elizabeth Taylor *at greater length* (but we never get to stare enough, the moment of staring always stops). One reviewer suggested that the movie should be called *The Amputee*.

Elizabeth Taylor's nearly fatal illness (the tracheotomy, the Sleeping Beauty moment) haunted *Cleopatra*'s production. The film project was a disease: in his diary, producer Walter Wanger called the film "a cancer that would destroy us all." Elizabeth Taylor described it in her autobiography as "an illness one had a very difficult time recuperating from." She writes, "The whole thing was sick: people spying, spying on each other, unseen factions." Taylor also connected the film to waste and vomit. "God, that was a filthy house," she wrote about Casa Taylor, the Roman villa she inhabited during the making of *Cleopatra* (a house so large she had a separate room for her wigs alone); "one day the sewer erupted and the whole kitchen was floating in sewage." During the making of the film, her stomach was pumped (she had over-dosed on pills); and after she saw the film for the first time, she vomited: "When it was over, I raced back to the Dorchester Hotel and just made it into the downstairs lavatory before I vomited." To say "*Cleopatra* is a piece of shit" is to offer an aesthetic judg-ment, and to make a reasonable if bitter assessment of the fan-tasies that Elizabeth Taylor's body has provoked during her career.

Though an amputee, *Cleopatra* was a blimp. According to Taylor, "And what ballooned the unbelievably Wagnerian, insane quality of everything was the insanity going on at the *Cleopatra* set every day." But there was a meaning, a moral, to the ballooning. The film's immensity represented Liz's independence and power, and the irreal, engulfing, and nearly psychedelic dimension that overtakes the viewer of *Cleopatra* and that overwhelmed its mak-ers: the outerspace on the other side of gender, an empire of signs, like the kingdom of toy boats over which Queen Cleopatra reigns. (The men in the movie fight real battles, while Liz plays with to-kens.) An ambulance was kept on standby when Taylor played her last scene, "lest Elizabeth collapse as the shock of postproduction reality set in." Was *Cleopatra* the sickness, or was reality the sick-ness? And do we, watching *Cleopatra*, inhabit reality, or are we the sick spies, like Liz's maid (in Casa Taylor) who buried a camera in her bouffant? Liz discovered the camera and fired the traitor.

I want to be alone. We envy the star for wanting our lot: soli-tude, invisibility. In *Cleopatra* she says, "Look at me!" but she also says, with eyes closed, during the ceremony in which she is made divine, "You are not supposed to look at me; no one is sup-posed to see me."

In *Cleopatra*, Elizabeth Taylor wore sixty-five different cos-tumes, each an event. The movement from outfit to outfit is a dramaturgy, though *Cleopatra* is to cathartic tragedy as an escala-tor is to a hike up a steep hill. We move and we do not move; the structure beneath us climbs, but our feet are motionless. In one remarkable scene, she changes costumes between quips: "Is it wise?" Dick asks Liz, who is wearing Costume #43, and when she retorts, "Is it wise?" (reaction shot) lo and behold she has advanced to Costume #44! History advances and does not advance.

Of the attention to Taylor's costumes in *Ash Wednesday*, critic Vincent Canby disapprovingly writes, "Mostly the film is interested in what Barbara [Liz] is going to wear next. This is not a male chauvinist's conception of a woman, but her hairdresser's, full of envy, awe, and superficial compassion." Canby condescends to the hairdresser's vision, but we should revere films like *Cleopatra* that speak to the hairdresser.

Liz won't admit us to her interior; Liz won't produce sensations of depth and authenticity. She conveys naturalness, but she is also distracted, glossy. Her stardom has become lumbersome. Elizabeth Taylor is the economic and aesthetic scapegoat for *Cleopatra*'s apparent failure to be dramatically convincing; she is blamed for stopping drama dead in its tracks. She is the enemy of *Cleopatra*'s ambition to revise history into a series of personal romantic encounters; but by flattening the film's historical ambitions, she tells a more real story. She shows us that *Cleopatra* is about women's bodies in 1961, 1962, and 1963, about gay men, about race, about power, and about waste.

Any glimpses of "truth" that we get in *Cleopatra*—the truth of queens, gowns, hats, corpses, scars, breasts, butts—we owe to Elizabeth Taylor's refusal to be "deep." For its lack of depth, I adore the scene when her maids give her a body rub while she lies on her stomach; we can see the side of her breast, but not the nipple, and her body seems so soft it is almost genderless, no sex in sight, just a blank surface, like the first scene in John Waters's *Multiple Maniacs*, when, seeing Divine from the back as an odalisque, we almost believe that Divine is a woman. In the early scenes of *Cleopatra*, the Todd-AO color process is so spanking and absolute that it audibly breathes, and Liz is supposed to be nineteen years old, not yet the weary diplomatic queen, not yet in love with Antony; when she stands next to her femmy brother Ptolemy and his loyal eunuch, her skin is so creamy I want to eat it—if I may confess my own unremarkable cannibalistic fantasy, my association of seeing and eating. To stare at Liz is to ask, like Oliver Twist, for more, and to receive it.

A reviewer wrote of *Cleopatra*, "At four hours it is the world's longest coming attraction for something that will never come." The film's edgy, bored foreplay teases us into wanting to come, but our desire suffers no release. Elizabeth Taylor is extravagant as a person (that is why she cost Fox so much money) and her body is literally an *extra vagance*: she has wandered beyond bounds, and we long to follow her into that far shoal of embodiment.

"Oooh, look, Liz has a gay son!" shouted a queen at a revival-house screening of *Cleopatra*, in response to the appearance of Liz and a little Italian extra on the Sphinx. In a later scene, Rex Harrison tries to teach the kid how to walk like a man, as if *Cleopatra* were a remake of *Tea and Sympathy*; Taylor watches the boy at Rex Harrison's School of Masculinity, and wonders why the boy is wasting his time. She is always, implicitly, winking; and she actually winks at the end of the procession into Rome, an expensive scene, when the crowd of extras expressed their love for Elizabeth Taylor, and their tolerance for her peccadillo, despite the Vatican's thundering protest, by shouting "Leeez! Leeez! *Baci! Baci!*" (Perversely, I imagine the extras are yelling "Lez!") Of the "Leeez" processional, *Newsweek* writes, "To top a ten-minute procession, costing hundreds of thousands, with a wink is fairly tricky business." Indeed, Liz is playing a trick. All the spectacle, as history, is garbage, and she knows it. When Rex Harrison as Caesar unrolls the carpet containing Cleopatra, and Elizabeth Taylor falls out of it, and arches her back like Maggie the cat, or as if it were the first scene of *BUtterfield 8* again and she were rising from a bad night's sleep, hungover, alone in her bedroom, no one watching, then the nonsense of narrative falls apart, and we are facing, without blinders, an extravagance.

In *Ash Wednesday*, someone asks Liz, "Was it fun?" and she replies, with a wistful morbidity that I admire, "No, not fun, but on the verge of fun."

I am not Liz, but I am on the verge of Liz. I can't arrive at Elizabeth Taylor. How would I recognize that arrival, except that I will have ceased to be? I may look forward to a life entirely founded on reveries that begin and end with Elizabeth Taylor, but I am also in the midst of that life, even as I call it a future life. I will never know a life innocent of her singular, specific beauty—a beauty of 1962 and 1952, a torpor I can locate and research and review, but never change. No one, least of all myself, can alter my relation to Elizabeth Taylor—utterly private, utterly historical.

With Liz's *Cleopatra*, I murmur, "You are not supposed to look at me. No one is supposed to see me."

14.

Elizabeth Taylor as Cleopatra has an Asian maid, but Hollywood couldn't cast an African American actress as Cleopatra, even though Leontyne Price opened the new Metropolitan Opera House at Lincoln Center in 1966 with a world premiere of Samuel Barber's *Antony and Cleopatra*—itself, like the movie *Cleopatra*, an expensive flop.

In *Raintree County*, Liz thinks she has forgotten her race (she goes mad because she believes she is black); in *Suddenly, Last Summer* and *Cat on a Hot Tin Roof*, she has forgotten homosexuality, or is forbidden to speak it.

Cleopatra's whiteness is the film's silent scandal—never mentioned, though the media scrutinized every other detail of the film's production and of its stars' conduct.

15.

After *Cleopatra*, Liz had to turn into a flop, to prove that Fox's investment in Liz-as-potentate was a miscalculation. After *Cleopatra*, she was never believable as anything except a "shrew" or a woman whom America compelled to lose weight. I find disheartening the photograph of a reduced lovely Liz beaming beside brain-dead Reagan after a stage performance of *The Little Foxes*; Liz's shed pounds seem a "figure" (as in full-figured) for the violent cutbacks and budget trimmings of Reagan's administration—the rhetorical emphasis on "spending cuts" and on stopping "liberal waste."

16.

Elizabeth Taylor's cleavage is "natural" (her body is built that way) but it is also produced. The camera emphasizes it; costume reinforces it. Her cleavage—as image—is a fact of culture. It is a darkness dividing two white shapes; it is a displaced cinematic representation of the vagina that even a scandalous film like *Cleopatra* can't show but that it wants, everywhere, to suggest; it is the schism of the Clift face after his accident, or of the doll with half-melted face that Taylor cossets in *Raintree County*; it is the ground of an income (and all grounds are divided); it is the place where the camera lingers in the later films, when she is no longer Elizabeth Taylor of the 1950s, and so the camera, still wanting to make a fortune off her, demands cleavage as signature, proof that she is still Liz. Her films make much of her breasts; but cinema is the art of cutting, and so wasteful films like *Cleopatra*, which required severe editing, care more about her cleavage, about the process of compressing breasts to describe a line, a space.

Cleavage is very 1960s: it shows off the new permissiveness. (Look! We can reveal most of Elizabeth Taylor's breasts!) Cleavage is not nudity. Cleavage is a promise: not sight, but on the verge of sight.

Staring at cleavage, I am not straight, but on the verge of straight. I pour resources of time and attention into her cleavage. I am not specifically aroused by it, but I am involved with it. It calls forth in me an elemental, curious response: it evokes, from my depths, a *yes*, a giggle. Her relationship to her cleavage—wise, indifferent—makes me want to walk into bright sunlight with a more positive attitude, makes me sick of equivocation and mirthlessness. Her cleavage, beyond attainment, beyond prose, is not sublime, but is what we bring to it, and is on the verge of me. Not me, but on the verge of me. I am not the only one who has looked at Elizabeth Taylor, not the only man or woman who has turned to her for the first, rudimentary lesson in how to imagine elevation, and how to endure division.

(1991)

MELANIE TIME

$\mathcal{T}$ime around a star is at once rigidly structured and loose, just as a star's utterances can be simultaneously prophetic and vacant.

In Wilmington, North Carolina, Melanie Griffith and Antonio Banderas, two stars in the first flush of a much-publicized romance, are staying in a huge beach house on Figure Eight Island. Antonio is recuperating between assignments (next he'll go to London to record songs for *Evita*, opposite Madonna); Melanie is here to film *Lolita* (she plays the mother).

What a house! What a view! Melanie says, "Last night it was so beautiful with the full moon coming down on the water. Huge. And so bright you could hardly look at it." She sips a ginseng-and-Evian elixir, prepared by an assistant: "It's all herbs. There's nothing bad for you in it."

The day is devoted to a photo shoot, on the beach. During lunch break, Melanie and Antonio kiss in front of the entourage. She wraps her legs around his. Entourage, for today, includes cook, Antonio's personal assistant, Melanie's personal assistant, makeup person, hair person, stylist, publicist, and one nice young man who just helps out. How long has he worked for Melanie? He smiles: "Awhile." Entourage time is vague, open-ended.

Cook's eyebrows need correction, so she is whisked away, by an assistant, to learn beauty fundamentals: "Eyebrows 101."

Antonio eats a piece of chicken, with considerable bravado, straight off the shish-kebab skewer. Melanie goes upstairs to shower, and changes into a grey satin slip, more negligee than dress. Bronzed Antonio, henna streaks in his long hair, jokes about impotence: someone once told him that drinking Evian compromised potency, but he's been drinking it for three years and has no problems.

A spare room holds clothes for the shoot, including rows of Manolo Blahnik shoes (some with masking tape on the soles), Alain Mikli sunglasses on the bed, and a rack of femme outfits.

In the background, the Korean cast recording of *Evita* is playing.

Melanie has begun to like classical music, under her beau's influence. "It's cool. I love it. Especially Mozart. I really like Mozart, and I like Tchaikovsky, and I like Verdi. . . . I find it's very soothing, in a very strange way; or else very energizing. Or calming. You know?"

This is the same star who said, in *Bonfire of the Vanities*, "Don't think, Sherman, just fuck," or "You know I'm a sucker for a soft dick."

∽

Antonio gives Melanie a pep talk after lunch, before her photo shoot resumes. "Mayl-ah-knee," he says. "Relax." She pronounces his name the same slow way: "Ahn-toe-knee-o."

Cellular phones connect the entourage in the house to the crew on the beach, so no one is ever in danger of losing touch. Chez Melanie and Antonio, everyone is in touch with everyone:

"Hi!" "Thanks!" "Do you want some food?" "Bummer!" "It was beautiful!" Easy to establish eye contact. Easy to be smiled at. Hours pass. The power goes out: that is the day's catastrophe. Without electric light, the scented "Diptyche" candles burn brighter, masking the smell of cigarettes.

The shoot is a success, except for the mosquitoes. All day the sun beats down. A member of the entourage calls sunlight the Big Gaffer: "The Big Gaffer provides the best light."

The line between *friend* and *help* is nebulous. Members of the entourage who seemed friends are, by late afternoon, emptying ashtrays.

∞

It is nearly sunset on the spacious deck. Melanie Griffith's attenuated body is draped in a floral dress: long tanned limbs, large high breasts. It takes work, to look like this: "You see where you have to work something, and you work it." Work and realness are two themes of her conversation. She doesn't wear much makeup, but there's a remnant smudge of lipstick on her upper lip, from the day's shoot. Her hair is dyed flame red, for the role of Lolita's mother. Melanie avoids comparing herself to her legendary predecessor: "I don't think there needs to be an issue about me and Shelley Winters."

Old-time Hollywood doesn't preoccupy her, though her whispery voice echoes Judy Holliday's (a resemblance put to use in the remake of *Born Yesterday*), and her mother is Tippi Hedren, ice-princess survivor of *The Birds* and *Marnie*. Melanie reflects: "I remember being at the premiere of *The Birds*, and having my eyes covered, when the woman got her eye pecked out. And I was so mad! Because I wanted to see so bad! But I knew it was a movie. . . . I saw *Marnie* when I was six. That's pretty heavy. . . . I was pretty fucked up for a while."

She doesn't want to talk about her mother, long absent from the limelight. "It's a tender subject. I don't ever want to hurt anybody. . . . I'm sure I wasn't a model daughter for her. I left home very young, and I was very independent and rebellious, and I'm sure that it's interesting for her to see me work a lot."

Melanie says, "Women are only stopped in this business from working as much as they allow themselves to be stopped."

With incantatory conviction she praises the wildness of her own daughter, Dakota: "My daughter is fearless. She is beautiful, and she is fearless, and strong, and wild. And I just can see that there's going to be no stopping her."

Melanie wears a ring: an ample, many-faceted sapphire, set between two large diamonds. "Antonio gave it to me last week. It's an old ring, from 1870. And he got it at Harry Winston's. It's beautiful, isn't it? Isn't it amazing? It's so beautiful." Her arms and hands and wrists are thin; she seems an impersonation of a princess. Exquisite, the quasi-deliberate composition formed by blue water, coral dress, red hair, blue gem. . . .

"I really love Antonio. I'm completely in love with him. I've never met anybody like him in my life. We're good together. And I don't feel like I have to justify that to anybody."

She resents the paparazzi photos, in a recent *People*, of the couple smooching. "We didn't ask for any of this press. We didn't take those pictures. We didn't print them in their fucking magazine. . . . How dare they complain about us putting too much out! We didn't put anything out. Nothing."

Mostly she's mad because *National Enquirer* insinuated, inaccurately, that she was pregnant. "I almost sued them. I called a lawyer. We were going to write a letter, threatening a lawsuit. But then Antonio and I talked about it, and we just thought, Fuck them."

The TV show *Hard Copy* shadowed Melanie and Antonio while they were shopping in Century City for her son's birthday presents. "Three days later we find out that we've been followed by *Hard Copy* the whole time, and we didn't even know it! It makes me feel that I've been spied on. Total invasion of privacy." Had she known she was being filmed: "I would have dressed better!"

⚭

Melanie speaks slowly, but her gestures and expressions dominate a room. One conventional name for this magnetism is femininity. But it is also fame, and an intricate knowledge of how people will react to her. She knows how to mold silence and still-ness, and she has a naturally flirtatious mien, drawing the inter-locutor conspiratorially close: "Can you come sit up here?" She likes to shrink distances.

But she also likes to rebuff. Many lines of inquiry are refused: "I don't want to talk about *Lolita*. Not yet. Because I'm doing it right now, and it's really difficult to talk about a movie while you're in it. I never do that. You know what I mean? It's kinda not fair to doing a good job." Her voice trails off into silence.

She used to go to coaches, trying to lower her purring voice, which has beguiling breaks and catches. She doesn't know the origin of her weird, Marilynesque croon: "People recognize me by my voice. People recognize me the minute I talk. It might have been an accident when I had my tonsils taken out."

Her perfume: Must de Cartier. "A woman named Helen Shaver, an actress, was wearing this perfume ten years ago and I said, what is that? And I've worn it ever since."

Melanie loves flowers. "Any kind but yellow." She differenti-ates the yellow roses in the living room from "those fake-looking carnation things, those bad-looking yellow flowers."

She doesn't dare label herself a star. And yet, discussing star-dom, her voice grows solemn, acquires authority and cadence: "People who call themselves stars quickly find out that that's not what it's all about. . . . You can't want to be famous. It doesn't work. You have to have something to back it up. People are only famous if they do something that other people admire. Or people can became famous if they pay enough money for it. They can try. They can become famous for a few minutes. I think that you cannot want to become famous. Fame is an illusion. It's some-thing that happens."

Defiance underlies her fragile demeanor: "I'm thirty-eight. I'm a woman. I'm a real woman. I don't want to feel like I have to look like I'm twenty anymore. . . . Sometimes a part of me wants to say, 'Yeah, use the airbrush around my eyes.' Another part of me says, 'Fuck it. This is who I am. This is real life. This happens to movie stars, too. I'm not going to live a life where I have plastic surgery every ten years.' " She reconsiders: "Maybe every twenty."

∞

She consulted Shirley MacLaine's medium. Through him, a spirit named Anton Ray—a five-thousand-year-old Egyptian—spoke to Melanie, and told her that *Working Girl* was one of the few movies of our time to communicate a message to a mass audience.

She met President Clinton. In the Oval Office, on his desk, he had a coin. He said, "This is a co-in." And Melanie said, "A koan!" Because of his accent, she thought that he meant *koan*. "Then he told me that Chelsea was really into Buddhism. So then I told Hillary about this great book that I read, *The Three Pillars of Zen*."

Melanie, dragging on a Benson & Hedges 100 and sipping ginseng elixir, has a vaguely wasted look, somewhere between healthy and traumatized. She reiterates the word *real*. "It's all very *real*," she says, describing daily demands. "I finished work last night at ten o'clock. I have to be at work at seven in the morning tomorrow. I worked all day today. I get, like, six hours' sleep. I have two children. I have a lot to deal with. You know what I mean? It's not a bed of roses. Jesus!" One senses wounds, masked by a sex-kittenish manner. *Real*, to Melanie, signifies pain. Describing a powerful film, she says, "That's probably the realest movie I've ever seen about spousal abuse. I cried so much in that movie, my assistant had to go get a box of Kleenex. Literally, a box!"

Are movies real? As she was once frightened by *The Birds*, so now her own kids are "freaked out" when they see their mother hurt on film: "I have to tell them in advance that's it not really happening, that it's only a movie."

She first met ex-love Don Johnson on the set of a Tippi Hedren vehicle, *The Harrad Experiment*: Melanie, a star who is herself the daughter of a star, and who clearly enjoys romances with other stars, has always lived near or inside cinema, but she tries to distance herself from its toxic desolations. Her motto: "Stay away from all of this star shit, and all the labels people tend to want to put on you. It fucks with your head."

∞

It is nearly impossible to gain access to a star, but once you have been admitted into the throne room, the hours pass slowly. Scent of a jasmine candle. Melanie saying "gazelle," Melanie saying "Audrey Hepburn," Melanie saying "Hillary," Melanie saying "scared the shit out of me," Melanie saying she needs to go upstairs to brush her teeth. Variously tinted wiglets in the hairstylist's bag of tricks. Antonio contemplatively rubbing his belly, Antonio saying "Franco," Antonio kissing Melanie. Smell of makeup. White vinyl skirt on a hanger in a spare room. Ashes in the clogged bathroom sink. Perfumed taste of Melanie's herbal elixir. Telescope and binoculars in the living room, and a grand piano on which Antonio plays a quick tune. . . . Star time, like entourage time, is curved, a boomerang; each instant is elongated yet disconnected. It is Sunday afternoon, on the back deck of a beach house in Wilmington. Tippi Hedren's daughter flashes an 1870 sapphire ring, blue against the blue-grey water. Everything seems new; everything, also, seems a remake.

Musing on endlessness, Melanie says, "The oldest woman alive is one hundred twenty right now, and she quit smoking three years ago. She eats, like, a half pound of chocolate a day, and it just made me realize, God, wouldn't it be cool to live, like, another ninety years?" She revises the dream estimate: "Eighty years?"

(1995)

200 WOMEN

*H*ere is a short conceptual book entitled *200 Women*, without pictures. Its prurience, considerable, is lexical and syntactic. Who is the subject? Who is the object?

For an 8mm animation course in the mountains I drew a cutout of Mae West and filmed her walking across a blank sheet of paper. Highlight was her gown's bell curve.

Sophia Loren performed in a preposterous, sepia *Aida*, her voice supplied by Renata Tebaldi. Sophia Loren struggled to bear children, ate spaghetti in Naples, starred in *Two Women*, was youthful and devil-may-care in a documentary on Joseph Levine, and bears consideration.

Doris Day grounds reflection, rode a swing in the credits of her TV show, was battered by James Cagney in *Love Me or Leave Me*, defends animals, lives near Carmel, and wears dresses with

French construction in *The Man Who Knew Too Much* while singing incestuously about what will be will be.

Patty Hearst rode in a car driven by kidnappers, had parents, appeared in *San Francisco Chronicle* photos, offered a cautionary tale, visited San Simeon, and knew Highway 101, which links cities in the South Bay.

Ida Lupino starred in my poem ("Ida's Glove"), directed *The Hitch-Hiker*, had a husband and a disease, saw Vivien Leigh in *Waterloo Bridge* and should have been considered for the part herself, was not in *Summer and Smoke*, and had Alexandra Del Lago aspects but was not pathetic.

Chance Wayne, hustler to Alexandra Del Lago in *Sweet Bird of Youth*, might also be friends with Montgomery Clift in *A Place in the Sun* when he wears an undershirt while working in the factory before attending a party in the presence of Elizabeth Taylor, who had near-death experiences and suffered comparison with Debbie Reynolds, who is not Doris Day.

Judy Garland sang "Hello, Liza" to her daughter Liza Minnelli, and knew Carol Channing but also knew herself to be Carol's superior. Carol Channing envied Barbra Streisand, who stole the part of Dolly in the film seen (and admired?) by Vincente Minnelli, husband to Judy and mother to Liza, whose sister, Lorna Luft, appeared in the movie *Grease 2*, not trumping Olivia Newton-John opposite John Travolta in the original. Olivia Newton-John sings "You're the One That I Want" as an argument for heterosexuality, and makes the act of loving John Travolta a divine pinnacle, an Eleusinian mystery, an anapest in an amphitheater. Brooke Shields appeared in *Grease* in its Broadway revival, graduated from Princeton, circulated with Bianca Jagger, was daughter to Teri Shields, wrote a book, and is not Tina Louise, co-star of *Gilligan's Island*, in which a character named Mary Ann appears, who has a family resemblance to Lesley Ann Warren singing "In My Own Little Corner" in Rodgers and Hammerstein's *Cinderella* on TV.

Peggy Lee confused audiences of her TV appearances at 7 P.M. and must have been rivalrous with Julie London, who is not Julie Newmar, star of *Batman*. Julie London always appears sideways on her record jackets, is not the only woman to sing "Foggy Day" with emphasis on the words "in London town," and appears on the compilation *Bethlehem's Girl Friends* in the company of Carmen McRae and Chris Connor.

Carmen McRae is not the sister of Sheila MacRae and is not the wife of Gordon MacRae. I am not sure who Sheila MacRae is. Probably a television personality, like Kitty Carlisle or Arlene Francis, who is not Arlene Dahl, though the art of distinguishing the Arlenes is as complex as parsing the MacRaes.

Among my neighbors as a child I numbered Charlene, Doreen, and Noreen. Noreen's laugh, louder and stranger than Charlene's, seemed to contain the words *gefilte fish*, though Noreen was not Jewish. No Arlene lived on our block.

Arlene Francis nursed no jealousy of Connie Francis, who nursed no jealousy of Connie Stevens. Connie Francis and Connie Stevens and Arlene Francis were three separate people with separate careers and separate erotic lives. Anne Francis appeared with Barbra Streisand in *Funny Girl* and was the star of the TV series *Honey West*, though Anne Francis lives in the Julie Newmar/Julie London category, where vocalism and TV fame blend to create a fog of anonymity and potential electricity that never crackles.

Susan Hayward played Biblical women like Bathsheba and was far superior in illumination to the Oscar-winning star of *Come Back, Little Sheba*, Shirley Booth, who echoes Shelley Winters: both played heavy losers. Shelley Winters, erotic braggart, lords it over Shelley Fabares.

Shirley Booth bumps into Shirley Jones, who left the musical category to star in *Elmer Gantry*, for which she won an Oscar. Mother to David Cassidy, she paid attention to Susan Dey in *The Partridge Family* and appears in milk ads with Florence Henderson, who starred in *Song of Norway*, the life of Grieg, and must endure the lexical nearness of Skitch Henderson, who conducted Anna Moffo in a New York pops concert in the late 1970s.

Who played Gidget? Originally, Sandra Dee, whom Stockard

Channing spoofs in the *Grease* song "Look at Me, I'm Sandra Dee." Stockard Channing stars in the movie *Six Degrees of Separation* and resembles my friend Shannon who played Juliet in a college Shakespeare production. Eventually, many women played Gidget, though Leslie Caron, star of *Gigi* and *Lili*, never did. Nor did Julie Andrews, star of *Darling Lili*, though she played the same part in *The Boy Friend* that Twiggy later won in the film version.

Diahann Carroll is not Diana Rigg, though both appeared to great acclaim on TV. Diahann Carroll's *Julia* is not the *Julia* of Vanessa Redgrave, sister to Lynn Redgrave, whose *Georgy Girl* included the song I heard in the garage of my third-grade friend Mark, with whom I saw a double feature at Cinema 150 and got eyestrain as a result. The beige dress of Vanessa Redgrave in *Camelot* could be the outfit of Mary Tyler Moore in *Thoroughly Modern Millie*, in which Beatrice Lillie appears. Beatrice Lillie and Gertrude Lawrence are not the same, though Julie Andrews played Gertrude Lawrence in the disastrous *Star!* The beige dress that looks like skin recently made a comeback in the hands of Miuccia Prada; my grandmother wore such a dress when she was mother of the bride in 1952.

Tura Satana in Russ Meyer's early sexploitation flick *Faster, Pussycat! Kill! Kill!* cripples a creep by driving over his legs. Tura Satana later became a nurse. Another nurse is Agnes Moorehead catering to blind Jane Wyman in *Magnificent Obsession*. Agnes Moorehead washes her hands so energetically it seems a Saint Vitus' dance, and has a walnut-shaped face, like Myra Hess, pianist, who plays Schumann's *Symphonic Etudes*, certain notes of it, with frightening lightness of touch, so the tones dissolve into their context.

Charlotte Brontë was the subject of Elizabeth Gaskell's nineteenth-century biography and was sister to Anne Brontë and Emily Brontë. The film version of *Wuthering Heights* starred the husband of Vivien Leigh, and the film version of *Jane Eyre* featured Elizabeth Taylor as the sickly Helen Burns. The Brontë sisters had minuscule handwriting, almost indecipherable. I read the Gaskell biography of Charlotte Brontë several years before I saw Elizabeth Taylor play Helen Burns.

Jane Fonda married Roger Vadim, who married and discovered Brigitte Bardot, who was a peer of Jeanne Moreau, whose lips are smoky and large as Simone Signoret's—rectangles, not ellipses. Jeanne Moreau's lips in *Mademoiselle* (screenplay by Jean Genet) are smudged and flattened by their criminal circumstance, as Bette Davis's lips are smudged when she plays the mother of Susan Hayward in *Where Love Has Gone*. Smudged lips are stretched, perfect, highly paid, and pleased by any technologies, including Cinerama, that bring them to the fore. Jeanne Moreau's mud-stained high heel in *Mademoiselle* need not fear the shoes of Audrey Hepburn in *Roman Holiday*; nor need Jeanne Moreau's shoe, clue to a murder, faze the ballet slipper of Judy Garland sitting on a stool as she prepares to sing "Born in a Trunk."

Joan Didion on the back jacket of *Play It As It Lays* makes me want to be a writer, as does Elizabeth Hardwick on the back of *Sleepless Nights*, and Jean Rhys on the back of *Sleep It Off, Lady*. Elizabeth Hardwick and Joan Didion write for the *New York Review of Books*, as does Susan Sontag. Susan Sontag was a friend of the French film actress Nicole Stéphane, to whom she dedicated the definitive *On Photography*. Nicole Stéphane, star of Jean Cocteau's *Les Enfants Terribles*, must have been a friend of Jeanne Moreau and might have been a friend of Arletty. Arletty and Colette might have known each other. I read Colette's *The Pure and the Impure* on an airplane and am not a child of paradise.

Victoria de los Angeles was not born in Los Angeles, sang Amelia in *Simon Boccanegra*, and recorded for Angel, which issued *Swan Lake* and *Sleeping Beauty* in a record with a green cover in the early 1960s. Angel also issued Elisabeth Schwarzkopf singing the Verdi *Requiem*; in the "Agnus Dei" it is difficult to tell her voice apart from Christa Ludwig's when they sing in unison.

Maria Tallchief created the part of the Sugar Plum Fairy in Balanchine's *Nutcracker*. Frank O'Hara idolized Tanaquil Leclercq, and Joseph Cornell made a jewel casket for Marie Taglioni, as well as pieces for Susan Sontag, Henriette Sontag, and Lauren Bacall. Henriette Sontag in the nineteenth century sang Donna Anna in *Don Giovanni*, as did Joan Sutherland, Leontyne Price, and Martina Arroyo in the twentieth. Joan Sutherland's repertoire included Mozart but did not center on it. She sang Clotilde to Maria Callas's Norma in London in the 1950s, and has a son named Adam, who collects her records.

Miss Jacobson, my sixth-grade teacher, wore a yellow dress. Miss Paul, my second-grade teacher, wore flat shoes, as did Mrs. Leaf, my first-grade teacher, and Mrs. Crandall, my kindergarten teacher. My fourth-grade teacher, Mrs. Nigh, was short, as was Mrs. Leaf, and my fifth-grade teacher, Mrs. Pratt, was tall, and introduced sex education while wearing a grey dress and pointing to her hips and saying, "I have wide hips, which made childbirth easy." I asked Mrs. Pratt what happens if the penis gets stuck in the vagina during intercourse, and she said that wasn't a problem.

Mrs. Rosendin, my seventh-grade typing teacher, wore her hair in a bun, and the school nurse in elementary school had an office down the hall from the school secretary, who handled tardy students and absences and also managed manilla folders.

Mrs. Hirose, my third-grade teacher, her hair in a ponytail, pulled down the pants of a boy who had been "bad" and spanked his naked rear end with a paddle she kept hanging from a hook in the classroom, while the rest of us watched. She sometimes wore leis.

I read the first chapter of Jane Austen's *Pride and Prejudice* in sixth grade and gave an oral report on the whole novel though I hadn't finished it. My favorite girl in sixth grade was Cheryl, but she was not Cheryl Tiegs or Cheryl Studer. Sixth-grade Cheryl resembled the daughter in *The Sound of Music* who went on to play a princess in *Lost in Space*. The princess moment took up two episodes and was a highlight of the series. My brother's first cello teacher, Cheryl, studied with Pablo Casals, and eventually became a nun, or tried to. She was a friend of my piano teacher, Lynn. Before Lynn I had two piano teachers, Mrs. Lincoln and Mrs. Shannon. Together, Mrs. Lincoln and Mrs. Shannon ran a music school, "Music Craft," in which I matriculated before kindergarten. Mrs. Lincoln was older or darker than Mrs. Shannon, who said my hands were too small.

Most things in the world are private. What I am saying now is no longer private. Once, I had complicated language, but the complexities unraveled.

My Sunday School teacher, Miss Forkash, had a pretty face, but I can't remember it. Her signature on a certificate attested to decent conduct or consistent attendance. I learned about God's will and atheism and cut class to read a volume of great American plays including a Rodgers and Hammerstein musical that never entered popular consciousness.

The noisy behavior of the other boys in Miss Forkash's class depressed me. She told us that Jews should let strangers— hitchhikers—into the house on Passover.

Metonymy, metaphor, allusion, and anaphora are friends of Elizabeth Taylor when she plays a Jewess in *Ivanhoe*. My mother's best friend, Marge, was not Jewish, though she had a tan and tolerated our contiguity: she lived in the duplex next door when I was born, and heard my infancy through the walls.

Shirley Temple, famous by the age of four, had curly hair, blew Deanna Durbin out of the water, and influenced the life of Margaret O'Brien, who is not Maureen O'Sullivan, mother of Mia Farrow, though Margaret O'Brien and Maureen O'Sullivan both played household roles. Mia Farrow must have known Mary Quant and Veruschka and Nico, though I can find no evidence.

Elizabeth Bishop, protégée of Marianne Moore, met Moore's mother, Mary Warner. Marianne Moore met George Platt Lynes, who photographed her and Edith Sitwell. Edith Sitwell met Virginia Woolf and Gertrude Stein, whose lover, Alice B. Toklas, met James Merrill, who met Alison Lurie, who lives in Key West, where I took a week's vacation and read the autobiography of Anita O'Day, who admired Billie Holiday although Holiday snubbed her. Diana Ross played Holiday in the movie, and, earlier, sang "My World Is Empty without You"; the backup band sounds tinny on the K-tel record.

Marilyn Monroe inaugurated her life as celebrity by posing nude. Raquel Welch never posed nude; neither, to my knowledge, did another siren, Jayne Mansfield. Hedy Lamarr played a nude scene in an early movie, and it would not surprise me if Greta Garbo did, as well. Did Clara Bow, too, and Theda Bara? What about Vilma Banky? Edna Purviance certainly never appeared nude; nor did Mary Pickford, Constance Talmadge, or the Gish sisters. Silence was not exclusively prurient. It is likely that Gloria Swanson played a nude scene, but unlikely that ZaSu Pitts did, though she committed an act of violent biting in *Greed*.

Jane Bowles's union with Paul Bowles was hardly a mere marriage of convenience.

Simone de Beauvoir was married to Jean-Paul Sartre. Janet Flanner was married to no one and dwelled in a hotel. I plan to read de Beauvoir and Flanner in the near future. Their sentences are strong.

Roland Barthes lived with his mother, Henriette Barthes, and Maria Callas's sister, Jackie Callas, remained close to her mother, Evangelia, though the more famous sister did not. Zsa Zsa and Eva Gabor were on good terms with their mother, Jolie Gabor, who employed Evangelia Callas.

Katharine Hepburn played Clara Schumann in *Song of Love*, and I played Robert Schumann's "Fantasy Pieces" while in love with Andrea in 1976. To praise her to my father I invoked the name of Anne Sexton: I said it was important to live wildly. That summer I did not read *Of Human Bondage* though I bought a copy.

Frieda Hughes, the daughter of Sylvia Plath, is now a poet; I saw her poems in *The New Yorker*. I wonder if Helen Vendler admires Sylvia Plath. I admire Helen Vendler, who is as trenchant and encyclopedic as Pauline Kael. I am glad that Helen Vendler praises the poems of Adrienne Rich, whose book, *Diving into the Wreck*, inspired me in 1977, though I doubt that she would countenance my writing.

Oscar Wilde's mother, Speranza, was a poet, as is mine. John Updike's mother is a writer. Literature runs in families, and often through the maternal line. My father is also a writer, but I have been more influenced by my mother.

My mother as a young girl was fond of Shirley Temple. I do

not know enough about the voice of Shirley Bassey to hazard an opinion, though Shirley Verrett's performance of Orfeo in the Gluck opera is magnificent. Shirley Verrett is virtually the god-mother of my friend Maurice, and I heard Shirley Verrett sing Desdemona and Aida in Boston in the early 1980s. Shirley MacLaine's psychic powers do not provoke laughter or skepticism in me; I read her first memoir while vacationing in Carmel in the 1970s, and, on that same vacation, saw *Red Sky at Morning*, star-ring someone who resembles but is not Katharine Ross, who ap-peared in *Butch Cassidy and the Sundance Kid*, the first M-rated movie I ever saw, on a double bill with *The Prime of Miss Jean Brodie*, starring Maggie Smith. The pallor of a nude female model's breasts in *Jean Brodie* had nothing to do with the dark-ness surrounding our car at the drive-in theater. That night a sib-ling had an "anxiety attack" (that is what we called it) and stood outside with my father by the concession stand while my mother and I watched the double feature.

In sixth grade I took Jean on a date to see *Airport*, starring Jean Seberg and Jacqueline Bisset. Later at that same theater I saw *The Andromeda Strain*, in which a flashing light causes a danger-ous epileptic attack. The date with Jean never led to a kiss, and yet she had a beautiful complexion, just short of ruddy—not in-congruous with the taste of a Lorna Doone cookie or the sound of Jacqueline du Pré playing Schubert just before her illness strikes. The body of her husband Daniel Barenboim, as I imagine it, has some affiliation with Liszt's "Mephisto Waltz" as heard in the movie *The Mephisto Waltz* starring Jacqueline Bisset and Bar-bara Parkins, whose appearance in *Valley of the Dolls* as Anne Welles, the proper New Englander, cannot interfere with my sense of Annie Sullivan's stay at the Perkins Institute for the Blind, where she learned the skills that helped her tackle the problem of Helen Keller, played by Patty Duke, who stars in *Val-ley of the Dolls* as Neely O'Hara, based on the life of Judy Gar-land, who was originally cast in the role of Helen Lawson in the same film, but was fired (she never acted again), and was replaced by Susan Hayward, whose role in *I Want to Live!* as the doomed Barbara Graham earned her an Oscar.

In that film, Susan Hayward on death row wears high heels as she marches to her execution. The prison corridor reminds me of the hallway joining the bedrooms in our ranch house in the 1960s. In the rumpus room or in my parents' bedroom I watched Shari Lewis and Lamb Chop; I preferred Miss Nancy on *Romper Room*. Miss Nancy and Shari Lewis were equally generous with their time: a half hour. But they returned, the next episode, for another half hour. The half hours added up. Lucille Ball gave many half hours, as did Vivian Vance. Lucy Ricardo's mother, Mrs. McGillicuddy, on *I Love Lucy*—played by Kathryn Card—had a grudge against Ricky Ricardo, who was certainly dashing enough to seduce women at the Copacabana, though these liaisons never appeared on the show. Lucy's daughter, Lucie Arnaz, played the Brooke Shields/Olivia Newton-John role in one revival of *Grease* on Broadway, I think, and must be known to Cher, as a client is said to be "known to Sotheby's."

I haven't said a word about Fanny Mendelssohn, the sister of Felix. Nor have I mentioned W. A. Mozart's sister Nannerl, or Yehudi Menuhin's sisters Hephzibah and Yaltah, or Vladimir Horowitz's wife Wanda Toscanini, daughter of Arturo. Wanda Toscanini Horowitz brought doughnuts and coffee to the fans standing on line to buy tickets to her husband's historic return to Carnegie Hall in 1965. I wonder if the doughnuts were glazed.

(1998)

AUDREY AND HER SISTERS

I read star biographies to find out how stars see themselves and how they see each other. Though I am interested in their behavior, I am more interested in the curves and austerities of their cognition. Huge gulfs divide a star in daily life from a star on-screen; the style in which a star executes an action (film role, household chore, errand, ambassadorial mission) is not the style in which she secretly contemplates her colleagues. Few writers have tried to describe ineffable instances of *stars perceiving other stars* and *stars perceiving their own stardom*. Such moments dominate the twentieth century, and so it is a mistake to consider a star biography as merely the linear tale of a performing life's progress. Rather, we may use star chronicles as springboards for philosophical investigations, however impromptu, into our own sight lines.

Audrey Hepburn, a biography by Barry Paris, offers a grid for dream inquiries into star consciousness. The pulse points that most fascinate me are relations between Hepburn and other female luminaries, including Colette, Edith Head, Deborah Kerr, Leslie Caron, Ava Gardner, Grace Kelly, Judy Garland, Elizabeth Taylor, Marni Nixon, Julie Andrews, Mia Farrow, Jeanne Moreau, Merle Oberon, Capucine, and Cher. I could advance a lesbian interpretation of Audrey Hepburn's oeuvre, though that is not my present aim: instead, I wish to inquire, modestly, into reverberations between Audrey's consciousness and the interiors of other stars.

Is it sufficiently well-known that Colette discovered Audrey Hepburn? Paris's account of the event is worth quoting in full:

> Colette, seventy-eight, was being propelled through the hotel lobby—sipping a liqueur and resplendent in her red corkscrew curls—when her wheelchair was blocked by a group of actors, technicians and their film equipment. The chair got tangled in some wires, and director Jean Boyer was cross about the interruption. But he fell respectfully silent when he recognized Colette, and shooting was halted while he went over to pay his respects. During that interaction and the time it took to get her chair sorted out, Colette studied the activity with her usual curiosity. . . . A girl in the background, oblivious to Colette, was taking advantage of the unplanned break to frolic with two of the musicians off to the side. She was dancing around them in playful fashion; she seemed graceful and awkward at the same time; she was extremely pretty. The old author's eyes narrowed. Suddenly she announced, "Voilà! There is my Gigi!"

There we have the origin of Hepburn's 1951 Broadway debut as Gigi, itself the catalyst for the beginning of her American film career in *Roman Holiday* (1953). After her Gigi lost Broadway's Tony Award for Best Actress to Julie Harris (for Sally Bowles in *I Am a Camera*), Colette sent the loser a photo inscribed, *For Audrey Hepburn, a treasure which I found on the sands.* That a major French writer should have helped launch an American film actress (whose weird thin androgynous beauty is a *nonliterary* treasure) invites me to imagine Colette's gaze, across the text/film divide, toward Hepburn, and to imagine Hepburn's reciprocal Orphean gaze toward literature and toward France, as well as toward wheelchair-bound plumpness and grandmotherly sapphism. This Monte Carlo hotel anecdote authorizes us to see on-screen Hepburn as if through Colette's desiring, fairy-godmother eyes.

A kindred encounter (patroness meets young star) couples Hepburn and legendary Hollywood costume designer Edith Head, famous for black bangs and her no-nonsense *jolie laide* (à la Diana Vreeland) attitude toward the women whose embodiment she managed. Head designed Hepburn's costumes for *Roman Holiday* as well as *Sabrina* (though Hubert de Givenchy was the true prime mover behind the *Sabrina* gowns). Head "marveled at Hepburn's ability to consume five chocolate éclairs at a time." Imagine Head watching Hepburn eat the éclairs; are the women sitting together on drugstore counter stools, and is Head eating, or merely admiring ingenue appetite? Head recalls: "Like Dietrich, Audrey's fittings became the ten-hour not the ten-minute variety. She knew exactly how she wanted to look or what worked best for her, yet she was never arrogant or demanding. She had an adorable sweetness that made you feel like a mother getting her only daughter ready for her prom." See Head leap to the maternal vantage; conjuring Hepburn as the only daughter, Head becomes the mother amorously alone with her genetic echo.

Hepburn's relations to star midwives (Colette and Head) are act one of the biodrama; act two features sororal tableaux of Hepburn and her Hollywood peers. Star affect (whether rivalry or love) is private; the presence of a reader/beholder makes it public. What's peculiar is not that Audrey and, say, Deborah Kerr, were friends, but that others knew that they were friends, and that others could thus perceive the friendship, spy on it. Take this moment, and the fact that I am here to pass it on to you: at the Oscar ceremony, 25 March 1954, as Hepburn "was rushing to change clothes, she ran into fellow nominee Deborah Kerr, just arrived—equally breathless—from her own Broadway hit, *Tea and Sympathy*. They wished each other luck and agreed Leslie Caron was going to win for *Lili*." They were wrong: Hepburn won for *Roman Holiday*. Skip ahead two years, once more at the Oscars: Hepburn, nominated again as Best Actress, this time for *Sabrina*, "lost to Grace Kelly for *The Country Girl* (who should have lost to Judy Garland for *A Star Is Born*)." Contemplate the star intertextuality, the ricocheting gazes of envy and admiration, between Hepburn, Caron, Kerr, Kelly, and Garland. Caron confesses that she and Hepburn felt "sibling recognition" whenever they met. Sibling recognition among stars is so intense, and so dizzying to me as I try to describe it, that I must, for clarity's sake, experimentally isolate two relationships (Liz/Audrey and Julie/Audrey), in order not to die in the crossfire of star glances.

Elizabeth Taylor herself wanted the part of Eliza Doolittle: reportedly, she said, "Get me *My Fair Lady*" to then-husband Eddie Fisher and agent Kurt Frings. I wonder if Liz knew that Audrey had turned down the part of Cleopatra in 1959. Audrey later said, "Oh come on, I'm not a movie star. Liz Taylor is a movie star." For a movie star, that's a surreal disclaimer, though it allows us to imagine Audrey looking up to Liz. When Liz and Audrey accidentally met at an Academy Awards bash hosted by Swifty Lazar, the two stars embraced, and then "Audrey pointed to one of Elizabeth's enormous jewels and asked, 'Kenny Lane?' 'No, Richard Burton,' replied Taylor, and both stars screamed with laughter." It blows my mind—I don't know a more proper way to say it—to imagine Hepburn pointing to Taylor's jewels, as if the two were simply women at a party, not symbolic figures cutting through cocktail chatter with the laser-sharp laughter of bacchantes. It also blows my mind to imagine that someone nonstellar (the journalist Dominick Dunne) was privy to this exchange. The moment I want to isolate, as if it were a "Kenny Lane" faux bauble, is Audrey looking at Liz's jewels, meanwhile possibly thinking, "Liz likes her jewels, and I like Liz, and I want to say something nice to her about them." Trying to describe these star intersections reduces me to bathos and inanity, but I remain committed to discovering a language that may liberate the potential energy compacted in such asides as "Kenny Lane?"

My Fair Lady was a wind tunnel of star identity blur. Julie Andrews deserved to play Eliza Doolittle, and why couldn't a technology or aesthetics have been invented so that both stars could impersonate the guttersnipe in the same movie? (Andrews so haunts Hepburn's portrayal that it's as if the rivals were simultaneously present in the Cukor film.) Julie had created the part in London and New York; because her original-cast album of the score sold 32 million copies, there were potentially 32 million "aggrieved friends of Julie Andrews" to resent Hepburn's theft. (Fascinating fact: Rock Hudson was considered for the role of Henry Higgins in the movie.*) Julie got her revenge when she won the 1965 Best Actress Oscar for *Mary Poppins*, her first movie role (Warner Brothers had refused her the part of Eliza because she'd never—until *Poppins*—performed in a film); Audrey wasn't even nominated for her work in *My Fair Lady*, an omission prompting Julie to say sympathetically to the press, "I think Audrey should have been nominated. I'm very sorry she wasn't." Hepburn couldn't sing: her songs were dubbed by Marni Nixon, who'd also ghosted for Deborah Kerr in *The King and I* and *An Affair to Remember*, and for Natalie Wood in *West Side Story*. If Marni Nixon's voice dominates Hepburn's impersonation, Hepburn was only imperfectly aware of the haunting—or tried to repress it: when Larry King in 1991 asked her who'd done the singing in *My Fair Lady*, she said, "I've forgotten the name, a lovely girl." In the same interview she confessed, "I did think the part of Eliza was right for me, but it was Julie Andrews's, so I had sort of an aching heart about it." Identities cross, compete, combine: Marni Nixon remembers, "It's funny. Alan Jay Lerner said in his biography that I dubbed *Gigi*, which I didn't. It was Betty Wand." Do you see how stars change places, a fair lady *mise en abîme* stretching from Betty Wand to Colette? We readers and

*Contemplate another virtual cast: Doris Day and Katharine Hepburn were considered for the leads as lesbian and crypto-lesbian in the 1961 film version of Lillian Hellman's *The Children's Hour*, parts that eventually went to Audrey Hepburn and Shirley MacLaine. Merle Oberon, too, haunts Audrey, for Merle played Audrey's future part in *These Three*, the 1936 film version of the Hellman play, and Hepburn eventually became lovers with Oberon's widower, Rob Wolders. . . . You can see how sticky, intricate, and historic are the veins of connection between fellow Hollywood players.

viewers can absorb this star intertextuality, and ponder it as if it were an architectural feature of our own hearts. The Gothic *My Fair Lady* drama culminated at the 1965 Oscars, at which Julie Andrews won Best Actress: Hepburn, standing in for Patricia Neal (who'd suffered a stroke), received "a warm 'consolation' reception when she stepped out radiantly—in gorgeous Givenchy gown—to present" the Best Actor award, but forgot to mention that she was onstage as substitute for bedridden Neal. As Neal recalls:

> I had been told that Audrey Hepburn would bestow the honor in my place and I couldn't wait to hear all the nice things she said about me. . . . But suddenly she was handing Rex Harrison his award, and she hadn't said a thing about me. It had to be a mistake. I pounded on the table with my good hand. 'God! God! Me! Not me!' . . . She was a fantastic woman, really. But I was so angry that she didn't say, 'I'm here in her place.' I couldn't say the words. I could only stick out my tongue.

Once-mute Neal articulates the starry compulsion to body-swap: *I'm here in her place.* A star is beautiful not only in herself but in her status as substitute for other stars, including ourselves. It is the custom of tabloids pithily to acknowledge the queer interchangeability of stars: consider such headlines as JULIE ANDREWS CHOSEN, AUDREY HEPBURN OMITTED; and AUDREY SNUBS AILING STAR.

As Audrey edged toward retirement, she suffered substitution; she watched from the sidelines, without sorrow, as other stars took her place. Because she wanted to end her film career, she responded *senza rancor* to her obsolescence. By the late 1960s, after Hepburn's second marriage, to Italian psychiatrist (and playboy) Andrea Dotti, she said, "Now Mia Farrow will get my parts, and she's very welcome to most of them." Note the varied stars who abut Hepburn, in the years of her fade-out. Jeanne Moreau wrote a part for Hepburn—in *Lumière*—but when she refused it, Moreau took it for herself. At least Moreau and Hepburn occupy the same echelon. Hepburn's role in the sleazy film *Sidney Sheldon's Bloodline*, however, had already been turned down by the likes of Jacqueline Bisset, Candice Bergen, and Diane Keaton; another part that Hepburn rejected went eventually to Carol Burnett. On *Bloodline, Variety* commented: "It's a shock to see Hepburn playing a role that even Raquel Welch would have the good sense to turn down." By accepting or turning down a role (and then seeing it pass to a cinematic sister), the star sinks into relation with sibling luminaries: these moments of giving the role to Mia Farrow or stealing the role from Julie Andrews comprise Hepburn's Hitchcockian inner gallery of hauntings, a montage of dream-sister portraits. By the 1980s, her favorite contemporary actresses were Michelle Pfeiffer, Meryl Streep, Julia Roberts, and Cher. Hepburn told the *Wichita Eagle* that she liked "anything with Michelle Pfeiffer in it. I like to watch movies in my *bed*—that's the best place!" Colette wrote in bed; Hepburn watched TV in bed to see (with wistfulness or love?) her sloppy inheritors. I linger on the rumor of that glance: sleepy Hepburn admiring another actress on the TV screen. Her companion Rob Wolders remembers that, while traveling for UNICEF in Turkey, "one night we turned on the television, and there was *My Fair Lady*. I had never seen it and was looking forward to it. But it was in Turkish. The combination of Audrey speaking in Turkish and Marni Nixon singing was too much. I had to turn it off." (Why hadn't he already seen it?) Audrey in bed, watching herself: such star self-inspection fascinates me. Once, in real life, I asked Vanessa Redgrave what she felt like when she watched herself on-screen. She said that she tried to be objective about herself, and that an actor grows accustomed to self-scrutiny. Her response didn't resolve my curiosity. I wanted to feel, on my pulses, the temperature of her self-regard. Reading biographies allows me to indulge my curiosity about star introspection. Usually, in reading cinema chronicles, I feast on the star's cattiness, but Paris's book reveals no unkindness on his subject's part. Instead, he inspires us to revere and pity her. Audrey Hepburn didn't consider herself beautiful; her father abandoned her, and she never recovered from the loss; her mother was cold and critical. Hepburn spent her last years working, as UNICEF spokesperson, to help starving children. On her deathbed, her last words to her son, Luca, were "I'm sorry, but I'm ready to go." When I finished this biography, I wanted to remain silent; I wanted to respect Hepburn's restraint by restraining myself, acquiescing to the demands of strangers, and giving to charity. On the last page, Paris suggests that the reader may wish to write to the Audrey Hepburn Hollywood for Children Fund or the Audrey Hepburn Memorial Fund for UNICEF, and he supplies the addresses. Thus the book, and the life, gesture toward action, away from the conceptualism and claustrophobia, however holy, of star consciousness.

Two final lists, to prove how suggestive and numerous are the coordinates of a star's mapped world. Among the people thanked in Barry Paris's acknowledgments are the beautifully named Christine Sixma van Heemstra, Yvonne Quarles van Ufford, Arabella Ungaro, Countess Lorean Gaetani-Lovatelli, and Camilla Pecci-Blunt McGrath. Some women in whose company Audrey's second husband Andrea Dotti was spotted by journalists (Paris calls the list a "Whitman's Sampler" of Dotti's possible infidelities): Lupua Yerni, Countess Coppotelli Latini, Dalila Di Lazzaro, Marinella Giordana, and Countess Iliana Coritelli Lovatelli. These names are condensed droplets of Audrey Hepburn's noun-rich *nebbia*. If moviegoing disperses this mist, I'll stay home and read biographies instead.

(1997)

LISTENING TO
ELISABETH SCHWARZKOPF

There must be a German word—opposed nouns clumped together in an unhappy hybrid—to describe my response to Elisabeth Schwarzkopf's voice. I don't know German, so I will invent the word. Worldlongingbitterness. Historyerasingbeauty. Hatredsublimity.

I listen to Schwarzkopf while I take early evening baths. Sometimes I also play Miles Davis, Chris Connor, Bev Kelly, Alfred Cortot, or Mafalda Favero—but best for baths is Schwarzkopf, because her faultless voice carries so well above running water, and because her precise pitch and narrow vibrato recall me to highest principles. The music comes from speakers in a far room, so the piano accompaniment fades into inaudibility, and Schwarzkopf's voice alone penetrates my sanctuary. I bathe to hide my body under a mantle of bubbles, and to renew my aesthetic vows: I want to attain the clean pure line, of which Schwarzkopf is high priestess.

Purity is a dangerous ideology, but I embrace it while under Schwarzkopf's sway. Her voice tries to stand apart from vulgarity and taint, including the stain of her own past.

∞

Until recently, one heard a lot about Maria Callas, and too little about Elisabeth Schwarzkopf—the other scandalous and charismatic soprano of the 1950s. The two were, almost, friends. There are fascinating pictures of the two divas dining together—able to be nice to each other because their essential repertoires didn't overlap. In one emblematic photo, they share a table in Milan, circa 1954. Callas—painted lips seductively parted, nails shellacked, eyeliner drawn beyond the lid, in the Medea manner—stares at the camera, while Schwarzkopf, too scholastic to waste time striking poses, looks away. Once, she gave Callas a voice lesson in the restaurant Biffi Scala, and diners and waiters looked on as the two sopranos explored each other's instruments. As Schwarzkopf's husband, Walter Legge, recalled, "Callas sang with full voice the notes that were giving her trouble, while Schwarzkopf felt her diaphragm, lower jaw, throat and ribs. . . . Within minutes Schwarzkopf was singing the same notes while Callas prodded her in the same places to find out how she kept those notes steady." Schwarzkopf claimed to have given up the role of Violetta after hearing Callas sing it; but, in fact, Schwarzkopf gave up most of her roles, focusing finally on only six—the Marschallin, the Countess in *Figaro*, Donna Elvira, the Countess in *Capriccio*, Alice Ford, and Fiordiligi. Such self-imposed limitation is characteristic of Schwarzkopf's art, which some critics call mannered.

Schwarzkopf, now eighty and living near Zürich, is undergoing a public reconsideration, but the stuff of the reappraisal is familiar to veterans of the vocal world. Schwarzkopf began her career in Nazi Germany. Debuting with the Deutsche Oper in 1937, she sang regularly during the war, but hit the international scene after the Third Reich's defeat. A biography of the soprano by British musicologist Alan Jefferson claims to clarify the nature of her Nazi allegiance.

Schwarzkopf has maintained, most famously in a 1983 letter to the *New York Times*, that she was involved with the Nazi Party only as far as she had to be to continue singing. According to Jefferson, on the basis of material he found in the soprano's ample yet heretofore unexplored *Reichskulturkammer* file, she was a *Führerin*, a leader, of a Nazi student organization for one term, and became a member of the Party in 1940. Her Party number was 7,548,960. To join, Jefferson makes explicit, Schwarzkopf "had to sign a form stating that she came from an entirely Aryan family and had never been in any way connected with the Jewish faith; then, eight days later, she made another detailed declaration about the racial purity of her parents and grandparents, completed in her presence by a Party official at the Deutsche Oper." Jefferson reminds us that Party membership was hardly compulsory for "Aryan" musicians: when Wilhelm Furtwängler led the Berlin Philharmonic Orchestra "only eight out of the 110 players were Party members."

Schwarzkopf sang for the Waffen-S.S. on the Eastern front, and she was a favorite of Goebbels and appeared in at least five propaganda films under his aegis. I have seen two clips. In one, she sings (in German) the end of act one of Bizet's *Carmen*: the gypsy persuades Don José, the officer, to unshackle her while a Nazi officer in the opera-house audience watches. In another clip, she warbles Schumann in a tranquil living room, while a servant moves anxiously to the window to watch enemy planes cross the sky.

After the war, Schwarzkopf's vessel hit choppy waters: she needed to undergo de-Nazification, and, according to Jefferson, she "fudged" by giving, on four separate occasions, misleading or conflicting answers to the Allies on the subject of her Nazi involvement. Jefferson alludes to intriguing rumors:

The main reason [she lied] was probably fear for her career, which had progressed very satisfactorily so far; but we do not know exactly what lay at the core of this fear, what precisely she was trying to hide or attempting to obliterate, if it was more than just her Party membership. Colleagues and others have spoken of Schwarzkopf's "protector" in the highest ranks of the Party, but while two names in particular have been mentioned with some confidence, this does not constitute evidence.

Blacklisted (along with Furtwängler and Herbert von Karajan), she was forbidden to perform, and was threatened with deportation to Germany from Austria, where she had been singing with the Theater an der Wien. Finally, however, in early 1947, her case was closed, and she was effectively exonerated.

By then she had met Walter Legge. She moved to London in 1947, and in 1953 they married. Legge himself had a legendary career as a record producer. For EMI, he supervised not only most of his wife's great recordings, but many of Callas's; he shaped his wife's phrases, and from the beginning he seems to have supervised the rehabilitation of her reputation. Under his wing (not without jealousy and skepticism among those in the music world who felt he exercised undue influence), she became a beloved fixture of the world's opera and recital stages. The Met, however, refused her: according to one person who was present at a Boston press conference, Schwarzkopf asserted that Sir Rudolf Bing, the general manager, had offered her the part of Tatyana in *Eugene Onegin*, knowing full well that she would come aboard only for a new production of *Der Rosenkavalier*. Bing eventually conceded, and in 1964 she gave New York her Marschallin. She continued to sing, with a darkened yet still superbly controlled voice, until 1979, when her husband died. Then came the fastidious master classes. Terrence McNally has put forward "master class" as shorthand for a has-been's sadistic pedagogy. Schwarzkopf, in master classes, seems to have been formidable: to a student struggling with how to place the consonant *t* in a Wolf song, Schwarzkopf said (according to Jefferson), "You killed it with your chin!"

∞

When Renata Tebaldi was asked how she spends her retirement, she replied, "I am honored." Schwarzkopf, too, has occupied her days absorbing accolades and approving CD remasterings of old LPs. She became a Dame Commander of the Most Excellent Order of the British Empire in 1992, and recently EMI Classics released the *Elisabeth Schwarzkopf Songbook*, a collection of three disks of lieder performances, chosen by the soprano herself; a CD version of the mono recording of Karajan's *Rosenkavalier*, remastered under Schwarzkopf's supervision; and a video documentary, *Elisabeth Schwarzkopf: A Self-Portrait*, in which the soprano, in voice-over, describes her career and her aesthetic philosophy but refuses to appear on camera. The *Self-Portrait* is a troubling document not only because it includes background footage of German trains, but because she seems so unrepentant.

In retrospective commentary, Schwarzkopf describes her attitude toward what she names, euphemistically, politics, as if it were not also the Holocaust: "I've heard people say, 'Oh, well, your parents should have made you interested in politics!' " But when visitors talked about events in Germany, her parents ordered her out of the room: "My father said, my mother also, 'Go away. Don't listen, don't listen. . . . you go, you go.' And nobody will understand, nowadays, that we lived this kind of sheltered life, concentrated solely on music and on singing. It was very special." The war years seemed a series of lucky breaks, she says: "Usually the good times in my life came out of the very bad ones." She caught tuberculosis while filming propaganda in Berlin, and so she went to the mountains to recover, thereby missing the worst attacks on the city. Her good fortune continued: "I could go straight from tuberculosis to the old Vienna State Opera and sing, and then the Vienna State Opera was bombed—that was another end—but it made me sing in the Theater an der Wien, which was ever so much better than a big theater for me. It was marvelous, the acoustics and everything. So that was also great luck."

Schwarzkopf remains morbidly conscious of the specifically German nature of her art. Recalling the protesters outside her first New York recital, she claims they were picketing against "the German," but in truth they were picketing against "the Nazi."

(Schwarzkopf's refusal to note the difference between German and Nazi allows one to remember that if *Nazi* nowadays is sometimes invoked as a metaphor, in Schwarzkopf's case it was literal.) Her New York debut was a success, and she says that she was proud to win friends "in America, not for myself, but for what we stood for, the German art." She asserts that when she sang at the United Nations, in 1959, she was proud "to confront our previous enemies, again with the German language, via lieder singing." And in footage from a master class, Schwarzkopf instructs a student whose German is inadequate: "Too bad you weren't born with the language. The most beautiful lieder come from German poems. I can't help it."

There is nothing wrong with being proud of German poetry and music. But it appears that Schwarzkopf took seriously what Goebbels told the Germans in 1933: "Musical education is a political message to the whole nation, no longer the private business of the individual."

One conventional way to describe Schwarzkopf's timbre is "covered." Her voice sounds caught in her throat or in her forehead—trapped somewhere, confined by its own smallness—yet also powerful and venal enough to cut straight through impediment. When Schwarzkopf covers the tone, she directs it on a muted detour through the mask, and I feel that just as she is converting the note from error into righteousness, so she is protecting me from knowledge of her past, and helping me convert my own vulgarity into an acceptable facade. This signature sound takes the aggressive impulse—the ambition to be a great singer, the ambition to be immortal—and polishes it into something palatable, lustrous; preoccupied with beauty, she has no time for evil, or she has mastered the technique of turning unpleasantness into a mournfully pellucid tone. In the great phrases she doesn't hit the note head on: it just appears, out of the vapor. One never hears the attack—just the released pitch.

I am sad that I never heard Schwarzkopf sing in person: I never witnessed that teal-gowned splendor she unfurled on the

recital stage, with her sumptuous hairstyle and imperial manner—
the gracious chatelaine, urbanely dispensing encore favors. I must
remain content with the discs, among which I have many favorites.
(I haven't heard the recordings she made during the Third Reich;
although she began recording in 1937, the origins of her career
are misrepresented on an EMI Angel compilation called *The Early
Years*, which includes performances from 1946 to 1955.) Her
"Four Last Songs" (Richard Strauss's "Vier letzte Lieder") are in-
dispensable. I know only the first version, recorded in 1953. (Some
connoisseurs prefer the later version, 1965, conducted by George
Szell.) I never tire of these songs, sung by anyone, and particularly
I never tire of them sung by Schwarzkopf, because, even in 1953,
not yet at her career's midpoint, she mingles the blooming (a
young woman's cantilena soaring above the orchestra) with the
autumnal (Strauss saying good-bye to the voice and to the world).

Schwarzkopf has certainly achieved immortality on the basis
of her renditions of Schubert and Mozart lieder (especially fine
are the versions recorded with the piano accompaniments of Edwin Fischer and Walter Gieseking). Slow tempi permit diminuendi nested within diminuendi, and microscopic attention to
vowel coloration. (*Tod*—death—is always a word that Schwarzkopf gives its full dark weight). But no matter how slow, how far
pushed toward the breaking point, her phrases always cohere; her
intense, small, forward tone seems *poured* through her cheekbones. I love her late (1973) recording of Schumann's *Liederkreis*,
a performance of which she didn't wholeheartedly approve. She
thought her voice sounded too old. I agree, but I love it old, con-
signed to vocal compromise, the songs transposed down, the signs
of Schumann's incipient madness everywhere evident in the hag-
gard, erratic harmonies. I love her Belinda in *Dido and Aeneas*,
singing "Pursue thy conquest, Love!" But, above all, I associate
her with the renunciatory soprano line in the last-act trio of
Rosenkavalier. No matter what soprano is singing the Marschallin, I always imagine it is Schwarzkopf saying (I freely paraphrase), "There are more things in the world than I could ever
dream, and until the dire event happens to you, you never believe
it will happen—but then it happens."

And what of this listener's history? I am an assimilated Jew, content to be assimilated, relieved to be religiously unobservant. I don't know any Hebrew, or have forgotten the little I once learned. My father, with his parents, left Germany in 1937. Other members of his family left, too. Others stayed. That story is not entirely mine to tell. But it is my Schwarzkopf story. Listening to Schwarzkopf, I feel at my most Jewish, if only because in listening to her I grow to feel quite intensely German.

I remember my father telling me about Beethoven's deafness and Beethoven's genius, and I associated the two—deafness, genius—with men like my father, who had ideas, who had troubles, and who came from Germany.

I wasn't born with the German language, but I imagine that Schwarzkopf and I share a creed—an infatuation with the legato line. Listening, I ride with Schwarzkopf into the Teutonic balm she offers, and I allow her sound to purify me. And yet I also let her timbre purify her past. Listening, I pity Schwarzkopf—because, I imagine, her voice sounds as if it might have pitied me. I pity her because she suffered, it seems, for her art—because one hears stories about how hard she forced herself to work, and how hard her husband worked her in the recording and practice studio. Even Karajan once protested to Legge, "Don't crucify the girl!" Jefferson reports that after one recital, Legge said to her, "You sang that last Wolf *lied* like a pig." Indeed, Jefferson notes that Legge "was quite capable of humiliating or insulting her in public when she said or did something of which he disapproved."

Another persistent rumor: Legge was Jewish. I can find no proof. Neither can Jefferson, although he reports that Rudolf Bing, alluding to Schwarzkopf, once said, "I can forgive her for having worn a Nazi uniform and for taking an American colonel as a boyfriend right after the war, but I cannot swallow the fact that she then married a Jew." The thought comforts: maybe she repented?

There are many parallel cases to weigh, if you choose to consider art and prejudice. A few names—and oeuvres—often appearing, of late, before tribunals: Philip Larkin, Ezra Pound, T. S. Eliot, Richard Wagner. Not to mention Strauss and Karajan, who were, with Schwarzkopf, on Goebbel's official list of artists blessed by God. I don't bring up the Schwarzkopf case because I think it exemplifies any principle, or because I think it solves—or even casts a significant degree of light on—the relation between ideology and art, or between moral conduct and creative genius. I am preoccupied with the Schwarzkopf question only because her voice has presented me with an ambiguity ever since I first heard her sing the Verdi *Requiem* on the 1964 Giulini recording. Her voice, with its sublimely projected vowels and its air of a world that will never be marred or crimped or diminished, asks me whether I live fully and honestly enough, and whether I have too quickly shut the door on lost experience. Her voice asks whether I have paid attention, whether I have been sloppy, whether I have obeyed the score, and whether I have served the music, even if I can't guess what the music means. Her voice demands that I make a stricter reckoning of my own life and see if it measures up. Her voice shames me into wishing I were cleaner, sweeter, and more concise.

Tonight, another unfocused summer evening, I will play a live performance CD (1955, Carnegie Hall) of Schwarzkopf singing the great aria from Mozart's *Così fan tutte*, "Come scoglio": "How like an unchanging rock are my affections." Her voice will seem the agent of a paradoxical salvation, and I won't know whether she is saving me or whether I am saving her.

(1996)

THE REAL DAWN UPSHAW

*B*ackstage at the Met, after a performance of *Idomeneo*, I'm primed to meet soprano Dawn Upshaw, whom I take, rightly or wrongly, to be a gentle paradigm of present-day opera—an art shorn of excess. More than any singer on the contemporary scene, she has renounced the behavioral peculiarities that, in legend, constitute the diva's tool kit. (And yet ordinariness, pursued as a calling, somersaults into extraordinariness.) The Anouk Aimée lookalike whom I spotted in Orchestra Row H is waiting in the Plácido Domingo line; I stand in the Upshaw line. When James Levine walks by, and a fan tries to buttonhole him in conversation, the maestro politely says, "Sorry, I have to change out of my wet suit."

Upshaw's unremarkable dressing room door opens (from the outside, it could be a parole officer's), and a thirty-four-year-old woman with lovely, sane, evenly spaced features emerges in sweater, turtleneck, and jeans, her face scrubbed clean of makeup, eyelashes glistening, as if she'd just climbed out of a pool.

Was she happy onstage tonight?

"Well, it was a good performance." She means that tonight was a good group effort. She deflects attention from her own gifts.

When I ask for an autograph she balks. Why should we go through the diva charade? But then she consents.

∞

The Carlyle, where we meet for high tea, is smoke-filled. Upshaw utters no complaint. Later she tells me she didn't even notice the smoke.

"I don't usually get to do this sort of thing," she says, when she scrutinizes the fancy menu. She is too busy for such indulgences. She's just come from watching a dress rehearsal of *Pelléas et Mélisande*. "I've heard so many people around the house rave about the show," she says. By "house" she means the Met, not her other, real house, a three-story Tudor in Mount Vernon, New York, where she lives with her husband, Michael Nott, a musicologist, and her two children.

Much can be learned from observing with what generous frequency Upshaw laughs in conversation: she laughs to set the interlocuter at ease, to insist that the afternoon will be jubilant. Much, too, can be learned from the laugh's robustness. It presents the wisdom of a contralto, not the effervescence of a soubrette. Talking, she doesn't plumply declaim her vowels and consonants but projects them with deliberateness. Her speaking voice is surprisingly low—deeper than her singing voice. One doctor suggested that she try to place her speaking voice higher, so as not to put pressure on it. Upshaw: "I tried for a while to speak 'up.' It's terrible. It's like trying to change your personality."

Discussing a transcendent climax from her rendition of Henryk Górecki's Third Symphony, she relates her philosophy of pitch: "My choral director in high school used to talk about pitch being like a circle. For each pitch he drew a line in the middle of

the circle, and said, 'You always want to sing in the upper half.'
Well, I like to take that a little further. An A is not just an A. It
has everything to do (if you're singing with other instruments)
with the colors of those instruments and where their pitches are
placed. I always feel like I find my niche with a pitch."

Upshaw's pitches—ecosystems—admit ambient colors (clari-
net, cello, triangle), as well as silence's nearby fingerprint. She removes vibrato and torques intonation because she wants to "rub"
against the orchestra. She says, "I love rubbing." Without vibrato, she can intensify the rubbing. She gestures with her hands,
to mimic the edged, amorous combat of two adjacent pitches. "If
notes are really close together and there's dissonance, in order to
hear what's going on you need to sing as clear a tone as possible,
and if there's too much vibrato, you're not going to tell where the
very, very center of the pitch is."

By exercising such control over intonation, she offers cogni-
tive clarity to the verismo-steeped listener: if vibrato represents—
or induces—psychological agitation, then Upshaw's pitches, washed
clean of yesterday's mannerisms, seem guarantors of tranquillity.

"I didn't have an incredible voice as a child. I had a very normal voice. Sometimes I used to tape-record myself singing along
with an LP, and I used to play it back and go, Yuck! So breathy! I
thought, I hope I never mature and get vibrato! In junior high I
didn't make it into the best choir. I never got the solo. Even when
I got to Manhattan School of Music I was not the big cheese in
the opera department. I don't think of my voice as being one of
those beautiful voices."

She has few regimens. "I try to drink twelve eight-ounce
glasses of water a day. Eight is pretty easy for me to do now. But I
have to work at getting twelve. I've gotten so much better at
drinking water." Sleep: "Ten hours is really great. Nine is essential. If I get less than that, I notice it in my singing." She sched-
ules two days' break between performances to rest her voice. And
she won't travel more than two weeks without seeing her husband
and children. "Something happens to me when I'm not with my
children. I start asking myself why I'm in this business, to a fairly
serious degree."

In search of quirks, I probe, and she confesses: "Another thing I do, which is maybe neurotic: I wash my hands a lot." Dietary peculiarities? None. She eats heartily before singing. "I'll eat just about anything. Once I felt like testing the gods and I had an ice cream sundae before a recital." She laughs. "And it was fine! I'm sure that doctors would say, 'There must have been a great deal of phlegm in the cords.'"

When she was pregnant, her voice changed: "My cords were feeling swollen, so that they weren't vibrating as easily. A woman's cords—they're different. They're filled with a lot of fluid, or can be. There hasn't been a whole lot of research. It's an unknown."

Once Upshaw walked into a tea party and one of her own CDs was playing as background music. She found the experience uncomfortable. Does her own voice give her goosebumps? "I only got goosebumps whenever I played oboe in junior-high band, or when I sang in choirs." If she can't give herself shivers, what does she think of her voice? She hopes it sounds vulnerable: "There's something beautiful about vulnerability."

Because sublimities of art resist description, we talk about housework. "We only recently got help with cleaning the house. That's been a real luxury. We started that at Christmas time. Well, I feel kind of guilty, to tell you the truth. I used to do all the bathrooms."

So even a year ago she was cleaning bathrooms?

"Oh, yeah. I still do. I do lots of scrubbing. I don't think of myself as some sort of queen. We have a very ordinary household."

It is a mundanity whose miraculousness speaks in every warm, glassy note she sings.

Next stop, Des Moines, Iowa: Upshaw is giving a recital at Drake University, with pianist Margo Garrett. In the afternoon, the two meet for rehearsal. First, Upshaw needs to warm up. "Unfortunately, you'll be able to hear me," she says. Indeed, we can. Her vocalise is like birdsong in Eden. The same cords that sing Mozart's Susanna are now crossing unscripted intervals; her characteristic timbre now exists independent of a composer's will. She warbles, drawing sound all the way downward from the top of her voice to its bottom—a quick, purging burr, a glissando that sweeps and tests every crevice of the instrument and pronounces the organism healthy.

She wears a flower-print shirt over loose black pants. Her hair, I'll wager, is the shortest of any soprano's in history. Short hair leaves room for the features to shine: "I like a lot of light on my face," she tells the stage manager.

At one point during rehearsal she steps forward and asks the three of us in the audience, "How does it sound?" She means balance—is she too loud, too soft? No singer has ever asked me to respond. It's an uncanny moment: as if a figure from a frieze looked down and asked what I thought of the frieze.

Rehearsal continues for two hours: the atmosphere that her voice catalyzes in the listener is taut languor, stretched to its measuring utmost. To accommodate the enormousness—Upshaw's voice filling the house, and I, in my seat, responsible for missing none of its overtones—I tilt my head to the side, as if sitting up straight would obstruct sympathetic vibrations.

She sways when she sings; rises on tiptoe to find a note; bends her knees. Pants reveal—and gowns conceal—the entire body's role in voice production. Upshaw often wears pants in recital, wanting to be comfortable, and not wishing to be distracted by the dress's glitz, and the "m'lady" traditions of gesture that go along with gowns.

Today she is, as usual, stringent with herself. After she sings a phrase that sounds perfectly wonderful, she frowns, clucks dismissively, and says, "Let's do it again." She has a dual identity: she is her voice, but she must also judge it, with the businesslike detachment of a contractor supervising construction. Her profession entails dissatisfaction with the self as it stands—a persistent desire to remake the moment, even if the moment is already over.

Singing a prolonged note, she flutters her fingers outward in the air, then stops, disappointed, and says, "The sound wasn't spinning." She hadn't achieved the desired iridescence. Traversing a phrase, she touches her ear, her cheek, as if to align the pitch, to push it toward a peak. Halfway through rehearsal she begins to "mark"—sing at half voice.

The rehearsal alternates between chatter and labor, without segue. Small talk: Upshaw compliments Garrett's glasses. The two discuss whether they will get dressed at the hotel or downstairs in the concert hall's unglamorous basement. Then seriousness overtakes the soprano's features; her stance shifts. Instantly she must allow the music to uplift her, and she must make a spectacle of her uplifted state.

To be in the presence of a vocalist leaping from speech to song may inspire the listener to effect similar transitions, upward, past crisis, toward conversion.

∞

That evening Upshaw walks onstage in a glittery green floor-length dress; vine-embroidered, it resembles the leaf-print scarf draped over the singer on the cover of her Grammy-winning *The Girl with Orange Lips* CD. Gel spikes her hair. And she is wearing full makeup.

She underplays the concert's sublimity by speaking, impromptu, between pieces. She provides a lightly feminist context for songs by Ruth Crawford Seeger, who, says Upshaw, "stayed at home," rather than devote herself to composition. "Luckily things have changed a little bit."

Afterward, at the reception, the only beverages are orange juice or coffee. An assistant brings Dawn a glass of juice. When a couple, holding white canes, hesitantly approach, the singer interrupts her conversation, touches them, says, "Hello, I'm Dawn Upshaw." Later in the reception a fan gushes, "I have an entire Dawn Upshaw CD collection," and the object of praise says, "I don't exactly know how to deal with that." A young man with shiny dark hair and bright eyes introduces himself: he will be singing for Upshaw at tomorrow morning's master class. She guesses: "You're a tenor?"

Her profession depends on supremacy. And yet because she's also a decent person, she must ignore her power. Earlier, when I called her recent Met broadcast "amazing," she skeptically said, disavowing mastery, "*Amazing* is a pretty strong word to use."

Upshaw flew here to Des Moines from Houston, where she's in the midst of rehearsing *Der Rosenkavalier*. Several times she has referred, in conversation, to this exciting event: "my first Sophie." How are rehearsals progressing? She says that the Marschallin, Renée Fleming, hasn't arrived yet. "It's hard to dig into the role without a Marschallin." Upshaw gestures—a tunneling, shoveling motion.

⌒⌒

In Texas, I ask a Houston Grand Opera publicist for dish. None is forthcoming. Only this sweet fact: "Dawn borrowed my library card to check out books for her children."

Her Sophie avoids the pitfall of coyness. The voice is smaller than I remember (later, she confesses fatigue), but when she soars into the last-act-trio's stratosphere, melding her line with the renouncing Marschallin's, I remember how the pianist Richard Goode described Upshaw's temperament to me: "She has a style that's deeply emotional but that doesn't have any of the traces of emotionality—a kind of art that doesn't break the purity of surface, though there's something very strong underneath." Searching for the right words, he quietly said, "The wavelength is a very clear and intense and genuine one. She wants to make herself transparent."

On high, exposed notes, she swells, hastening toward the ineffable. And yet, of the role, she cautiously admits, not wanting to seem ungrateful for the opportunity to sing it, "All my life I've been saying, 'I really want to do Sophie, I really want to do Sophie,' and now I'm working on it, and yes, it's great music, but to be quite honest, I'm a little disappointed." She has had her fill of "green" girls—Zerlina, Pamina, Despina.

Deferring to the leading lady, during curtain calls, Upshaw kisses her Marschallin's hand.

Backstage, Upshaw hasn't changed out of her frilly white gown. She hugs me, then says, "Oh, I'll get goop on your jacket."

(By goop, she means makeup.) I don't mind; I hope she gets goop on me. Accustomed to admiring vocal plenitude from a distance, I relish the chance to be touched by any goop that could, by proxy, signify song.

∞

"I understand there's beautiful rain that comes down in the first act," says Upshaw, the next morning, at brunch. Because she's offstage, she's never had a chance to see it.

She says, "Would you be interested in trying this spinach-artichoke dip?"

She explains the pleasure that singing gives her, in terms a nonsinger can understand. The closest approximation is swimming laps: "When I stop, I'm tingly. Do you know that kind of tingle? Especially I feel it in my face, but I sort of feel it all over my body. There's something so calming about using my energies that way and feeling like I'm using every part of my body."

Inevitably, describing a singer, I am describing a body. And so I ask her height.

"Do I look like an Amazon? I'm five seven."

I still want stories of indulgences. She has only one to offer. "Once I left a hotel because I could not stand the decor." She laughs. "It was a huge Best Western place for people who come for conferences. It's the first time I've ever done that. I felt really guilty. But I just thought, I have to be away from my family! There was a lot of noise in the halls. It was homecoming weekend in this college town. And the room was orange and purple."

Once, when Upshaw was in a hotel room, warming up for a concert, a woman knocked and said, "I'm a mathematician. You sound like you have a very nice voice. I think there's a lot of promise in it. I hope you'll continue. But I'd really appreciate it if you wouldn't sing right now, because I'm trying to work with numbers." Upshaw said, "Sure." And she stopped. The soprano explains, "It would be annoying to me in a hotel if I were next door to a singer. We all have personal relations to individual voices. Sometimes you can be picky about what you want to hear."

Indeed, I am picky about what I want to hear, and I have personal relations with voices. I revere Upshaw, above all singers of her generation, because of her voice's thought-charged clarity, and its resemblance to the light of ordinary days. She offers a rare amber—the variousness of our historical moment, crystallized in a tone that never advertises its own charms but unceremoniously uses its merit to advance specific heartbroken or uplifted meanings. When she sings, the word's weight predominates.

Upshaw performs contemporary American music (Jacob Druckman, John Harbison, Earl Kim, Joseph Schwantner) with the same idiomatic, sincere ease she brings to Mozart, Bach, Gluck, or to Ravel, Poulenc, and Messiaen. Musically, "she switches gears faster than any truck driver on the highway," says Eric Stern, who collaborated (as conductor, arranger, and pianist) with Upshaw on a quirky, stirring album of American musical theater songs, *I Wish It So*. Stern rhapsodizes: "Her sound when singing the vernacular is unlike anything I've heard. Lyric soprano singing is dying in the theater. The theater could benefit from the colors of Dawn's palette." However, belting onstage seven times a week would quickly wear her down, and she admits to hazarding, on *I Wish It So*, low notes that she wouldn't comfortably try at the cavernous Met.

If European art songs could be distilled to an adjective, says Stern, then American art songs could be distilled to a verb. And Upshaw sings with a verb's giddy intransitivity: she sends force spinning forward—the unnamed vector of a woman intent on leading a spirited and magnanimous life.

What careers resemble hers? In conversation she invokes Elisabeth Schumann and Jan DeGaetani as idols. The annals of song are rich with peculiar undertakings, and it would be rash to claim that Upshaw's path is unprecedented.

I wonder if she has a dark side. Harbison guesses that anyone who responds to Rilke as strongly as Upshaw does must have hidden aspects. Sometimes I sense darkness on a tone's fringes—

when a good clean note admits a sad word's meaning, or when she cooperates so fully with her musical context that serenity begins to suggest surrender.

By any standards, Dawn Upshaw is a phenomenon; but she would be the last to agree with such an effusive judgment. ("Dawn is allergic to hype," Goode says.) Reviews have been unanimously laudatory; colleagues and associates profess complete admiration. The one criticism sometimes made of Upshaw is that, at this phase in her career, her timbre can't purvey gloom, grandeur, or high drama, and may seem, to certain listeners, overly radiant. I, for one, have a high tolerance for radiance.

In opera, she is often typecast, because of her light lyric voice, but in recital and recording she can venture into exotic, dramatic postures. She is interested in experimental programming, and in thematically arranged recordings over which she has great control, like *White Moon*, a collection of ethereal works by Purcell, Villa-Lobos, Crumb, and others. She can imagine a career in which self-generated, unconventional projects are the norm.

Not single-handedly, she is changing the assumptions that underlie classical music—challenging its protocols, dissipating the cult of personality, removing false formalities, and shattering the boundary dividing the dead composer from the living. Without apology, she sings the works of her contemporaries. Thus when she essays Schubert or Mozart, they, too, seem new-minted, unsentimental. Like all expert interpreters, she respects the score, but not as if she were Norma walking into the pyre.

In every phrase Upshaw sings, one notices her refusal to be haughty, her insistence on acknowledging music's affinity with the everyday. Is it difficult, given the pressures she's under, to maintain serenity? Not, she says, when she keeps her mind on reality: "The reality is that I love music, that I want to serve the music and the words, that I am especially thrilled to have a certain control of my own work, and to make in some areas my own choices completely about what I want to do, and that I have enough people supporting me who are interested in hearing me or working with me or hiring me that life is good right now. That's the reality."

Art song and opera have never specialized in reality. Upshaw smuggles into her performances a new, contraband substance: the ambiguous timbre of the real.

(1995)

MY EVENING WITH
ALEC BALDWIN

I meet Alec Baldwin, star of *The Shadow* and *Malice*, at the Surrogate's Court on Chambers Street, New York City, where his new movie, *The Confession*, is being filmed. Today, it "wraps": shooting ends. He gets a brief vacation, and then he begins rehearsals for the New York Shakespeare Festival's *Macbeth*, in which he plays the hero, opposite Angela Bassett.

Alec is a smart guy. He uses words like *template*. We hit it off.

He's on the tall side, and he gives an impression of godly bulk. His eyes, a beautiful blue, are rather small, but they shine. He's wearing a snug blue Nino Cerruti suit. He has thick wrists, thick fingers. His shoulders are huge, his head large, his gait unmeandering. He knows where he wants to go and he goes there fast, dispensing witticisms or words of encouragement to crew members as he passes them. I overhear people saying, "Alec's wonderful. Fun. Divine." Everyone's excited. It's a big day for Alec. His movie is being wrapped.

It is extremely difficult to talk to a star, even if the star is making an effort to be nice. One does not wish to intrude; even simple eye contact seems rude.

"Do you have makeup on?" I begin, noticing beige cover-up around the corners of Alec's eyes.

"Some," he says. "Why?" He's sitting on a director's chair. I am standing inches from him.

"I'm just curious. I've never been on a movie set." I ask what he puts in his hair.

"Thick cow-snot KMS jelly, a kind of airplane glue, like they use in professional aviation programs. I have Chinese hair. I have stick-straight hair. I don't have fabulous body to my hair like you do. You have really great body."

I did not make this up. Alec Baldwin really said I have great body.

I ask about his clothes.

He admits, "My brother Billy is more the classic fit. I'm a lit-tle misshapen in the couture department. I'm big. I can't wear all the clothes I want to wear." He mentions Ralph Lauren. "He's your size in real life. Have you met Ralph Lauren?"

"I haven't met anybody."

"He's a very tiny guy, really small. He has a man's head on a boy's body."

Some clothes are sent free to him, but his wife, Kim Basinger, star of *L.A. Confidential*, gets more. "My wife gets a phone-booth-size box of clothes once a month from some designer that wants to give her the clothing."

I wonder if Alec hates the press. He says to me, "Why do you do this for a living? Do you feel a burning need to tell the world about other people?"

"I feel a burning need to meet stars."

That stumps him.

Alec is required on-camera, and so I talk to his stand-in, the handsome Todd Etelson.

Five people were interviewed for the job. Todd proudly says, "Alec personally picked me."

When Alec returns, I ask what developmental stage his two-year-old daughter, Ireland Eliesse, has reached.

"The princess stage. Her ass gets shined all day long."

He clears his throat frequently. He speaks with a raspy, low voice.

He says, "I'm not Clint Eastwood." Sure, Alec gets fan letters, but "not a million a day, like Arnold Schwarzenegger."

I don't ask him many questions: I let him go on. He likes to talk, and I like to hear him talk. But I think Alec is impatient with the way the interview is proceeding. He says, "Got any more searing questions to ask me?"

So I ask him about beauty, his own. He confesses, "My weight goes up and down radically. If I ate reasonably, and drank a lot of water, and worked out every day, and didn't eat fattening desserts, cake, I would lose weight quickly. I have a very high metabolism. For me to keep my weight down is such a premium for my work that I'm thinking of hiring a cook—getting somebody who can cook all my vegetarian meals."

Alec, seeing my vinyl jacket, asks if I'm an animal-rights person. I point out my leather pants. He doesn't seem to object to leather. Fur is another matter.

∽

After the film wraps, and each actor receives a round of applause, and Alec gives a speech in praise of the crew, he disappears into a wardrobe trailer parked outside the courthouse. I fear our interview is over, though he never said good-bye. I skulk around the set and have words with his coproducer, Corrinne Mann, who reminds me of a pretty Joan Rivers. As I'm speaking to Corrinne, she says, "Excuse me, I have to put on my lipstick." I watch her apply it.

She's not comfortable speaking into my tape recorder, so I turn it off.

What's the wildest thing she's seen Alec do?

"You have it all wrong," she snaps. "He's a family man. His priority is his family. After that, it's his work. He likes to take risks with the material he chooses." Then she adds, "When he was wild, I didn't know him. Ask his brothers."

As if I could telephone a Baldwin.

I want to broach the subject of Alec's charisma, but I do it clumsily: "Are you in awe of Alec physically?"

She hits my arm.

I agree to guard her shopping bags while she wanders off, but after a while I grow impatient. I'm bored, standing in one place, guarding Corrinne's bags. I decide to abandon them. Fortunately, no one steals them.

Finally Alec emerges from the wardrobe trailer. He points to a waiting limo and tells me, "We're going for a ride. Sit in the front, my friend." I sit beside driver Fred Liberman, whose home base is Phoenix. Stipulated in all of Alec's film contracts is the requirement that Fred be his driver.

Alec sits in the backseat, directly behind me. He suggests that I face forward and hold the recorder over my shoulder. But I want to look at him. So I turn around, and get queasy from the reverse motion out the rear window.

We're driving to a restaurant (I think it's a seafood place) where he's meeting co-star Ben Kingsley. Alec looks tired now. He's wearing glasses, like the pair he wore in *Prelude to a Kiss*.

He's not too tired to tell another story. "I remember saying to my wife, we'd be sitting and watching TV, and I'd say, 'Who made this TV? This is the biggest piece of shit, this TV. I want to go out to the store and buy a good TV right now.' And she'd say, 'It's brand-new. It's a Mitsubishi.' I'd go into my bedroom and say, 'Who made this TV? This TV is a piece of shit. We've got to get the cable company in here. Obviously we have bad cable service.'" Then he realized the problem was his vision.

He won't wear contact lenses. "The idea of jamming something in my eye is—"

"Totally gross?"

"I'm really a weenie at heart."

I disagree. Alec Baldwin is not a weenie.

He grows wistful, talking of Marlon Brando: "What made Brando Brando was that he figured it out young. He still had all the juice and the meat and the muscle of a young guy and he put it all together. To put it all together when you're twenty-five years old: what an advantage! To still be young, and good-looking, and sexy: and you've got the secret. You've got the secret formula, the Kentucky Fried Chicken formula in your back pocket, and you're just knocking people on their ass. Most people don't figure it out until they're forty, and by then you're not a young, beautiful *thing* anymore." He says "thing" with a mixture of disdain and longing.

Recently there has been speculation that Alec wanted to run for office. To deny the rumor, he tells a long story about a revelation—the moment it struck him that if he went into politics, he might never act again. The thought appalled him. "This bolt went through me, this hallucination, this spasm. I'll never go on the set of a movie and generate and pull up from my balls and from my soul some moment of great truth and beauty and intimacy with another person and maybe capture it like a firefly in a jar, catch it on film? I'll never do that again? And I started to cry. I sat in my house and I started to cry. Tears were running down my face."

He is raising his voice, pushing the scene to its climax. It is a powerful soliloquy, though tears are not yet running down my face. We're parked now at the curb outside the restaurant. Alec ends the story: "Is going into public service a worthy thing to do? You bet your ass it's a worthy thing to do. But to give up what I'm doing? This? It's beyond belief what I'm doing! I'm going to do *Macbeth* at the Shakespeare Festival!" He is shouting. The car is virtually shaking. "People say, 'Are you going to go into politics?' No. Not 'no.' *Hell* no." He pauses. "I've got to go."

And he's off.

Fred—the driver—and I are seared by the performance.

I ask him, "Does Alec always talk like this?"

Fred says, "Yes. The homilies! The similes!"

Driving me home, Fred tells me how loyal he is to Alec. The other drivers feel the same way: "We'd all take a bullet for him. You talk to any of the other guys."

Alec buys pizza every Friday night for the entire crew.

He sends Fred out to do research to find the best pizza. Fred emphasizes, "Domino's is never an option. Pizza Hut is never an option."

I wouldn't take the bullet for Alec, but I'd work for him. Think of the pizza.

(1998)

MY RIDE WITH ROBERTO ALAGNA
AND ANGELA GHEORGHIU

*S*uddenly I have the luck to ride from Manhattan to JFK Airport in a white stretch limousine (whose vanity plate ostentatiously says "MUSIC") with opera's gossip-provoking couple, the Sicilian-French tenor Roberto Alagna and the Romanian soprano Angela Gheorghiu.

I meet them in the lobby of New York's Four Seasons hotel: they are at the check-out desk, about to leave for the airport, to take a Concorde back to Europe. She has black hair (with a little white or gray at the roots, up front) framing a pale, matte face; she wears a black, fur-edged stole, a black, tight skirt, and a black, angora sweater. Her look, without exaggeration, might be called *la belle dame sans merci*. She has intense, darting, restless eyes and a slight overbite that lends her smile a kooky wistfulness. He is tightly built, an inch or two shorter than she, with a roundly cherubic face, a beard, and reddish-brown hair puffed out into the kind of buoyant (blow-dried?) style that men in the opera world often favor. He is clothed as one might have expected Ramon Novarro or Douglas Fairbanks, Jr., to have dressed, were they opera singers: double-breasted blue blazer, tie, vest, grey trousers, and pointy black ankle boots. He looks the sort of man who plays, on weekends, a lot of soccer.

To set the tone, I compliment his aria disc, and I praise her *Traviata*. I say that she seems, vocally, a genuine reincarnation of a nineteenth-century Violetta Valery. "That's what I always thought," says the tenor. She smiles, as if she already knows the magnitude of her splendor but will tolerate its polite reiteration.

While waiting for the car, we stand under the awning. The two hum to each other. It's hard to tell whether these are passages of music or a private, shared baby talk. She sings into his ear. I ask the couple whether they sing this way, to each other, in public, because it's healthy for their voices to keep the cords vibrating. They say, "It's unconscious." Their temperaments require unremitting song. Why should they abstain?

Occasionally she speaks to him in Romanian but mostly they use French and Italian with each other. Because of my linguistic deficiencies, and the absence of an interpreter, we must resort to English, which gives their utterances a quaint charm: opera singers, international wanderers with a surplus of tongues, have the knack, when they are confined to one language, of stretching it to the idiosyncratic, imperious limit.

I put the tape recorder on the floor of the car and sit beside the chaperoning record-company executive. Gheorghiu imitates the sound of the car—the motor's *r-r-r-r-r*—and we're off.

When did they meet?

She is characteristically brief: "We met in '92, in *La Bohème*, in Covent Garden. That's all." Silence. Her pauses reinforce the uncanniness of the fact that a soprano is speaking, not singing. She has enormous poise and self-assurance, and holds herself with a stillness reminiscent of Greta Garbo, Lady Bird Johnson, and Yvonne DeCarlo.

They met but "nothing happened" at first—no fireworks, no romance.

"Just with eyes," says Alagna, laughing. "And heart." He laughs

once per sentence: a good clean masculine chuckle, it "pings."
She laughs less frequently.

The names Alagna and Angela are virtually anagrams, and
like synchronized swimmers, the two behave as doppelgängers,
interrupting each other, speaking sometimes in quiet unison. They
confess to spending hours and hours after every performance an-
alyzing the other's work. In English she declares, "We are complementary." And he adds in French that hearing her sing, or
singing with her, is like a relationship with "a mirror," and that
together they are "invincible."

Alagna, a self-avowed autodidact, learned how to sing from
records; Gheorghiu had a more conventional training, studying
at the Bucharest Music Academy. She decided by age fourteen
that she wanted to be a singer: without a trace of governessy pride
she says, "It was clear for my family, for my teacher, and I was
very, very happy. It was natural. I have my voice from God, you
know?"

She describes the voice of her lover: "He has musicality. Instinct. Fantastic. And details. Million details." He characterizes
her art with the same rapture: "Fascinating voice, because the
color is very dark, and at the same time brilliant. *Fantastico*."

"The same for him," she says.

"She is very sincere," he confesses. "I think, today, Angela is
the best soprano. For me."

"For me, too," she reveals, and laughs. "But it's true."

Let's say you want to prepare a meal, the tenor suggests—an
analogy for how an opera company assembles its season: "If you
cook dinner, it's better to see what you have at home. If you want
to cook a duck, but you have a chicken, it's impossible, no? If you
have a lyric soprano, do *Traviata*. Don't do *Aida*."

I ask Gheorghiu what she has learned from listening to
Callas's performances of Violetta.

"Oh, I don't know," she says, with deadpan or ironic indifference. "I never heard of this name. Fortunately."

In turn I ask Alagna what he has learned from listening to the
records of Beniamino Gigli.

"I like the quality of the voice—the emission. Relaxed. With the throat open. The same for Nicolai Gedda: I like very much because the throat is very open. I like everyone. I like Pavarotti, I like Carreras, I like Alfredo Kraus, I like everyone. But my favorite singer is Angela Gheorghiu."

She laughs, says "Baby," or something else, not quite audible, yet sweet and cooing, and then admits, "It's true."

I ask about the difficulties of performance—how they steel themselves. Just to be onstage, they admit, is a task, requiring a fortitude earned with ascetic self-control. As the career progresses, a performer grows more and more nervous, because an audience's expectations intensify. "We are normal like you," says Gheorghiu.

"What are the normal things you do?" I ask.

"What do you mean," she replies, her voice falling, not rising.

"Shopping, sports, raising a child, buying a house," I suggest.

"We have a daughter, four years old."

"What is her name?"

In unison they say, "Ornella."

Alagna: "We like to do—"

"Normal things," says Gheorghiu.

"Walking in the country," chimes the tenor. "I like very much *la natura*. And she likes shops."

"We have a lot in common," she says.

"Where did you get your shoes?" I ask. "Both of you. Your shoes are amazing."

She looks down at her formidably chic pair and says, "Oh my God. Probably . . . I don't know."

"I buy these in Vienna," he offers, gesturing toward his black boots.

"No," she insists. "*Forse* in—"

"Vienna."

"I don't remember. Maybe from London."

"From London," he avers.

The shoes are probably Italian, suggests the chaperone.

"No, no, no," reiterates Gheorghiu.

"I think I buy these in Vienna," the tenor thinks.

"Non ricordo," concludes the soprano.

"In opera," I ask, conscious of the question's possible irrelevance and temerity, "do you use your own hair?" (I mean: as opposed to a wig.)

"Yes," she says, firmly, for this is a matter of principle.

"And you, too?" I ask.

"Yes," he replies.

"Of course," she says.

"Of course," I say. Everything in the organized life of an important singer is a matter of course.

"And my beard, too," he adds.

"Is that permanent?" I ask.

"No, not permanent, I change many time," says the tenor, who at the hirsute moment appears a few years maturer than the boyish, clean-shaven figure in his debut CD booklet photographs, including one in which he wears a brocaded vest.

He specializes in vests. He calls them by their French name—*gilet*. He has more than one hundred.

"Who are your best friends, as a couple?" I ask.

"Best friends?" she repeats.

"Business?" he asks.

"Either," I say. "Business or whatever."

"For me," says the tenor, "it's God."

"We have a list," says the soprano, suggesting enormities.

"Lots of friends," I say.

"Many," she says, again with a tone of fatigued definitiveness.

"Too much," he sighs.

"Do you have an opinion about the United States?" I ask.

Alagna translates for Gheorghiu.

"Do you have a feeling . . . ," I repeat.

"I have a feeling," she says with sudden quickening excitement. "Ah!" She can barely contain herself: the energy is Verdian and on the verge of rhythm. "New York is so—" She searches for words. I wish I knew Romanian. She begins, "It's a little bit, how do you say, not clean."

"Filthy," I add.

Praising his place of origin, I offer, "Sicily is beautiful, isn't it?"

"Beautiful," he agrees.

"Have you been?" I ask her.

"No, not yet. So hot there."

"Yes," he adds. "It's very hot. It's impossible for Angela in July or June. It's better for her to go in September."

"Do you think there's anything in your temperament or vocal endowment that's Sicilian?" I ask him.

"I have a Sicilian temperament," he opines.

"What's that?"

"It's terrible." For example, he heard a rumor that someone at the Met once didn't hire him because of a suspicion that he didn't have a big enough voice, and this error infuriated him.

"This is more than ridiculous," she sneers, at the idea that anyone would accuse Roberto of having a less-than-ample voice.

"Ridiculous," he repeats.

When the interview is over, and we have arrived at the airport, I tell the driver, who may require the reminder, "These are opera stars!"

Gheorghiu says to the chauffeur, "Can you understand a little bit French or Italian? Not at all?"

The driver says, "I missed some of the jokes."

"Sorry," says Alagna.

"What a shame," continues Gheorghiu.

The driver assures her, "But I picked up the rest."

"You can imagine?" she says.

Everyone can imagine.

(1996)

ENRICO CARUSO'S SON

$\mathcal{I}$ have no special love for the voice of Enrico Caruso, perhaps because it does not need me to rescue it; classic, impervious, it awaits eternity—it has already arrived at eternity—and demands no fan, no patient posthumous acolyte, to alchemize it. The Caruso voice (as his son Enrico Caruso, Jr., describes, with the collaboration of Andrew Farkas, in *Enrico Caruso: My Father and My Family*, a story as pathetic, plodding, and perverse as any I have read) is a pure column of air; without flaw, it assails low and high notes alike with machismo, sometimes sobbing, sometimes finishing off the breath with a punctuating snarl. When impersonating a Jew *(La Juive)* or an African *(L'Africaine)*, the voice might feign abjectness, but it is always confidently public—aimed toward the receiving phonographic horn rather than toward a frailty-seeking inward ear. Therefore I need the son's sad tale so that I might find pathos in the Caruso voice; so that I might pretend to be Enrico Caruso, Jr., who, learning of his father's death, and separated from him by an ocean, listened mournfully to records of the great man, just as we now are listening to them; so that I might hear Caruso as his son heard him, and thereby eroticize him.

Poor Enrico Caruso, Jr. "Caruso is not Caruso," the critics said, when the son attempted a singing career. *Enrico Caruso* poses as the father's story, but the great tenor dies nearly halfway through the book: the remainder is concerned with the son's botched, entirely human ventures—and these chronicles of a son named Enrico Caruso trying and of course failing to imperson-ate a father named Enrico Caruso are much more fascinating than any stories of the priority-hogging tenor. Enrico Junior's mother, Ada Giachetti, listed as "n.n." (unknown) on his birth certificate, ran away with the father's chauffeur, Cesare Romati, when the boy was still young, and so his only memory of the divine Ada was of an unknown woman appearing "at the top landing, the *voile* of her beautiful gown floating behind her as she descended the stairs." He was raised by a governess whom he called, with the callousness of youth, simply "Lei" (she). The mother tried to kidnap back Enrico Junior (nicknamed "Mimmi") and his older brother Rodolfo ("Fofò") but to no avail; and so Mimmi and Fofò were raised by the father, who shuttled them off to cold academies. Mimmi's first memory of his father is a reminiscence of not-remembering: "I had no idea who he was: he was a total stranger." The only photo of his parents together that Mimmi ever saw was a snapshot published in a 1905 *New York Times*.

Desire rises from such absences. Listen to Fofò's recollections of his Papa: "The stubble of his day-old beard hurt my lips. Yet this slight pain made me want to return my father's embrace." Stubble! Remembers Fofò: "Every so often I would feel the hair on the back of his hand as it passed lightly over my cheek, and the light tickle gave me the sensation of the most welcome and sweetest caress." Fofò also had the curious privilege of enduring surgery at the same time as his father: Caruso scheduled an op-eration on his vocal cords to coincide with a procedure on Fofò's nose, "so that father and son could convalesce together." How thoughtful. *Enrico Caruso* is not a tale of vocalism, but a story of weird thrills and deprivations. Enrico Junior remembers playing horsie with his father: "Lying flat on his back, he would toss me high in the air with his powerful diaphragm." Another memory of delirious closeness to the remote vocalist: Mimmi recalls drooling on Caruso's "beautiful embroidered vest, leaving a large damp spot on the yellow floral design." I suppose the glory of being allowed to drool compensates for the indignity of Auntie Rina (sister of Ada, and sometime lover of Caruso) regularly slapping little Enrico so hard that the metal back of her ring "would clonk against my cheekbones"; after the assaults, little Mimmi was required to say, *"Grazie, Zia."* The value of these anecdotes: they encourage us to attend, in Caruso's recorded voice, to the implicit presence of the son who listens, the son who has been slapped, the son tossed high in the air on the lifting pillow of the father's diaphragm.

One can't ignore the presence of filth and disease in *Enrico Caruso*, a book that might as well have been titled *In Search of Lost Father*, or *My Father and Myself*, or *Myself as My Father*. Paradoxically, Enrico Junior must embed the legendary tenor in rankness for the rosy voice to become worth its weight; and therefore the book overflows with fabliaux of rottenness. A moment of closeness between father and son inevitably includes shame: "I remember one morning going to his room to greet him and finding him in the bathroom, sitting on the toilet. This didn't bother him in the least, though I was deeply embarrassed." Somewhere in this story of a son's shame and a father's shamelessness lies waiting a moral, an oxymoronic formulation about listening, cisterns, crevices, and exposure. The son reports that there was no toilet paper in Naples during the era of his father's childhood. In San Francisco after the earthquake, Caruso drank "the nauseatingly oily and warm water from the radiator." The father, rapt in the task of crafting a *presepio*, was oblivious to "the heat or the flies circling his hot pot of foul-smelling fish glue." Caruso's hot pot! One of the tenor's favorite dishes was "tripe and gelatinous gristle with garlic and oil." The grotesquerie grows truly Guignol when it comes to details of the singer's sickness and death. Ailing

Caruso "sang the entire first act of *L'Elisir* wiping the blood from his mouth as one handkerchief after another was passed to him by the chorus and the Adina of the evening, soprano Evelyn Scotney." When pus was drained from the tenor's abscess, "the pocket of liquid beneath the incision burst with such force that fluids hit the opposite wall." And when a portion of Caruso's rib was removed, a doctor remembers that "out poured the foulest pus I think I have ever seen and smelled." Greatest voice, foulest pus: why do the two seem complementary? Caruso's dead body, preserved like a potentate's or saint's, became an object of pilgrimmage, contained in a "rolltop, glassed-in sarcophagus." Unfortunately, the Caruso chapel over the decades was not well tended, and unthinking pilgrims appropriated it as an "outhouse": "at the moment the authorities are not furnishing the cemetery with proper hygienic services (urinals and commodes) to serve either those working in the cemetery or the visitors. So what better spot to use than the side of the Caruso chapel?"

Filth is an important part of the Caruso story, because *Enrico Caruso* is a parable of mysterious origins, and of a son's profound conviction that he does not belong to his father, that the presumptively unbreakable trajectory of patrilineage has deviated, gone awry: "To this day it puzzles me that I am the son of this great and wonderful artist." So has any son or daughter the right to wonder: why am I so-and-so's child? *Where I began* is inevitably a tale of uncleanliness. To counterpoint uncanny rankness, the narrative occasionally genuflects toward the clean. Caruso liked to bathe several times a day; he splashed himself with 4711 cologne, and his favorite soap was Carnation by Roger & Gallet. (I hadn't known that carnation was considered a masculine scent.) After brushing his teeth, Caruso rinsed with Eau de Benedictine, and then scraped "the mucus off his tongue with a one- by five-inch piece of flexible celluloid." Although he never had serious vocal trouble, any magnificent singer's image inevitably summons the specter of throat problems, of obstreperous phlegms: there was once in circulation a product called Cough Drop of the Stars, its box decorated with the faces of major Met luminaries, including Caruso—as if, by sucking a lozenge, you could supernaturally enter the Golden Horseshoe's stratosphere.

The story gathers momentum after Caruso dies, and Mimmi loses his inheritance and must go to work. He changes his name to Henry de Costa and serves a stint as an Italian-speaking salesman for Real Silk Hosiery Mills, Inc.; under these auspices, he sells hose to such stars as Kirsten Flagstad, Grace Moore, Helen Hayes, Kitty Carlisle, Tallulah Bankhead, and Tito Schipa— "who complained in a long letter about the color of the stockings he received." Then the son dares to take up the father's profession. Caruso Senior had discouraged aesthetic vocation in his family, saying, "If you can't sing better than I can, don't sing. Beside, one singing Caruso is enough." So Mimmi takes a humbler path; he appears in obscure Spanish-language films *(El Cantante de Napoles* and *La Buenaventura)*; as a guest on *Ripley's Believe It or Not!* show; and as star attraction in such venues as the Kitty Davis Theater Restaurant (a supper club in Miami Beach) and the Town Barn in Buffalo. Enrico Junior's career as singer at least wakes his absent mother, Ada Giachetti, from her long South American slumber; phoenix, she rises to steal, with her unshakable charisma, the show of *Enrico Caruso*.

Whatever happened to Ada Giachetti? Ada Giachetti and her sister Rina Giachetti, both of them lovers of Enrico Caruso, were accomplished opera singers with major careers. Upon setting up a common-law marriage with Ada, however, he forbade her to perform. Imagine her chagrin, then, when her sister Rina continued to sing opposite Caruso in such operas as *Tosca*, *Butterfly*, and *Aida* at Covent Garden! The feud between Rina and Ada makes for absorbing reading, as do the accounts of their years away from the limelight. Rina ended up retired in Rome, reading penny dreadfuls and smoking cigarettes. Ada moved to Buenos Aires, where she lorded it over the locals, and occasionally performed. One impresario remembers a "grand old lady" singing "Vissi d'arte" in a cabaret there. Writes Enrico Junior: "He praised her singing and asked, 'You have been an opera singer, no?' She told him with pride, 'Yes. I am Giachetti.' " A complex utterance: *I*

am Giachetti. The speaker declares an identity she assumes everyone knows, even if it is an identity now and forever obscure—
obscure, that is, until she unfurls the faux and yet convincing boa
of *I am Giachetti.* The son, understandably, needs Ada's point of
view in order to articulate his overwhelming desire for Father (a
craving that overpowers speech and threatens the doctrines of
Papa's law): pondering whether Ada attended any of Caruso's performances in Buenos Aires, Enrico Junior speculates, "I have
often wondered what passed through her mind as she sat in the
elegant auditorium listening to the familiar, caressing voice. Did
she find its beauty changed? Was Caruso singing better? Were his
interpretations deeper, truer?" Enrico Junior imagines his lost
mother Ada listening to her lost husband Caruso. For the bereft,
fantasizing son, the improbable scene is the richest.

Singing is labor. To sing is to submit one's body and pro-
ductions to the harshest scrutiny; to offer one's flesh to a terrible
purgation, akin to Iphigenia's. The score, or the conductor, is
Agamemnon; the audience is the sacrifice-demanding god. In
communication with her faraway son, Ada Giachetti reveals the
mythic, cruel stringency of the vocal regime to which the first
Caruso himself was held subject, even if we imagine that he es-
caped it because of his natural gifts and his feted state. On seeing
one of her son's films, in Buenos Aires, Ada wrote to him for the
first time in fifteen years. How did she find him? She sent the letter to his Hollywood studio, Warner Brothers. After quickly dispensing with maternal pleasantries, Ada, ever the connoisseur of
instruments, got down to the business of mastery: "I have seen
and heard your films, however I found that you still need to
study to have more *finesse* in the attacks. The voice however is
beautiful and I am proud of you because beyond a beautiful voice
you are a handsome young man as you promised to become
when you were a baby. You know? They all say that you are my
image, especially the eyes and the mouth and the expression of
your glance." Later, responding to some records cut by Enrico Junior, Ada critically observed, "You have a beautiful voice and
most beautiful high notes, however you must close a little more

the middle and must soften and perfect your diction. At certain points it is too colorless and lacks brilliance, and those are the marks of a trained singer." What a hard school the Carusos and the Giachettis attended and perpetuated; Ada Giachetti voice-coaching by mail her abandoned son, whom she was never to see again, is a scene as unhomelike and scary as imagining Judy Garland contacting Liza Minnelli, from beyond the grave, through a medium, and informing her daughter that she sang flat in Las Vegas on Friday night.

Caruso lives on; Ada and Rina Giachetti, alas, do not. Did they ever make records? I doubt it. But Caruso's possible sublimity—the phrase is Wordsworth's—lies not only in the splendor of his recorded, hence immortal voice, but in his former proximity to such figures as Ada Giachetti, who possesses the cachet of the ancillary and the adjunct. Ada, Enrico's shadow, sheds glamour—the magic of the repressed—on the too-well-remembered Caruso. We need to forget him, or need to remember his forgotten aspects, so that he might become possibly sublime. And therefore I present the following coordinates of the obscure realm in which Ada and her sister Rina dwell, and in which Caruso himself was potentially citizen. Consider: the now unknown Rina Giachetti sang in the now unknown *Mazeppa* by Minhejmer. Consider: Rina Giachetti was praised as a "vibrant Ricke" in *Germania* opposite Francisco Vignas, in Pistoia's Teatro Manzoni. Consider: in Portugal, Rina Giachetti sang the lead in *Cabrera* by Menendez, as well as starring roles in Puccini's *Edgar*, Leopoldo Mugnone's *La Vita Bretone*, and Catalani's *Loreley*. Consider: in Naples, Rina Giachetti sang the world premiere of D'Erlanger's *Tess*. Do we call her an unremembered entity, a has-been, unillustrious as the penny dreadfuls that fed her imagination during her eclipse? Or do we choose to crown her with the diadem of numen that she, too, deserves? Without Rina and Ada there would be no Enrico Caruso; they helped improve his technique and advance his career. When we remember Caruso we must resummon the leading ladies who sang with him in Buenos Aires: we must revive from dust the curiously named Adelina Bertana, Gilda Dalla Rizza, Tina

Poli-Randaccio, Hina Spani, and Geneviève Vix. What rococo names, their splendor magnified because they are uncelebrated—and yet they once sang with Caruso, who himself at that early time in his career occupied the realm of the doomed-to-be-forgotten. Just as Ada Giachetti sang the title role of *Maruzza* by Pietro Floridia, so Caruso sang in such vanished operas as Carlo Sebastiani's *A San Francisco*, Fornari's *Un Dramma in Vendemmia*, D. Lamonica and G. Biondi's *Celeste*—and in the world premieres of Giordano's *Il Voto* and Mascagni's *Le Maschere*. For every star there are a thousand imitators and a thousand failures. For every performance we cite as historic, there are multitudes of dirty dressing rooms, empty theaters, and cracked high notes. And sometimes, behind a star, there lies a well of unlettered ignorance. It is important to know that Caruso, himself a museum, never visited museums or read books; that Caruso, whose reputation consolidated the gramophone's, seemed to have owned no records by singers other than himself—the only two his son could find in the father's collection were "The Whistler and His Dog" and Harry Lauder's "Roamin' in the Gloaming." Whenever, in the future, I hear the voice of Caruso, securely transferred to CDs, I will think of Ada Giachetti saying "I am Giachetti" after her doubtless wobbly performance of "Vissi d'arte" in a Buenos Aires cabaret, and I will think of Enrico Caruso, Jr., (opera's "Little Ricky" Ricardo?) selling Real Silk Hosiery Mills hose to Tito Schipa, who dared to complain.

(1995)

A FAN'S APOSTASY

*Q*have a tiny uvula: that's why I can't sing.

A uvula is "a fleshy projection hanging from the rear margin of the soft palate."

Perhaps it was removed, with my tonsils, in 1963.

My boyfriend has a huge uvula.

Anita O'Day, jazz singer extraordinaire, has no uvula: that's why she can't sustain tones. She compensates.

Imagine the size of Joan Sutherland's uvula.

Recently I dreamt that I broke Jessye Norman's shoe—a pump—in half. I thought she'd forgive me but then I realized she valued her shoe, didn't consider it dispensable.

This is an essay about grandiosity: how I have given it up.

I have given up opera.

For years I've wondered whether Anna Moffo tuned in, Saturday afternoons, to the Met broadcasts. Now I think I have the answer: of course she doesn't tune in. She has other things to do on Saturday afternoons. Anna Moffo is tired of opera, too.

I am older than Anna Moffo was when she recorded *Thaïs*. I am as old as Maria Callas when she recorded *Carmen*. I am at the age when a career can end.

Snow, outside, is falling, as I write, and a woman across the street is staring out her window, parallel to mine, at the snow, which falls sideways, not straight down; the angle of descent, oblique, may be a result of wind, or gravity, or it may be an optical illusion. For an instant I think the woman is watching me, not the snow. Maybe she is watching snow and me, parallel descents.

∽

Opera is a form of religious experience. It allows the listener to identify with largeness, with torrents of sound, and the stories associated with those waves.

I used to love to close my eyes and let godhead in the form of a soprano voice engulf me.

Now I am interested in quietness and silence. I listen to Chet Baker and Blossom Dearie. I like the sound of a drum when I can barely hear it. I like the sound of Chet Baker's voice because he can't sing, gives almost no emotional inflection to the standards. I like the sound of spit in Miles Davis's trumpet in the 1950s, before his comeback.

Charlie Parker's sax occasionally resembles a woman's voice. Franco Corelli and Charlie Parker have something in common. I had a dream, recently, about Franco Corelli. I dreamt I loved his voice. And when I woke up, I remembered, "I *do* love his voice!"

Opera presents long lines. Every other art form truncates, divides, stutters. Only opera bases its effects on extension, prolongation.

∽

"Sing!" a piano teacher told me, decades ago. I didn't know what she meant. She sang along with my playing, to give me the idea.

What does it mean, to "sing"? It means: to continue. To go to the next note, without a break, without hesitation, except when hesitation is necessary, expressive, or itself a means of imposing continuity.

I tend to hesitate. I tend to stop, stammer, repeat myself. I tend not to go on to the next note.

Once, a piano teacher told me, "Don't stop before you play each note."

Later, another piano teacher said, "Take care of every note."

For decades I have been trying to put together these two apparently contradictory pieces of advice.

Sometimes, to take care of a note, you must move directly into it, without caring for it. You must forget the note, ignore it, move through and past it.

To take care of a note, you must "blend" it. This was my teacher's word: blending. One achieved "blending" by "scooping" the keys. The physical gesture of scooping the key blended the sound into the overall phrase.

I dreamt that the first joints on my fingers finally became flat, spatula-like, large, and independent: a true pianist's fingertips, capable of adhering to the keys, not slipping off them and flubbing the masterworks. Horowitz had these fingertips. Look at the photos.

My fingers' first joints may not be large and flat, but I have one habit of the true musician. When I listen to music, it fills my body. I don't make extravagant gestures, or wiggle. But my nostrils mildly flare at the appropriate moments. I listen like a true connoisseur, or like a sensitive teacher, at a master class, eager to inculcate principles of bel canto, but unable, at this point, to demonstrate them with her own voice.

Another piece of piano wisdom: don't bang. Banging is the enemy of beauty. A piano must simulate the sound of a human voice. If you bang, you sound like a drummer.

The great blenders and scoopers: Edwin Fischer, Myra Hess, Dinu Lipatti, Artur Schnabel, and Walter Gieseking.

My parents listened to serious vocal music: the *Messiah*, Bach's B Minor Mass. My parents were Bach people, not opera people.

My parents owned one complete operatic recording: *Don Giovanni*. I never once heard them play it.

Opera was a fettered effulgence lying to the right or left of my childhood.

Instead of opera, I had piano: a one-boy operation. Piano didn't involve the mouth or the throat. It involved only the hands.

Taking Kiri Te Kanawa's voice into my ear is not the same as moving my fingers through a Chopin waltz.

However, listening to Kiri Te Kanawa, and playing a Chopin waltz, are both forms of amateurism: amatory behavior, pursued avocationally, and, often, in solitude.

I assume you've played an instrument, or listened, with unspeakable pleasure, to music. I assume you've tried to describe your pleasures, and failed, as everyone fails, because pleasures can't be described, only pointed to.

The pain of playing Chopin: the stiffness of my hands; the ineptness of my phrasing (the punched-out notes of the melody, the missed pedal points, the insufficiently voiced chords, the trill that won't let go and ruins the tempo); the inability to employ a true rubato; the soreness of shoulders and forearms, a soreness that prevents Chopinesque mobility; the sensation that someone in the room is listening and finding fault; the knowledge that it is too late to play Chopin decently, so I might as well quit; the knowledge that no one is listening; the wish for someone to hear this marvelous phrase, and the certainty that no one will; the wish to show off, and the wish to hide; the wish for a different body; the realization that my body has altered, in this wishful instant; the fear that I'll never regain my former, mediocre, acceptable body. . . .

At the last moment, before my first climax, I stopped. I was ten or eleven years old. I reversed the jolt, prevented it, lest it ruin the furniture. And yet, in a reduced form, it happened anyway. I felt the shudder. I felt the sensation of frozenness, which I would thenceforth associate with all heightened aesthetic experience: liberation achieved, yet also rescinded: joy (or release) taken back, at the moment it is bestowed. The pleasure, the intoxication, is revoked, at the instant it is most intensely given.

Long ago, I vowed to place opera above all the other arts; to place the soprano voice above all other voices; to believe that climaxes were audible and able to be incorporated by a listener; to believe that one needed to train a voice in order to acquire power; to subordinate my body to a grand release initiated by someone else's voice, itself subject to another's music.

My apostasy is larger than merely a flight from opera.

I've left behind ecstasy itself. I've left behind stars.

And yet if one abandons a form of aesthetic experience, it returns later, in ambush.

On a whim I'll play Victoria de los Angeles singing a bit from Gounod's *Faust*, the part where Marguerite asks the pure and radiant angels to carry her soul to heaven, and I'll want to die, or to live differently, on a higher plane. I'll want the operatic angels to rescue me, and I'll want to organize my life so that punishment can take the form of vocal climax, so that my own regimens of behavior and willpower will perform a puncture in my soul, equivalent to what Victoria de los Angeles inserts into my ear and listening physiology, courtesy of Gounod's expert if unsurprising harmonies, and courtesy of the religio-erotic prod of Marguerite's aggressive masochism.

Now, writing, I can't hear an orchestra. I can't hear a soprano.

Damn this moment's distance from the operatic. Damn the fact that I'm not Marguerite.

I am often in the position of trying to breathe life into scenes and images that are dead to me.

I am often dead.

I've always been grateful to opera for dramatizing my periodic movement from life to death, and for making death seem the higher ecstasy.

Now I am interested in the opera of driving a car, the opera of taking the subway, the opera of deferred gratification, the opera of massage parlors, the opera of sunset at the piers, the opera of whisky, the opera of silence, the opera of palm trees, the opera of bathtubs, the opera of the daily splash of eau de cologne, the opera of inanition, the opera of stupefaction, the opera of amnesia.

I wish to correct a misperception: that we can meaningfully define the limits of "opera."

One beauty of a category like "opera" or "poem" or "religion" is that the term horrifies and expands, it colonizes and allegorizes, it metastasizes.

I am interested in the opera of the waiting room, the opera of the electric chair, the opera of the stirrups and the probe.

Every medical procedure deserves its opera.

Every sex act and sex classification deserves its opera.

On a recent winter evening in New York I went to Danny's Skylight Room to hear Blossom Dearie. She sang her standards: "I'm Hip," "Bruce," "The Ladies Who Lunch," "Everything I've Got." Seated a few feet away from me was Dame Kiri Te Kanawa. During a run of Strauss's *Capriccio* at the Met, she braved the cold New York night to hear Blossom Dearie sing. Perhaps Kiri was picking up pointers for a future crossover album.

Kiri didn't clap very ardently. A couple of light hand taps after some numbers. After other numbers, no response at all.

She was husbanding her energies.

I didn't introduce myself to Kiri, or acknowledge her identity. Clearly, she wanted to be left alone.

She wore an elegant checked jacket (Hermès?), black pants, black top, and a bulky watch.

Blossom wore three strands of pearls (fake?), a brown velvet top, and dark pants.

I liked watching Kiri listen to a jazz singer who manages with meager vocal resources.

From the experience, I deduce these maxims:

permit juxtapositions (Kiri, Blossom); permit reversals (opera watching cabaret); make no snap judgments about the origins and destinations of operatic instincts; refuse compartmentalizations; if you're agonizing over an aesthetic problem that you can't solve, widen the frame.

(1998)

IV

THE LOCOMOTIVE EMPRESS:
12 IMPROVISATIONS

NOSTRILS OPEN TO EVERYTHING

Did you know that Elizabeth of Austria-Hungary was called the locomotive empress because of her addiction to travel? I share that vice: I wake up each Friday morning and take a three-hour train ride to a distant province, to get my head examined. I've been in psychotherapy for seventeen years. The great side effect of travel is the chance to visit terminal bathrooms—the ones that forgive vagrancy.

Last night in New York, I heard a transcendent essayist lecture on preferences. She described Coleridge as a "profound junkie," and said (quoting Jules Laforgue?) that Baudelaire had "nostrils open to everything." May my nostrils be open to everything!

In a dream last night I took a final essay exam in school. My teacher was fat and queer and important, and in an earlier dream her buttocks had fallen on my face. Using my finger as pen, I wrote my answer in blood or chocolate.

There's stubble on my cheeks this morning because I forgot

to shave. The image of my own whiskers arouses me, as does the act of writing, though, unlike the Marquis de Sade, I don't enjoy inflicting pain. I try to limit my pornography purchases to one magazine a week: each costs six dollars. My preference is *Honcho*, because its models look like teachers professing the art of everyday ecstasy.

In a letter, Keats wrote, "I feel my impulses given way to would too much amaze them—I live under an everlasting restraint." The rose of thought this morning is blooming, unrestrained. Two decades ago a teacher told me that I looked like Keats, because I'd cut my triangular wedge of frizzy hair into a cap of Caesarian curls. Keats was a mere five feet. This morning I want to write a treatise about short men, vampirism, and the paradoxical beauty of the erroneous. Keats wrote, in a letter, "I was never afraid of failure." I want to fail in the most beautiful way, to write something so like a parallelogram it baffles every critic and excites the raven-haired young androgynes.

BBC called me two days ago, asked for an interview. I said not today, how about tomorrow? BBC said tomorrow was too late, the public quickly loses interest. Fickleness. At a movie about a has-been star's diaries, a cute performance artist with imperial features sat next to me: I cast longing glances at his wrists because they were bony, hirsute hybrids of youth and decay. His art, conceptual, involves taking off his clothes. He has become a locus of my thought, although his breath smelled, not unpleasantly, of smoked whitefish.

Too many books I want to read, I wish I could condense them into pills and swallow them: I long for the collected letters of Lord Byron, Mallarmé's fashion magazines, manuscripts about nineteenth-century dandyism and department stores, and the new biography of Barbra Streisand—and maybe one day I will meet Streisand? I ate dinner two nights ago with a writer who grew up in the same building as Barbra. The writer and I talked about hook noses and plastic surgery and ethnic identity and homophobia and Plácido Domingo and Renata Tebaldi, while I ate, too slowly, my cassoulet, down to the fatty *lardons*. In a different conversation at dinner I tried to figure out whether Robert

Schumann was an aesthetic radical, and a pianist (who, coinci-
dentally, has the same German-Jewish surname as the first guy to
whom I ever gave an *emotional* blow job!) said that we remained,
in 1995, unwitting heirs of Romanticism.

You see, I spend most of my time on the train. Last night en
route I read a trashy novel about a psychopath, and, from a
magazine devoted to ephemeral vanities, I cut out a picture of
couturiere Edith Head receiving an Academy Award for Best
Costume Design, 1955. I love Edith Head because of her surname, Head, a sex act as well as the prime body part, and because
of her secret indispensability to history. I clip moments from
evenings, and eminences from magazines, but I don't have a
proper scrapbook in which to paste the pieces.

On the train in the seat ahead of me this morning a serious-
looking guy with black-silver curls and an earring is reading tales
of Nathaniel Hawthorne. I'd love to snuggle up to him and discuss American parables of good and evil, but the train just
stopped at some ignominious waterfront town, and the alluring
reader—stranger, *semblable*—disembarked. I've found a blood-
stain on my denims: residue of last week's paper cut. Would
Edith Head approve? Would the Marquis de Sade? Would
Baudelaire? Would my father?

(1995)

POWER & AESTHETICS

At breakfast I am thinking about power. Last night's dream: I followed President Clinton into a school bathroom. Or he followed me. I used the urinal. No liquid emerged: wouldn't you be self-conscious if the president were listening? Then Clinton and I strolled down a long hallway toward a police-woman training area, where novices kicked imaginary opponents, as in *The Silence of the Lambs*. Now the president wore just undershorts. Chagrined, I noticed his flabby chest. Meanwhile the First Lady, in inauguration finery, skipped up the schoolroom steps; beneath her fancy frilled blouse, she sported an inappropriately casual denim skirt. I thought, "She is no better than her daughter."

Is it unusual to dream of undressed presidents? Clinton resembles Kirk Douglas's son, Michael (star of *The American President*). In real life, a year ago, at the Union Square Café, I followed Michael into the men's room, where I caught him standing at the urinal. He turned around. Trapped! A fan, I observed a star in the process of elimination. This moment possessed a rare electric charge: I'd captured a powerful symbolic man, in medias res, committing a necessary embarrassment. I let him finish his business. Could he tell I was gay? Was he afraid I'd make a pass or take a picture?

In the film *Disclosure*, Demi Moore took Michael in her mouth: sexual harassment. His face contorted with ambiguous pleasure. (My grandmother, sitting beside me in the theater, didn't flinch.) In the Union Square Café lavatory I mentally revisited this cinematic scene, and wondered if the real Michael Douglas was thinking, "I have been seen in desire's thrall on-screen, and now I'm relieving myself in public, and a stranger, probably queer, is watching." Did Kirk, viewing *Disclosure*, regret or relish his son's on-screen sex act? Did Michael, as a fledgling teen, see Kirk in *Spartacus* and think, "I want to grow up to have a sexy and internationally visible CinemaScope chest, just like Dad"?

As I write, I am listening to a recording of Roland Barthes's voice teacher, the French singer Charles Panzéra: Henri Duparc melodies—"Extase," "La vie antérieure"—balance the lachrymose and the clinical. The name Panzéra (the *p* of *powder* and *power*) recalls the opium-dream box of Guerlain Shalimar talcum powder I discovered while visiting my boyfriend's grandmother. She kept the perfumed dust beneath the bathroom sink. How old was the talc? Where did she buy it? Did she use it daily? I surreptitiously applied the precious powder; I spent so long at my toilette that the grandmother in the kitchen apparently asked my lover, "Why is Wayne still in the john?" I was voyaging to Shalimar. Though I worry that I'm immature, at least I'm not, like Barthes, a middle-aged bachelor still living with his mother. Incidentally, on this Panzéra recording, his wife, Madeleine Panzéra-Baillot, plays piano accompaniment: when Roland came for voice lessons, might she have brought from the kitchen a plate of powdered-sugar-coated lemon cookies, which, forevermore, he would associate with pedagogy and musical exquisiteness?

Last week in a frigid clime, a specialist in lyric poetry recited to me the following Hölderlin couplet, dear to Heidegger: "The spirit's thoughts are,/Quietly ending in the soul of the poet." The scholar was trying either to humiliate or to flatter me; I can't tell the difference. His eye had an Ancient Mariner gleam: the look of a man so involved in his own narration, he pays no attention to his helpless, hypnotized audience. I thought, "Every time someone makes a pass at me, I accept."

Digesting my café au lait and my toast with raspberry preserves, I am still musing about power. Long ago when my teacher lifted her hospital gown to flash a hysterectomy scar, I smiled weakly, and praised the successful surgery. I brought the requested gifts of dollhouse furniture, and together we listened to *La Traviata* and *Macbeth* and *Don Carlos*, as we planned our imaginary collaborative book about Verdi's Oedipus complex.

I want more coffee, so I can continue to brood about aesthetics. Thirteen years ago when my mother's retina detached, and she had laser surgery, I flew across the country to offer comfort; in her bedroom, I recited my new, first poems, which reminded her of Dylan Thomas. (In those days I wanted my parents to think I was an alcoholic, so I ostentatiously drank ample snifters of cognac before sleep.) One poem concerned cows falling down hills in China. Another described a phantom Byzantium in which my father, an appealing hobo, wandered. Soon thereafter, at Thanksgiving, I accidentally dropped an entire hot cooked turkey on my mother's bare foot. Luckily, an eye surgeon was our supper guest—the very doctor who, decades earlier, one midnight, excited me by stripping to his undershorts on our mountain-climbing trip. On his advice, my mother put the scalded foot under cold running bathwater.

(1995)

AN UNWRITTEN POEM
BY HEINRICH HEINE

*M*y father, born in Berlin, described his own upbringing as "Prussian," and I remember with longing the militant way he attacked the octaves in the fifth Chopin Polonaise: his stubby, flawed pianism struck me as patriotic. He seemed to be praising a Germany that had tried to destroy him. Chopin was an exile; from Poland to Paris he fled. And in France, dying, he dreamt of a vanished nation, just as my father, playing parlor music in California, conjured a flame-encircled Berlin.

Right now I am listening to an old record of Dietrich Fischer-Dieskau singing Schubert's "Death and the Maiden." My father bought me this album nearly two decades ago, along with an LP of Witold Malcuzynski playing Chopin polonaises.

Yesterday, while early snow fell on my obscure yard, I practiced the polonaises, using the very same edition that was once my father's property: I stormed through my favorite—number three, in A major, nicknamed the "Military"—with a frenzy so heroic that afterwards my wrists ached. Later, in the gym locker room, I saw four young swimmers shaving each other's bodies, in preparation for the morrow's race. (They stood under one shower nozzle.)

Last night I succumbed to a bathetic, inappropriate nostalgia for the German tongue, of which I am entirely ignorant. And yet the opening melody of Brahms's Third Symphony describes my latent Germanic temperament; and the unexpected key change in the Schubert song that Dietrich Fischer-Dieskau is now singing ("The Wanderer"?) recalls the forest near my father's Berlin house, of which I've seen only one black-and-white photo—a glade I have been sentimentally revisiting for three decades, the twigs sharp under my naked feet. And I don't need to explain to you that Schumann's split-personality affliction, portrayed in *Carnaval* (performed, on a disc I treasure, by Solomon, who met an untimely death), imitates my imaginary incestuous tango with an absent Teutonic father.

Schubert might have loved to kiss me. My conversation's aphrodisiac medicine might have extended his abbreviated life. (These words don't revoke the decrees of history, the whims of microbes.)

My next perfume purchase will be Route du Thé. The scent recalls apple blossoms, black tea. When I splash it on, I will think of a colonial ship's unsavory hidden cargo. My current cologne is Annick Goutal's Eau d'Hadrien. Observe: I model myself after emperors.

In last night's dream, a lesbian bookseller handed me an unwritten Heinrich Heine poem, "Mirror," and asked me to translate it into English. We discussed problems of labor and management, and I pledged fealty to the powers-that-be. She complained about striking workers; despite the bleeding ulcers on her lips, I accepted her kisses. Why did a lesbian want to seduce me? She must have noticed my resemblance to Caligula.

Yesterday, in real life, outside a rare-book library, I kissed an African American man on the lips, while, across the plaza, snow fell on my college's marble dining hall, the names of World War I battles—Cambrai, Argonne, Somme, Ypres, Marne—carved on its frieze. Then we stepped inside the archive to look at the pornography scrapbooks of Carl Van Vechten, famous for promoting New York's "Harlem Renaissance." I felt sorry for the photographed genitals: they had nobility, but none of the models were smiling.

(1995)

THE FOOD GROUPS

*O*ver a Thai lunch—curried chicken—I mentioned Germany to a literary friend who describes herself as a staunch atheist Jew and who once wanted to be a movie star because she had a crush on Laurence Olivier in *Wuthering Heights*. I said, "I love writing for Germans, and yet I fear that I am betraying my father. He fled Germany; and now, at the end of the century, I am back in Germany. At least my words are." After lunch I excused myself and went to the bathroom so I could get rid of what I'd eaten; symbolically it is crucial that I evacuate my body in some fashion after each ingestion of food, so that my vessel remains pure.

The friend I kissed outside the rare-book archive sent me a postcard from the Anne Frank museum, on the back of which he wrote, "I remember your orange scarf, and the expression on your face when we opened the scrapbooks and saw the outsized cocks."

Though I am a writer, I decided yesterday, after looking at a sofa fabricated from telephone books, to become a visual artist. I will buy a Polaroid camera and take pictures of my intimate body parts, especially my anus. I will place these photos on the labels of old opera discs (Caruso, Galli-Curci). I will buy a stiff-backed notebook at an art-supply store and compose collages of recipes for aspics and variety meat stews from the paperback *Joy of Cooking* my mother mailed to me when I lived, impecunious, in Baltimore, and juxtapose these beef-marrow-stained recipes with Polaroids of myself urinating into a beautiful ceramic birdbath in my backyard. The Polaroid of my nipple will line up with the spindle hole of the 1906 purple-labeled Victor *Lucia di Lammermoor* Sextette.

Unfortunately I have no appetite this morning: my lover was sick to his stomach in a San Francisco hotel room, after eating cassoulet and drinking Perrier-Jouët champagne, and so I decided to devote myself to austerities, and to forget my family, whose oddities preoccupy me to an unfashionable and unfathomable extent—particularly the eccentricity of my father, who lectured me, last week, about the sundry food groups (vegetables, fruits, bread, grains, beans, meat, dairy, and fat). Since that conversation I have been painfully conscious of every particle of fat I consume, including the teaspoon of possibly rancid cream in this morning's coffee.

As we ate our oversauced ravioli, my father told me, for the first time, that his aunt died in a concentration camp. I'd known about the two sets of imprisoned cousins, but not about the aunt, whose name, I think, was Hedwig. Listening to my father, I wondered, with a narcissism that shocks me as I recollect it now, "Would Hedwig have loved me?"

Last night on the train home I read Renaud Camus's novel, *Tricks*: its descriptions of sexual encounters kept me aroused for a full unsatisfied two hours. Camus recounts the carnal episodes without emotion: only the small talk, the unzipped fly, the round buttocks, the music (Glenn Miller) playing in the background, the *X* the two penises composed as they crisscrossed on the lovers' abdomens. Immersed in *Tricks*, I remembered the photographer who took a full roll of photos of me, nude, when I was twenty.

Somewhere in my basement I have these images: I will use them in my future collages—juxtaposed with transcribed fragments from one of the first poems I read as a child, Langston Hughes's "The Negro Speaks of Rivers," and a ripped piece from the cover of the Tchaikovsky *Swan Lake* album (green glade through which the ballerina glides) my parents gave me one early Christmas.

Today I will ask my psychiatrist for how many more years I must take the magic green and yellow pills I have been using to regulate my moods; and I will tell her that, yesterday, I ate an onion omelette with a glamorous poet whose name is a month in spring. I treated the *primavera* poet to lunch because sentimentally I remembered loving, in college, her floral scarves and her poem—about flirtation and Michelangelo—which I read on the plane back home to my mother and father, who did not yet understand I had the soul of a poet, though I fantasized that they envied the miraculous lump of arousable flesh I hid like a dowry in my chinos, bought for ten dollars at a used-clothing store beside the deli where I ate a Boursin-and-roast-beef sandwich with the girl I then loved, an Italian who was writing her senior essay on the paintings of Kirchner and who told me (courtship banter) that she carried a knife in her purse to protect herself against predatory men.

(1996)

ON CIVILIZATION'S DISCONTENTS

This morning, while listening to my ambiguous idol Elisabeth Schwarzkopf sing Hugo Wolf lieder, I try to forget last night's dream of two nude hermaphrodites (women with penises) who ran a hotel in a cowboy region. To escape them, I jumped out a second-story window.

I want white patent leather shoes for spring; or a white shiny waistcoat. If other men appear in white shiny fabric on New York streets *before* I do, I will have failed at my mission: to become as armored and beautiful as a woman's handbag.

My great-aunt, Alice Gutfeld, moved from Berlin to Caracas in 1937, and then to California. I met her when I was born, in 1958. At that point, she was partial to capacious black purses, 4711 cologne, and Marlboro cigarettes. She spoke with a thick German accent, and praised Munich, her favorite city. She called herself a "freethinker": an atheist. I don't think she cared much about Judaism.

In the stairwell of the gymnasium, on my way to the locker room, I pretend I am Elisabeth Schwarzkopf in 1955 entering a hall to check out the acoustics a few hours before her evening performance; I try a phrase, sending one of the Marschallin's honeyed apostrophes through my mucuses. "No, the sound isn't vivid enough; I must step forward, toward the lip of the stage," I say to myself.

I love Schwarzkopf's avoidance of the cutting and the ugly; she will go to any lengths to cushion the attack of a note in her middle-upper range. Her mouth is a nectar factory.

I want to talk about the rotundity of my buttocks but don't have anything particular to say about them. Except: *I see myself as if from the rear.*

I just finished reading Freud's *Civilization and Its Discontents.* I have a strong superego, and it speaks with a German accent. I wake up most mornings feeling vaguely doomed. I brought my copy of Freud to a screening of Scorsese's reissued *Taxi Driver* and noticed that there were more guys than girls at the theater. Robert De Niro had a decent body when he took off his shirt, but not the kind of torso that dominates my fantasies. After the movie I saw a hermaphroditic man waltz with an imaginary partner at the edge of the subway tracks, and I was afraid that he was a madman about to leap to his death before the oncoming train. He had waxen skin, the rheumy eyes of the blind, and no secondary sexual characteristics that I could detect: was he a eunuch? He seemed the embodiment of the apocalypse, though he held a briefcase just like any ordinary American working man.

My great-aunt Alice Gutfeld's father manufactured candy in Berlin in the early twentieth century. This will mean nothing to you, dear reader, unless I can explain Alice's roseate, ethereal complexion, and the unrealistic images I have long harbored about the moral purity of art: I have always believed that a devotion to the minutiae of one's craft constitutes a holy calling. I am a jester, but I am also a priest of art. Can you hear, in this sentence, the vibrations of my vocation?

I own a pair of skintight bronze rayon pants that gild my decent yet slight thighs, transforming me into a baroque cherub, or the James Bond "Goldfinger." These trousers are not fashionable. They are merely extreme. They stand on the edge of fashion's undocumented continent; they look out toward Prospero's island, and are perhaps the drowning boat en route to it. I have been seduced by Shakespeare. He harbors a divine aggression toward his own language; he smashes words together, barbarously close daggers overlapping, as if the juxtaposed syllables were copulating dogs.

Schwarzkopf's voice soars over my sentences, this Sunday morning, providing the context for my defiling ruminations. Her pitch never wavers; she finds the timbre she desires, and she sticks to it. The pitch continues, extends into space; depending on my mood, the note is a silver platter holding Moses' tablets, fresh from the Mount, or else it is the pool in which Narcissus, nude and on the brink of a blinding pubescence, stares.

(1996)

REISEPASS

Eight light purple clematis flowers—a vine on my fence, in my North American backyard, where I am now writing—can't explain the Third Reich passport my father's aunt managed to obtain, to leave Germany. I like irrelevant juxtapositions, out of which I try to squeeze some sense. For example: as if constructing a collage, I place these present flowers against the *Reisepass* I found in my basement, amidst moldering memorabilia, and ask the flowers to explain the *Reisepass*, the *Reisepass* to explain the flowers.

One hundred years ago, Alice Gutfeld—the great-aunt about whom I have so much to say—was born in Berlin, a city I have never visited, a city for which I retain a culpable nostalgia. In the *Reisepass* identity photo (the date is 20 October 1937: is this the date on which the photo was taken, or the date of her departure?), she is a woman at the beginning of middle age, with flushed wide high cheeks, two short comma-bobs of hair straddling her face, large watery grey inquisitive eyes, an austere Peter Pan collar, a flowered plain dress fastened by two tiny buttons. I can't read any expression on her face. She has the stolid, philosophical look of someone who does not yet know she is about to be pushed off an airplane.

I found this resonant *Reisepass* in a cardboard box. Also in the box I found her Venezuelan identity papers—her *Cédula de Identidad*. In these official photos (27 December 1939) she is heavier, her hair is thinner (I wonder: why didn't she get a wig?), but I can read no substantive difference in her demeanor. No clues tell me how she experienced the transplantation from Berlin to Caracas. I know she considered herself lucky to leave Germany, but for the rest of her life she would speak with admiration about its architectural splendors, and her German accent always seemed to my childish ears a sign of a secret aristocracy to which I might also belong, if I behaved.

I am sitting in an American garden but I am studying the silent *Reisepass*.

With the *Reisepass*, I found, in the box of Gutfeld artifacts, a Spanish-German dictionary, a few old forks (of no special value: why were they saved?), a menorah (missing one prong), a guidebook to Munich (she returned as tourist in the 1960s), a road map to Venezuela, and photographs of her trip to the United States, in 1952, when she attended my parents' wedding.

What other sacred objects did I discover in my basement? Objects from my California childhood. I found a book about witchcraft: the crumbling paperback included instructions on how to sanctify one's hands, in preparation for performing spells. I found a gingham plaid shirt and denim overalls—costume for my role in a children's production of *The Wizard of Oz*. I found homework from grammar school years—including a play I wrote about a belle who flees the South, during the Civil War, and undergoes a sex change. I found collegiate love letters from a soulful poetic stud: he praised my warm brown eyes. Was he lying? I found a letter from my grandfather, telling me never to forget the Holocaust, and also hoping that I wouldn't "turn snob" now that I was a student at a fancy Ivy League college. I found some old unpaid psychiatrist bills. I found nude photos of myself, age twenty—artful, as if I were a bell pepper or a piece of sea glass. (I mounted one of these photos in a *Così fan tutte* frame—my buttocks surrounded by the Mozart score's first bars.) I found a photo of my boyfriend—taken eighteen years ago—in which his shirt is provocatively unbuttoned, and yet he looks as innocent as the young Tadzio in *Death in Venice*. I found love letters from the first girl I ever slept with—the first, and one of the last. (She taught me the beauty of pressure—a breast, as warm as rye bread, pressed against my neck; an arm, weighty as a bunch of green grapes, pressed against my forehead.) I found a wedding picture of my parents, in which my mother is wearing alabaster butterfly glasses, and my white-tuxed father, plump-faced and nervous, stands next to Alice Gutfeld, who has flown from Caracas (or California?) to New York to witness the ceremony. In the photo the wedding party poses before a fake shrub. I found a photograph of my parents on their honeymoon (accompanied by the erstwhile Alice): her arm is locked in my mother's, as if attempting to steer the marriage toward a nonlunatic destination. I found a photo of Alice's cousin, who survived a German concentration camp, and who, in the photo, is stocky and unsmiling and smoking a cigar on a New York sidewalk. I visited this cousin only once: long enough to see the number on his arm, to eat the rice his wife cooked, to see her tattooed number, and to hear them urge me to join my university's Jewish organization—advice that I dismissed, for I was (and I remain) religiously apathetic, devoting my life to aesthetic and erotic nuance but not, alas, finding time to study the Jews' long, sad, glorious history, and my position within it—far on its outer edge.

I have spent a long time looking through the basement boxes. I am glad to be in my garden now, a thirty-seven-year-old man wearing boxer shorts whose bright pattern is yellow hippie flowers, from the era of free love. I grew up wanting to be a flower child. Perhaps I have achieved my Aquarian goal. This morning is humid, and nearly summer: the smell of mildew, rising off the *Reisepass*, distracts me from my new friend, the clematis. How many days will the frail flowers last?

(1996)

AUGUST HYPERAESTHESIA

The windowsill flower with aggressive red pistil stares at me like Fanny Brice. I am an American clown with a prominent nose. I am overstimulated from too much coffee; my kitchen table is stained; I don't know how to begin to explain my enervation and hyperaesthesia.

Hyperaesthesia: "abnormally great sensitivity of the body or mind, especially of the skin."

A great poet said, "No ideas but in things." Fortunately I have no ideas, so I can only give you things.

I am no longer a selfish writer. I had been a narcissist until today at noon, and then I converted to generosity: I realized how many millions of books lay fallow in the world and decided I didn't care if mine figured among the ignored. The fate of a book is to be forgotten, and so I can fornicate with my own anonymity.

I hate my spontaneity, but more so I would hate lack of spontaneity, so I must give you immediacy, my only cordial.

Red flowering plant on the windowsill, you have uncounted buds the color of a prom dress.

I saw a lawyer friend exiting a porno store; he looked "caught in the act," and to change the subject and deflect attention from his recent porno escapade he started chattering about a recent trip to Paris and a specific sublime restaurant, and I mentioned Elizabeth David's recipe for salmon steaks cooked in a muscadet of the Loire.

At the gym I saw a guy doing sit-ups: "crunches." He wore baggy shorts. I peered up them, saw no genitals. He kept them hidden, like a good tease. He looked like an anesthesiologist with a huge salary, so I'm surprised he didn't have the money to pay for a baldness remedy. Maybe he tried it for a few years and then capitulated, said, "There's beauty in baldness."

Sometimes I fear I behave like a stereotype—but what kind? Do I conform to any categories that you know? My favorite stereotype is the ecstatic—Bernini's Saint Teresa in orgasmic ecstasy. Scholars believe there is little difference between hysteria, religious exaltation, and orgasm. Thus I occupy many camps at once—I am a borderline manic-depressive with a sense of humor but I am also a sexologist and a faux saint. I shave and then splash blue astringent tonic on my face like an obedient witch (Joan of Arc) and then apply the lanolin of the gods, a weird beige potion that I imagine was made from the testicles of religious heroes of yore, the ones whose exploits are not reenacted on TV sitcoms.

I pray that my body stays presentable for another three years, and that I can overcome my natural repugnance to the taste of dirt. I woke up with a strange sensation that I'd swallowed a cupful of sand. I rinsed my mouth and found nothing—so how can I explain the illusion that my tongue is coated with grit, like the powdered grape-flavored candy that in my childhood I sucked from straws?

For the last few days I have been afraid of the written word. I avoided newspapers and typewriters. Now I am in love again with sentences, and I hope I don't suddenly want to jump out the window and crack my skull on the pavement nine floors below.

Tonight I have a date to meet the star of an upcoming film

about heroin. She is pretty but has to battle her overprotective mother, who doesn't approve of the film's subject. I will try to persuade the mother that heroin is metaphorical, but the mother may argue, "I don't plan for my daughter to be a *metaphorical* movie star, so she'd better star in a picture about a *real* elixir, and it'd better not be some poison that's disemboweling American prowess!"

Next month I will tell you about my mother and how she almost ruined my life but then magically turned me in the right direction—so I could simulate sanctity. Ah, but before I shut down I must tell you about my stomachache—and my desire to buy a grey chenille couch and sit on it while eating vanilla éclairs above the sooty yet also skyblue street, and my fear that I spend too much time dissecting the texture of my feelings and not enough time living mutely inside unthinking pink capillaries.

No, that's not what I meant to say. I wanted to tell you about the power of the mind when it meditates on dust; or about the 1950 movie I saw the other day, *Halls of Montezuma*, about America's navy in WWII, and dirty men's wounds; or about the Picasso show, all the portraits of his many women, how fortunate he was to have multiple wives and mistresses so he could become a visual virtuoso, adept at splitting features into disjunct tribal planes; or about a show of African art at the Guggenheim Museum (Frank Lloyd Wright snail) and the lovely European-looking man whose chest and shoulder hair rose above his baggy shirt as he stood admiring a mask—carved by whom? None of the masks had individual signatures.

(1996)

DESIGN

At a department store last week I slipped on a Dolce & Gabbana black sheer undershirt tight as a body condom or pantyhose mashing my chest hairs together. "How does it fit?" said the clerk, when I emerged from the changing room. "Too claustrophobic," I lied. In truth the garment had redesigned my modest pectoral muscles, turning them into small scallop shells.

Men who are not athletes or striptease artists may be unfamiliar with clothing that hugs the flesh, but I encourage you, whatever your girth or ambitions, to enter the realm of the tight-fitting, even if no one ever sees the garments. Invisible clothing is the most sublime.

Wearing the autoerotic Dolce & Gabbana undershirt was like embracing a prosthetic inflatable doll: but I was the doll as well as the real person hugging it.

The secret of intimate wear is not what the body declares to the viewer, but what the body announces to itself.

The T-shirt was a conversation. I have only one psyche but the garment performed parthenogenesis on me; it doubled me. It chatted with my chest, said silly and wise things to me. It didn't have a personality or a history. It didn't use dialect. But it tilled new ground on my body.

Of course I did not buy the ridiculously expensive shirt, but I learned from it to rise to this new level of narcissism that isn't sloppy or irresponsible but has a covert philosophical rigor I pray you can see.

This experience has encouraged me to take the first few feeble steps toward redesigning my body. One hundred jumping jacks. One hundred sit-ups. One hundred push-ups. A mile in the pool. Alone in my studio I dance to Miles Davis's *Blue Haze* until I sweat and my pulse races and I transcend the usual dull velocities.

In college days I bought a tight tiger-striped punk Lycra spandex V-necked jersey because I sought transformation and a conversion experience like the sort that William James describes in *The Varieties of Religious Experience*.

I will never tattoo my flesh, however, nor will I pierce my nipples or my cock, despite my admiration for porn star Jim Buck's Prince Albert.

One friend wears a backless dress that shows butt cleavage, and this is her best artwork. She is an ambitious designer.

Another friend rents a hotel room, invites famous artists to screw him, and photodocuments the acts. He is an ambitious designer. Like me, he is in the business of composing and distributing manifestos.

We are not callowly bourgeois. We deplore exploitation of workers. But we are interested in nudity and more importantly want to talk about our interest in it. Amateur philosophers, we wonder where the body ends and begins.

When you don a slinky T-shirt and it speaks slithery serpent words to your skin, your moral obligation is to repeat those incantations. The undergarment said to me: *Shed dishonesty. Redesign circumstances so that you can feel naked in public even though you are clothed.*

I would like to remain in the present tense, but it is necessary, as always, to zoom into the past. On a trip to Japan in the 1970s I took a bath with a beautiful redhead girl whose pubic hair was a small round "thought bubble," as in a cartoon. She said, deceitfully, "You have a nice body." A male tympanist lay naked beside us (it was a huge communal tub), and I thought, "He has a man's body but a girl's name." How like a codefendant in a legal suit his penis seemed. . . .

All my life I have wanted to be a grown-up man writing and smoking alone in his room in his underwear, like the mannequin simulation of an old pathetic nut in the Ed Kienholz sculptural installation I saw at the Whitney Museum of American Art: loser, reading on a seedy hotel cot, hand in his briefs. Plexiglas separated my curious gaze from the interior of the fabricated cubicle—not a real room, just an artwork.

And in Japan I rode a swan boat with a chubby teenager who spit when he spoke. As he described his precocious sexual rendezvous with married women, I watched the oars lap the water and the haze of the humid day settle on the lampposts and the Buddhas, and I wondered whether I had the sort of body anyone would have designs on. It wasn't really a male body. Not yet. It had male aspects but mostly it was musical and formless. I vowed to read Plato and practice my minor scales and stop masturbating and then eventually I would become the kind of body I desired. On the afternoon of the swan-boat ride I was wearing a tight striped jersey that stank from perspiration, and my hair had no design at all, its kinkiness had not been managed, reformed, or secured by a metaphor.

(1996)

ENVY

$\mathcal{S}$ince birth, I have suffered envy.

For years I misunderstood it: I called it love. Now that I know envy's proper name I can punish it into a litany.

This morning I envy the art dealer with a shaved head who fed me grilled salmon last night: I envy his beach house and his abdomen.

This morning I envy the novice filmmaker who knows the hidden semiotics of illness although he is growing old. I envy his drunk father and his oversized nipples; I envy his distaste for nostalgia and his friendship with six-foot-tall AIDS activists.

Oddly I do not envy the photographer who took a picture of an ectopic pregnancy scar, although her pomegranate-colored hair is so beautiful it makes me want to say "pearl."

I envy the skinny woman who wears feathered toques. I envied her first husband—until they divorced. Now I envy her second husband's jogger thighs and his confident knowledge of Bordeaux vintages.

I do not envy his daughter, although she sleeps in a crib that reminds me of Della Robbia terra-cottas.

Envies shift, like rotten riptides. Yesterday noon I envied the journalist who forked soft-shell crab into his mouth while we sat on an emerald-green banquette, but by sunset I envied the deejay who attempted suicide and then survived to write an essay about it.

If my envies stayed the same, I could end them. I could drown them in champagne or smother them with compliments.

Instead, each day, I must devise a new battle plan, a fresh choreography, to conquer the object of envy.

My first envy was my brother: he played Fauré's "Après un rêve" on the cello so sublimely, at a mere age eight, that I broke into a murderous sweat, listening.

My second envy was my sister: she balanced the bottle of formula in her baby fists as if she were a tiny Ondine, feted butterfly-ballerina.

My third envy was my body: it had no interest in me, even though my thoughts sounded like Tchaikovsky. My internal monologues were Russian empire ballroom music, but my body didn't care. It stood apart from me—luminous as a candle in a Georges de La Tour painting. I coveted my mean flame.

My fourth envy was my mother: she was a pale, cruel genius, and I was her effeminate serf. I envied my underwear when she laundered and folded it. I envied her legs when she didn't wear nylon stockings. I envied her solicitude for the orange "rumpus room" carpet: she told me to vacuum it and I envied my obedience. I vacuumed.

My fifth envies were my mother's parents: I envied the ocean liner they rode from New York to Paris on their Jazz Age honeymoon. I envied my grandfather explaining Latin etymologies, my grandfather singing "Tit Willow" from *The Mikado*. I envied my grandmother eating chocolates and having a hairdo that resembled cotton candy.

THE LOCOMOTIVE EMPRESS | 225

Those envies—five Furies—are antique. I have frozen them. Now, new envies follow me.

I envy the smell of lard down the hall because it comes out of a poet's apartment—the bard who has a Machiavellian five-year-old son who withheld his "turds" for five days to protest against toilet training. I envy the son's blond curls, and I envy the father's poem about the nightmare hallucinations of Jewish survivors.

The opposite of envy is renunciation. I renounce the curls. I renounce the underwear my mother laundered and folded. I renounce my body luminous as a candle in a Georges de La Tour painting. I renounce my brother's "Après un rêve." I renounce the novice filmmaker, the oversized nipples, the catastrophes.

(1996)

BEES

*L*ong ago a bee stung my earlobe. Here is how it happened: I was poised on an unmoving bicycle and I lost my balance and fell into the home of bees, a flowering bush loaded with little red berries like gumdrops or pimples.

Stung, I began to scream; my mother—who was gossiping across the street in the kitchen of a neighbor lady I will call Dalila—came running to my aid, and smeared unguents on my swollen earlobe, flushed from the bee's kiss.

I wish I could tell you more about the bee itself, but the thought of bees leads me down the inevitable path to Dalila. Every morning my mother went across the street to Dalila's house to chat and drink coffee with the other neighbor ladies: this matutinal confabulation, a feminine mystery, was a ritual of our suburban cul-de-sac. My mother hated the heavy cigarette smoke in Dalila's kitchen, and the bad, burnt coffee—but every morning she returned for another gossip session.

Dalila always wore the same black dress: I remember her abdomen pressing against its shiny fabric.

Dalila's daughter had pierced ears at an early age. This seemed a sign of licentiousness. I wondered whether she would end up working for the circus.

I considered my bee sting to be a variety of ear piercing. The stinger entered my lobe and created a tiny hole, through which I might, like Carmen, hang a gold ring.

Once, a few years after the bee sting, I saw Dalila at a tawdry downtown theater, at a screening of the Walt Disney cartoon, *The Jungle Book,* a full-length feature I didn't take seriously. She was wearing, again, the one black dress. I observed the rotund stomach and thought of a plump bee hugging its own stinger, enjoying its private resources of nectar.

Dalila looked like Anna Magnani, laughing, exhibiting an enviable excess of animal spirits. I didn't want to sleep with Dalila—I had no notions, yet, of sexual intercourse—but I liked to brood about how she mistreated her children. The sadism of neighbors attracted me. I heard a rumor about the night that Dalila went to use the bathroom and sat on her daughter, by accident, who was already on the toilet. I imagined Dalila placing her maternal heft on the helpless, prior body of her daughter, peeing in the dark.

Soon thereafter this daughter—unmarried—was discovered to be pregnant; when Dalila got wise to the situation, she kicked the girl out of the house. It was a public spectacle. The mother twisted the daughter's arm—they were fighting on the front lawn, and all the neighbors gathered to watch. Someone finally called the police, and an officer came to separate the combatants.

So when the bee stung me, and my mother came running across the street, from Dalila's kitchen, to apply a salve to the wound, I wasn't thinking about the sting, or the pain, or the bee I'd killed (its stinger lodged in my lobe), but about the chatty, cruel voluptuousness of neighbor ladies.

Years after the sting, I retained a fear of bees. And so I avoided nature. I eschewed canoes, parks, picnics, hikes; I hated the elements. Then adolescence came, with its erections and cigarettes, and my dread of bees gave way to curiosity. I stood aloof from bees but I began to wonder about their possible gorgeousness, and I grew to love objects and agents that once seemed noxious. Now I am no longer averse to bees. In fact, this morning I am disguised as a bumblebee: black leather pants, yellow turtleneck. But my penis is not my stinger. No. My stinger is my vocabulary. I put words together to attack your earlobe, to make it swell, so someone may come running from across the street and press a cold or warm poultice to the aggrieved place.

(1996)

BEDS

$\mathcal{M}$y childhood bed was a narrow, small, twin affair, the mattress uneventful; the only excitement was the green electric blanket, which matched the green shag carpet. On that bed I listened to Schumann symphonies, read *Anna Karenina*, and masturbated, but never had "real" sex.

In college I encountered traditional dormitory beds, with inexplicable (menstrual?) stains from previous users. On one of those lousy beds a man I mistook for a saint held my hand for hours in the darkness.

Now I live in two different cities, so I need two beds. To prevent identity confusion, both beds are the same; when I wake in one house I can imagine I am in the other. To overcome afternoon ennui, I lie flat on my stomach on the white waffle cotton cover and imagine I am becoming a minor bodhisattva.

In Rome at a *pensione* near Sant'Andrea della Valle (Tosca's church), I slept off jet lag in a bed huge and flat as a banquet table. I felt like Lola Montes in the Ophüls film—a circus aristocrat opulently offered to viewers.

In a farmhouse in the Dordogne, the middle of my mattress was a soft declivity or canyon big enough for two male bodies to fall into. I read Montaigne's essays each night and then put the book aside and fell asleep for eleven uninterrupted dark hours, the shade closed over the one window high up on our monkish wall.

In an old French Provençal village, Venasque, I ate olives and cherries for lunch and then dozed in a room that sunlight penetrated at three o'clock, baking my feet. Evenings I rose from convalescence to eat crème brûlée or rhubarb *clafoutis* at a nearby auberge.

On Cape Cod, sea air woke me as I lay in the bed of my boyfriend's parents (away, they'd lent us the cottage): sunk into the slack, oft-used mattress, I read *Tender Is the Night* and remembered a hotel bed in Nice, beside a window overlooking that lucent city of *fruits de mer* and rosé consumed outdoors in midday heat.

In Miami Beach I slept soundly on a bed flecked with crushed mosquitoes. During the day, marimba music played over the swimming pool loudspeaker, but nights were quiet. The bed was a typical American motel bed—flat, plain, dull, but useful if you want to forget who you are. Before sleep the first night of my stay, I ordered a Mexican beer from room service. A friendly black man in a suit delivered it. The next night, I ordered a Campari and soda. The same man delivered it. By now I felt I knew him well. He said, "It was beer the first night, and now you're moving to Campari." He implied I was undergoing a progression.

One final bed (I will be writing about beds for the rest of my life): in Paris, at a cheap hotel on the Left Bank, I slept on a mattress hard and pious and unyielding as the church my room looked out to, St.-Germain-des-Prés, the oldest in the city. The sheets didn't stay tucked tight. I woke every night in a sweat. That was the year of the inedible boudin blanc. Every night before retiring I'd test my inadequate French on the Algerian concierge. Every morning a swarthy maid served me a soft-boiled egg. In photos from that trip I look unattractively pale, sickly, with my dyed red hair and my blue suede gloves and my black patent leather cowboy boots. It was the coldest winter in memory. My skin tone resembled custard cooked with greyish-blue skim milk.

(1996)

WHITE WINE

The pleasure of white wine is its transparency; I would like my language to match white wine. I drink it in order to become abstract, to forget, to become a cipher, not the dreary particular person whom the Fates have clumsily molded.

White wine is a misnomer. Actually it is amber, yellow, gold—the color of the sun. If red wine is presence, then white wine is absence. If red wine has ambition, then white wine is lazy and slack and endures the monotony of its celibacy. White wine has no genitals; it is what a well-known pair of French philosophers have called the *body without organs.* Drinking white wine, I participate in a bleached rite: I enjoy the fantasy that the rouged dregs have been removed and that all my glass has the luxury to hold is a blankness the color of an indifferent scorched hedonistic afternoon on the sand dunes, among sea roses, the drinker searching vainly for Egyptian obelisks and sarcophagi and finding only topless sunbathing women reclining like Cannes film stars on towels, and naked men like eunuch sentinels guarding the fortress of the latrines.

I drink white wine not entirely to erase my life but to pretend that I am erasing it: whisky or gin or vodka will obliterate consciousness but white wine will merely shed a bridal veil over candor, clouding objectivity. I drink white wine to acquire the relationship to oblivion that a child cultivates toward its "transitional object," its book or blanket or bottle or stuffed bear.

White wine isn't mother's milk but is closer to the maternal than the paternal—if we must split the world. I suppose white wine resembles, in viscosity and color, that unspeakable fluid whose hue and scent are hay, and whose expulsion from the body determines health and happiness. Each morning we wake to this insistence: *make wine*.

None of the above generalizations applies to chardonnay, only to sauvignon blanc and to certain of its virgin sisters, including *green wine*, a Portuguese attraction that fizzes on the teeth and induces in the evening a delusion that colonies have not yet been colonized and hemispheres have not yet been divided.

(1996)

V

AESTHETICS

ON PAPARAZZI

$\mathcal{I}$ love paparazzi. Perhaps I should qualify that statement. I know none personally. I've never been accosted by one. I've never stood on the blitzkrieg flash's receiving end. (However, at press events, I've been bumped against, jostled, and pushed aside by jutting telephoto lenses.) I assume—wrongly?—that most paparazzi are pushy men, and I don't like to be pushed around; nonetheless, I love paparazzi. They resemble (in a cheerfully debased form that remains true to the high original) a kind of perverse artist I've long held dear—the artist who does not merely represent a desire, pilgrimage, or inquiry, but performs it, and thereby crosses the risky borderline between mimesis and praxis. Such border crossers (Montaigne, Sade, Proust, Freud, Stein, Artaud, Leiris, Cornell, Schneemann, Sherman, Goldin) use their bodies, memories, organs, fantasies, and friends as more than fodder. In fact, I'd be hard-pressed to name any contemporary writer or artist I respect who doesn't to some extent put forward his or her body as the work's ground. This offering of the body is hardly essentialist; rather, it acknowledges that for the practice of art to mean anything now, it has to hurt. It can hurt the viewer. But first, the process of coming into the artwork, of arriving at it, must wound the artist, and I demand to see the wound.

Paparazzi are not a spectacularly wounded bunch. Indeed, after the tragic death of Princess Diana, they have been branded murderers.

We use the word *paparazzo* rather carelessly: I use it because it's snazzy. Despite the scapegoating pleasures of saying "paparazzo" when we mean "taker of candid celebrity photographs," we should understand that the paparazzo is a fiction, not a vocation; it is a complicated cultural construction, composed certainly of recognizable behaviors but also of misty projections. Like *flaneur*, *sadomasochist*, *vegetarian*, or *abstract expressionist*, *paparazzo* is a description of a practice but is also a refined, phantasmatic field of images, allegiances, and disavowals.

But let's pretend for a moment that the word *paparazzo* uncritically identifies certain photographers deemed to be an unethical, combative, pathological species. How are paparazzi connected to the exemplary artists I've praised? Paparazzi may not wound themselves, but they are artists of cauterization. Their images do not leak, spill, break open. Paparazzi record actions—invasions, sightings—that are entirely sealed off by the image thus produced: the paparazzo picture doesn't parasitically render a *something else*, philosophically outside the frame of what the picture can hold and prove. As a porn film records not just the sexual act in question but the fact that someone was there to capture it (not just the genitals, say, but the fact that *here are genitals I've stolen from the Real to bring to you on video*), so a paparazzo photograph (often called a money shot) steals a vision of celebrity and renders the instant of theft with a necessarily scrupulous and self-impugning candor, an openness about its own unsavory means that goes so far as to be self-wounding. The paparazzo can condemn only *himself* (the paparazzo, in myth, is always male) with the image he has pilfered: the image is proof of the perforation, the laceration he has committed in the fabric of the decent, the private, the civic. Though the celebrity is the one ostensibly invaded, the paparazzo is also making vivid—making documentary—his own abject status as *voleur*, voyeur, render of veils: he is publicizing his abrupt ejection from the civilized.

There is thus something beautifully self-staining about paparazzi photos: while the star's privacy has been invaded (though many paparazzi shots are consensual, the star cheerfully granting the photo op), the paparazzo has willingly taken an ontological pay cut. By exhibiting, selling, circulating the image, the paparazzo says, "Here, I looked where I was forbidden to look. I did it for you. Observe my debasement. The money I receive for this photo allows me to transvalue my 'lowness,' and turn my sleazy profession, my bottomed-out vantage point, into a new 'high,' higher than yours." A paparazzo photo reveals the photographer's love of lucre, and is in that sense a representation not only of his star prurience (perverted hunger to see a famous person in a private moment) but of his cash fetishism: "Only for a tidy sum did I, paparazzo, so lower myself." We're observing, therefore, a fiscal performance. No surprise: art is often a fiscal performance. Warhol never hid from the viewer the role of money as one catalyst of the overdetermined painting; neither, I suppose, did Rembrandt. Stars are even more conspicuous about their indebtedness to money. For example, Elizabeth Taylor in *The V.I.P.s* (1963) dramatizes her salary: the large sum she was paid to star in the film is all she is required to impersonate. This tautological task doesn't waste her artistry, but seals off the film from the debris of the non-self-reflexive, the non-Liz. In Liz's performance of the acquisition of money, there's no messy supplement, no didactic overlay, no civilization: only money, sumptuously embodied, showcasing its embodiment.

From the show of paparazzi images recently on view at the Robert Miller Gallery, cocurated by Olivier Renaud-Clément, Amy Wanklyn, and Franca Sozzani, I gleaned two lessons. (Half of the show was devoted to work of the classic, vintage paparazzi, especially Marcello Geppetti and Tazio Secchiaroli, each of whom, at their best, I do not hesitate to compare with Weegee; the other half was a selection of post-1967 fashion and celebrity photographs—much of it by women, including Pamela Hanson and Elisabetta Catalano—that borrowed stylistic features from the earlier work.) The first lesson is the supernatural beauty of the female stars from the great era of Cinecittà and *la dolce vita*. One feels that the paparazzo arose as a species of photographer in the fifties not to lay siege to famous people generally but to respond to a new form of glamour—the drama of such faces and figures as Sophia Loren, Brigitte Bardot, and Anita Ekberg. Hands down: Ekberg dominated the show. In a 1958 photo taken by Secchiaroli, her face is entirely blanched by a flashbulb that has obliterated and blackened the Roman backdrop. As the gallery's Alexandra Rowley commented to me, Ekberg's face in the snapshot has a *commedia dell'arte* abstraction, a single mood or humor dominating the mask. That mood is rage: in one Geppetti photo, she aims a bow and arrow at him. (She's been caught in her stocking feet on the pebbly driveway of her Roman villa.) Because beauty can't be described, there is almost nothing I can say about a face like Ekberg's, except to note that it is unusually wide; that she seems absolutely in command of the inevitable effect that her heightened beauty will have on any sane beholder; that she seems to have adopted an attitude of patience toward a world that will need a long time to absorb all the meanings and shades she puts forth without apparent premeditation or artifice, although the fact that her face is on display for us, and that she made a career out of such displays, signals the knowledgeable decisiveness of her self-presentation.

The second lesson of the show: a paparazzo photograph is a reaction shot, and therefore indirectly foregrounds the traumatizing agency and desire of the seemingly invisible paparazzo. (The paparazzo has a few traumas of his own, not the least of which is the star's antipathy toward his presence.) The reaction that the paparazzo photograph reveals is often anger: the photographer has "gotten a rise" out of the usually composed star (the star may have her boyfriend or bodyguard chase after the photographer, who then takes pictures of the pursuer, or she may herself do battle with the intruder). At the very least, the star will project condescending toleration, itself a reaction to a paparazzo who has had the bad taste to make his presence felt. In many cases, other paparazzi (they travel in flocks) will appear in a shot that ideally, for commercial purposes, would have isolated the star from any appearance of a press conference. The most engaging photos—the ones that highlight the paparazzo's morally ambiguous, scarifying art—acknowledge the omnipresent nest of lenses around the star's body. In Mario De Biasi's 1956 picture of Brigitte Bardot in Venice, she kittenishly poses for a constellation of cameras that collectively recall the accidental mutant in David Cronenberg's *The Fly* (1986): Bardot's beauty itself is a kind of supranormality that elicits camera attention, but the truly freakish scene stealers in the photo are the camera organs. No distinction can be drawn between the cyborg-paparazzo's face and his technological prosthesis. The photographic apparatus is the emblem of his moral decrepitude; he wears it like a Pinocchio nose, or the mark of a branding iron.

The most poignant photo in the show documented the rage not of the star or the paparazzo, but of an unseen viewer: Marcello Geppetti's 1960 image, captioned JAYNE MANSFIELD LYING ON THE GROUND AFTER HAVING BEEN ASSAULTED BY A WOMAN JEALOUS OF HER BEAUTY, illuminates the uncivic drives that form the quicksand on which a star must walk. These desires are ours, not the paparazzo's, and as long as they do not lead to actual assault, they are nothing to be ashamed of—except to the extent that most art objects are things to be ashamed of, which is why we love them. I wish that Geppetti had taken a photo of the woman who assaulted Mansfield; I also wonder how Geppetti knew the motive of the assault. Did the unnamed woman confess to her jealousy before or after pushing Mansfield onto the ground? Was there something particular about Mansfield's style of beauty that led to envy rather than happy identification? I hope, for the purposes of my argument, that it was not the paparazzo himself who knocked over the star.

(1997)

WARHOL'S TOILETRIES

A few hours after dawn I went to Rite Aid to research Andy Warhol.

I was pleased to be up and about so early in the day.

I discovered objects, variously priced, brightly boxed.

I bought two rolls of Polaroid film and went home and took pictures of the interior of my medicine chest. They came out ugly and unfocused. To take a good Polaroid is more difficult than is commonly acknowledged.

I visited Rite Aid because I'd seen Warhol's cosmetics and toiletries on display in a vitrine at the Whitney Museum's show, "The Warhol Look/Glamour Style Fashion."

If he used these products to prep his face for his Polaroid drag "Self-Portrait," 1981, then the toiletries are source materials for art. Otherwise we are in the happy, confused position of simply looking at toiletries.

Warhol's toiletries are now dusty and dated. They don't look chic. Some still have price tags: Duane Reade. I know Duane Reade. But the tags aren't artful allusions to Duane Reade. The tags are tags.

I can never get enough of a celebrity's toiletries, because I can go anywhere with them.

Here is a list of his toiletries (a similar inventory appears at the conclusion of Bob Colacello's *Holy Terror: Andy Warhol Close Up*).

Gelly's Color Enhanced Styling Gel.

Fostex 10% benzoyl peroxide cleansing bar.

Glycel Cellular Treatment Activator by Christaan Barnard, M.D.

Senoket natural vegetable laxative.

Neet lemon-scented cream hair remover.

Propa pH Acne Cover Stick.

Aspergum (orange flavor).

Vidal Sassoon Hair-in-the-Sun Hair Protector.

Glycel Cellular Night Creme by Christaan Barnard, M.D.

Clinique soap.

Vitamin A capsules.

Lecithin.

Aapri Apricot Replenishing Lotion.

H pour hommes Fixateur.

Preference L'Oreal Permanent Creme-In Haircolor, 9A Light Ash Blonde.

Lubriderm Lubath for dry skin care.

Maybelline lipstick, shade unspecified.

Clinique dramatically different moisturizing lotion.

Citrus aftershave balm.

Face Pack Liquid.

Visine Eye Drops.

Neutrogena imperial bath size soap (dry skin formula).

Grey Flannel cologne.

Liquifilm Tears.

I am fascinated by the Liquifilm artificial tears. They introduce the theme of fake pathos, a person unable to cry yet able to look clearly and unsentimentally—to the point of pain—at objects and at famous and rich people, who can be, as Warhol knew, objectlike, because they spend much time in the company of commodities, and so grow, deliriously, to resemble them.

Here is an edited list of my current toiletries and cosmetics. Melatonex dietary supplement for a natural sleep cycle; Elastoplast (fabric stretch plasters); Brioschi; Neo-Synephrine Mild Formula Nasal Decongestant Spray; Kiehl's Ultra-Moisturizing Concealing Stick #2; The Body Shop Under Eye Cream; Trazodone; Grey Flannel deodorant stick.

I've done an artful thing. I've listed toiletries.

Warhol did an artful thing with his toiletries, too. He saved them, and he became a museum that allowed them to be exhibited and pondered and written about.

Looking in someone else's medicine cabinet, or in one's own, produces epiphany. But if one never speaks or writes about the experience, never photographs the objects, never displays them, then the toiletries, like bodies not stellar enough for porn, sit unobserved, unframed, unfetishized.

I pity Warhol's toiletries, puny and useless, but I feel more sorry for toiletries that never make it into art.

The Whitney show features a wall of publicity shots of Elizabeth Taylor, collected by Warhol.

Liz knows a thing or two about toiletries.

Her scents are sold at Rite Aid.

I am interested in the ordinary fan who cuts out Liz pictures but never makes a silk screen to justify, retroactively, the industrious clipping and collecting.

I am interested in the Warhol who never graduated from fan to artist.

I am interested in the drag queen who doesn't have the looks, ambition, genius, and good timing to become Candy Darling.

I am interested in the lazy nobody who dreams of stardom but never finds a cooperative patron to film a screen test.

Warhol's toiletries pose (but do not answer) the question of the slob and the shut-in, the question of whether one who lives outside of the art act may take aesthetic credit for using makeup and collecting star pix.

If we want to follow Warhol's example, we must not only pay attention to beauty; we must attend to plainness and anti-glamour, to ignored bodies and slapdash outfits.

I'm thinking of Richard Billingham's photo of his mother, Elizabeth, published in *Ray's A Laugh*. She wears a floral print housedress that no fashion magazine editor would find beautiful. I am not a fashion editor, and I find it beautiful. On the table before her is an unfinished jigsaw puzzle and a pack of Sky cigarettes. Her arm tattoos rhyme with the patterns of puzzle and housedress.

The photo turns Elizabeth Billingham into a Superstar. She's no longer just a puzzled woman with poorly parted black hair; she's a performer, collaborating with Richard the photographer.

Looking at the photo, I think, "I always knew there was something arresting about a listless woman in a housedress. Others might have said she was unglamorous, but I knew she had a lazy, easy stylishness."

I once knew a lady who looked like Elizabeth Billingham. Her name was Meredith, and she lived across the street from me when I was a kid in the early 1960s. Meredith's Superstar status was a secret. She had all the qualifications to be a Divine or an Elizabeth Billingham, but there was no one to discover her, to send her into the art orbit, to lend her the legitimating context of performance. (In exchange for the privilege of looking at an early photo of Meredith, taken during college, before her descent into booze and desuetude, I agreed to strip for her bullying son. He was seven, I was five.)

Warhol owned a velvet evening gown once worn by Jean Harlow. The dress qualifies as a source of cultural interest. But what if nobody signed or designed it, and Harlow never wore it, and Warhol never collected it? What if I saw it in Elizabeth Billingham's closet? What if I—with my mania for authorization and legitimacy—never saw the dress at all? Do garments unseen by curators and critics still participate in art?

I don't want to lift fashion into art. Clothing doesn't need the boost. It offers its own pleasure, which is the joy of useful material in the process of being used, like cardboard boxes before

Robert Rauschenberg discovered them and turned them into artifacts, or the pleasure of the orange cotton turtleneck I'm wearing while I write this essay, a turtleneck you will never see.
Unexceptional, it keeps me warm, and gives me adjacency to the
presence of orange I've seen verified by magazines this season.

Because Warhol owned the bottle of Liquifilm Tears, we can
interpret it. We can see it as a symbol of his affectlessness. We
can say, "Warhol couldn't cry real tears. He turned himself into a
mannequin." But if the bottle of Tears were sitting mute in your
medicine chest or on a pharmacy shelf, would it give you a significance shiver, an aesthetic tingle? (It might.)

Like Warhol, I take objects literally. I take the bottle of tears
as a bottle of tears. The advantage of literality is that I can go
somewhere else with the tears. I can think about Warhol weeping
or not weeping. I can think about his bodily fluids. I can think
about vision, the need to lubricate the eye to keep the retina honest. I can think about Elizabeth Bishop (now connected to Elizabeth Billingham and Elizabeth Taylor) and her "Sestina," with its
references to "equinoctial tears," and "the teakettle's small hard
tears," and the teacup "full of dark brown tears," and the "buttons like tears," and the "little moons" falling down "like tears."

Looking at Duchamp's *Fountain* (urinal), or one of its repro-
ductions, I take the urinal literally: "Urinals are really beautiful."
I don't think, "Isn't it interesting that Duchamp brought a urinal
into the museum?" Instead I think, "Urinals are pretty. Their
porcelain is shiny." Similarly, looking at Warhol's *Blue Liz as
Cleopatra*, I don't exclaim, "Wow, Warhol transformed a found
image." Rather, I muse, "*Cleopatra* was a great movie. With every
passing day this is becoming clearer to the general public. I'm
glad that Warhol foresaw the truth, and made the truth blue."

I want to encourage any attempt to look seriously and play-
fully at clothing, to talk about it with the slow care usually re-
served for art and literature. I want to see clothing turned into
discourse: not into languages already coined by the trade, but
into whatever kinds of speech we want—litany, gossip, complaint, diatribe, digression, autobiography, commandment, description, psalm, testimony. . . . Clothing astonishes not because

it's more aesthetically resonant than other objects but because it's ordinary as can be—enigmatically self-explanatory, like sex and waterfalls and forests and other wild habitats. Some clothes are ingeniously or expensively made. Some provoke envy or fatigue. Most clothes are shorn of commentary, and therefore open to all comers. Let pour upon the following Warholian indelibilities the cold water of your awe: the wig, the Liquifilm Tears, the blow job, the Empire State Building, the wrecked car, the face of the Most Wanted Man, the voice of Diana Vreeland. . . .

Clothes are interesting because they are passive and wilting; they need a body to fill them up, just as pellets, to become sea monkeys, need immersion in water. Warhol's wig depended on him. Abandoned in the vitrine, it looks like a flattened jellyfish, a spent broom, an apology.

Like Warhol, I am interested in nude photography not because nudes look good in art but because nudes look good: such an attitude—such a resistant, impious addiction to things as they are rather than to things as they are represented, if there is entirely a difference—might seem to give short shrift to artfulness, to the large-souled paintings of Richard Diebenkorn, also on display at the Whitney. But Warhol's Liquifilm Tears cleanse the sight: after seeing his toiletries I am newly attentive to Diebenkorn's *Ocean Park* series, willing to absorb its lessons about color, subdivision, and duration ("suspend time whenever possible," the paintings advise). Warhol has put me back inside my clothes and my tears; he's extended me a gift certificate for an hour or two of embodiment, though the penalties for abusing the privilege are dire. One needn't love Warhol in order to acknowledge that he made looking at the evidence (clothes, genitals, cremes) as philosophical an endeavor as Cézanne looking at the mountain, or Troy Donahue looking in the mirror.

(1997)

IN MEMORY OF MY FEELINGS

I am a jockey with a sprained ass-hole I am the light mist
in which a face appears

—Frank O'Hara, *"In Memory of My Feelings"*

distrust narratives of origins—*here is where my desire began*—but I feel repeatedly compelled to concoct them. 1977: a college sophomore, naive, addicted to obfuscation, I visited the Jasper Johns retrospective at the Whitney Museum with my friend, a violinist with the eyes of a Bellini madonna. Before this exhibit, I'd seen little contemporary painting. But I loved transcendence, and I loved the Bellini-eyed violinist, and I wished to impress her by unfurling my art-historical intuitions in front of masterpieces. I wanted to be straight, to be a guy. Could the museum help?

Together, we rode the Johns retrospective like a Tunnel of Love. We clutched each other; we talked about the pilgrimage of our perceptions. The frothy discourse we generated glued us together, made us feel a couple. Often, in those years, I grew hysterically verbal in the presence of a woman I loved and wished, in my own queer way, to court. In retrospect I detest those flights of fancy, even as I recognize that, without the sympathies of women whose intimacies I pretend were mere preludes to my eventual coming out, I'd never have tapped those wishes I now, with false confidence, disregarding ambiguity, call "queer."

And yet—a contradiction?—a few weeks before seeing the Johns retrospective, I'd stumbled into a genial shrink's office and spoke for the first time about what I humorlessly called my "homosexual feelings."

I'm curious about how one Johns painting in particular summarized the paradoxes of my position vis-à-vis *art* and *desire* (I can't explain the gaps and antagonisms between these two seemingly neighborly terms). The painting that galvanized me was *In Memory of My Feelings—Frank O'Hara*, a work I consider influential within my own history primarily because it prompted me to read O'Hara, whose exuberant fluidity and candor would push me toward the gestures I now consider my own and could not bear living without. But even before I'd read O'Hara—even while, in the Whitney, I stared at the Johns painting, my companion as rapt as I—the terms of my engagement with art were permanently shifting. Although I viewed this painting within a threadbare regime of transcendence; although I scoured its surface for signs of how I might improve my soul; and although I assumed that Johns was part of an enviably straight cultural program, *In Memory of My Feelings* secretly fed me intimations of a quite other mode, uncloseted and rhapsodic, a mode I am still trying to attain.

In 1977, though, it was not the possibilities of gay figuration that excited me. Now, with hindsight, I can willfully decode his works, but back then I didn't linger over the possibly queer significance of his numbers, targets, balls, skin, and his allusions to Hart Crane and to Tennyson (the master of *In Memoriam*, so apposite to *In Memory of My Feelings*). It was because the painting was *abstract* that I solemnly worked myself into white heat. Beholding this canvas, I was at once greeting queer feeling and—in retrograde motion—refusing all premonitory traces of that identification. Desire's fulfillment, then, lay in seeking refuge from the figure and from representation. I decided it was wonderful to love paint's voluptuous accretion, to read—minutely—the brushstrokes for signs of foiled, thwarted interiority. The jism of paint! It was fun to blur my eyes in front of the abstraction and tip myself over the edge into hallucination. I found in Johns what I would soon relish in Mark Rothko: a nebulous field that would tolerate my extremes of projection, my excesses of interpretation.

Yet Johns's art is rigorously antisentimental, just as O'Hara's poetry displays his "feelings" but remains critical of mystified ideologies of the self. Though I poured my own "feelings" into *In Memory of My Feelings*, the painting now seems to me rather drab and silent. In its laconic gravity I must have deciphered a hidden glamour; I must have appreciated the fork and spoon, dangling; I must have loved the way these dining utensils topped or supplemented the two-part canvas (mysteriously hinged in the center), reminding me that life was material, plain, oral. Certainly I must have relished the painting's playfulness. . . . Honestly, I can't remember. Now, looking at a reproduction, I can't even decipher the letters—numbers, too?—on the canvas's lower right-hand corner.

In 1977 I hadn't yet written poems, and I hadn't more than glanced at O'Hara's oeuvre, and I hadn't heard of his friend John Ashbery, whose *Self-Portrait in a Convex Mirror* had been published just the year before—but this painting, as I reconsider it, suffuses me with elegiac impulses. Frank O'Hara died in 1966; this painting dates from 1961; I first saw it in 1977. Now, in 1993, I appropriate it as a memorial for O'Hara—as the melancholy afterimage it might always have tacitly implied it would become. Read against an unspecified abstract field, the phrase "in memory of my feelings" reports emotion's death and disappearance: how impossible it is to be sincere, and how grievous the impediments that thwart any artist who dares to depict desire without dissimulation! O'Hara did his best to ignore those impediments: he threatened to bring us farther than we'd imagined possible to the taboo Jerusalem of "feeling." And that is why the spectacle of O'Hara's insouciance and all its fond, revolutionary corollaries seems now, more than a decade after the advent of AIDS, and nearly three decades after his death, so irretrievable and utopian. In 1993, looking back at the various scenes (Pietà scenes, Fire Island accident scenes, hospital scenes, bedroom scenes, tearoom scenes, museum scenes) splayed for me like spokes around this painting's hub, I want to say: *think of all I didn't know in 1977; think of how this painting might have counseled me, if I'd known how to listen to it; think of what this painting refused, with its magisterial abstraction, to tell me.*

Sixteen years after the retrospective I write these sentences in memory of my heterosexuality. There is much to memorialize; it will take a lifetime. I write today in memory of 1977, when I hadn't yet given up seeking apotheosis in the artwork's surface. I write in memory of my delusion that in front of a painting one might dissemble a love affair. I write in memory of a time when I surrendered to a painting's mesmerism in order—perversely—to lay claim to my own fugitive interiority. I write in memory of the hinges—as if one could open the canvas and find nested within it an ulterior, "sincere" painting. I write in memory of O'Hara, and of the power of words (but only if they refuse compromise) to unlock the several, contradictory hearts, all the competing narratives of what happened in 1977, before I'd named my desires. I write in memory of the art that helped me to find the names and also helped me to forget them.

(1993)

MORTIFYING MAPPLETHORPE

New York's Guggenheim Museum contains an annex, a covert Robert Mapplethorpe Gallery, beginning with a dull hallway, and leading into a sober exhibition space, which, like the masterpieces of its namesake, seems consecrated to the unusual and the mortifying. At least one recent show—Joel-Peter Witkin's photographs of corpses, amputees, and hermaphrodites—holds a grotesqueness sufficient to remind the visitor of how sweet, how antique already, the infamous Mapplethorpe images have become. At least his models were alive.

Circumstance has forced Mapplethorpe's art into the unhappy position of being exemplary—of the racially objectifying gaze, of homoerotic curiosity, of free speech triumphantly exercised against tyrannic censorship. No artist—and Mapplethorpe was a fine one—deserves such treatment. He was just a fellow who worked assiduously to take pictures of what obsessed him; the nature of his preoccupations, and the movement of his photographs from a Manhattan demimonde into international notoriety, had everything to do with luck and with the shabby splendor of an era still so misunderstood that I urge us not to generalize about it but only repeatedly to observe its random peculiarity, and, in noticing how extreme and lacquered were Mapplethorpe's documents of it, to allow ourselves a shudder of envy, before we turn away.

I don't wish I were Robert Mapplethorpe—most times when I read biographies of famous artists I wish I were they—but I give him credit for getting somewhere first. He was among the first to promote and document a certain radical transvaluation of the rotten, the rejected; the meaty, the monstrous, the mathematical. (To the company of Byron's "Princess of Parallelograms" we should add the type of the counting-house trickster, the stud-libertine for whom quantity is quality.) I approach the corpus of Mapplethorpe, and the life under consideration, with a bias, a predilection for what Susan Sontag once baptised "the pornographic imagination." And if photography—Mapplethorpe's, at this moment—incites my regard, it is because some great specimens of that relatively new art are indistinguishable from pornography. I want to see weirdness documented. I don't fistfuck, but I find photos of the act instructive. If I attend a photo show that lacks nudes, I consider the visit a waste. A prurient interest in seeing sex, and an aesthetic interest in seeing photographs, can't be easily dissociated from one another. I agree with the painter Ellen Phelan, who said, defending Samuel Wagstaff's habit of pursuing handsome artists (including Mapplethorpe), "A lot of people get driven around by their sexual interests, and there are worse bases for aesthetic judgments." In some circles, that measuring stick of taste is called the "peter meter."

Patricia Morrisroe's eponymous biography insists that we find in Mapplethorpe's early life the seeds of his later leanings. Interesting to hear that child Robert "killed his turtle, Greenie, by impaling the pet on his index finger," but this act doesn't make him Satanic—merely unreverential of animal spirits. (In childhood I allowed a turtle to die, and I don't practice coprophagy.) His father "spent his career examining the insides of electrical appliances to see if they passed safety regulations"; his mother was "a fanatical housekeeper and often cleaned to the point of exhaustion." She also smoked—so heavily, the children reportedly "reeked of nicotine." Housecleaning, chain-smoking, appliances: these period appurtenances and afflictions, surely as a tuna fish casserole topped with corn flakes, speak Cold War America. "His father once forced him to eat burned eggs while he sat on the toilet seat." As a young collegiate subject to hazings, he was ordered to crawl into a bathroom on hands and knees and "eat excrement from a toilet bowl," though the offensive stuff turned out merely to be "mashed bananas and chunky peanut butter." He first masturbated while reading *Lady Chatterley's Lover*. Art-historical parlor game: hypothesize the circumstances of the first time Cézanne masturbated. (Or Nadar. Or Duchamp. Or Arbus.)

About porn, Mapplethorpe averred, "There's nothing worse than wanting to see something and having someone stop you." The budding artist frequented a blind newsdealer who sold skin magazines. Mapplethorpe was nearly nabbed stealing some: "For weeks afterward Robert had nightmares of the blind newsdealer, and he would wake up, sweating, in the middle of the night." (Is the sightless vendor a portent of the grim reaper, coming to claim the allegorical figure whom Thom Gunn has labeled "the man with night sweats"?)

Not yet sexually self-aware, Mapplethorpe visited Greenwich Village "to stare at homosexuals" and "to bask in their malevolent aura." Transplanted to New York's nervous, ambiguous Chelsea, he quickly realized that sex would become his great subject. He made sculptures from jockstraps, and hung near his bed a "masturbation machine"—a "mirror with dozens of white lights that blinked off and on, like a carnival roulette wheel." He formed one provocative early piece by taking "a pair of his blue jeans, stuffing the crotch with several socks, and wiring the pants so the groin pulsated." Another collage from his fleet apprenticeship was entitled *Tight Fucking Pants*. He encouraged Sandy Daley to make a vérité film called *Robert Having His Nipple Pierced*, later shown at New York's Museum of Modern Art; and in a Daley movie about Patti Smith's menstrual period, he changes her sanitary napkin.

The relationship with the "surrealistically rude" Smith proved catalytic. (Robert, too, would later be characterized as "lyrically selfish—that's when you're selfish to the point where it becomes a kind of poetry.") Smith earns my admiration for describing her poetic method this way: "I'd sit at the typewriter and type until I felt sexy, then I'd go and masturbate to get high, and then I'd come back in that higher place and write some more." Worse advice has come from the mouths of writing teachers.

Mapplethorpe's philosophy: "sex is the only thing worth living for." Redefining the enduring and the transient, he declared, "I was never into quickie sex. I've only slept with maybe a thousand men." He liked some partners to eat his excrement, and "was careful not to wash beneath his underarms because he believed perspiration odor was vital to his sex appeal." His haunt was Keller's, on New York's West Street, "a social gathering place for men interested in biracial sex; whites were known as 'dinge queens,' blacks 'dairy queens.' "

If we now think of Mapplethorpe as a sexual warrior who made museums hospitable to raw gaiety, his work was in reality nurtured by underground skin industries, and his achievement was to build a credible bridge between the divergent milieux. He did a cover photo for the gay S/M porn magazine *Drummer*, and it was through this far-left-of-center gig that he discovered some of his first models. And yet he was hardly alone in traversing libidinal frontiers. For example, at virtually the same time as Mapplethorpe's early experiments, artist Vito Acconci was publicly masturbating "under a wedge-shaped ramp" in New York's Sonnabend Gallery: "He called the piece *Seedbed*, and his sexual fantasies were incited by the presence of the gallery-goers." What Morrisroe coldly calls Mapplethorpe's "homosexual obsessions" paralleled the chimeras of other artists, though others might not have pursued their eidolons as indefatigably.

The root of his rigor was a reverence, deep as Thoreau's, for the real; that is why he photographed fistfucking. "I recorded that because it happened to me. . . . In fact . . . the *fist* in that picture belongs to an art director for one of the better art fashion magazines . . . they were friends of mine." So the darkly venturing fist can be traced to a world of influential men. That fist belongs to—J. Edgar Hoover? Roy Cohn? Truman Capote? The daisy chain doesn't stop. A hostile critic in the *Village Voice* will write that the famous photo of a black man in a suit "with his fly open and his elephant cock sticking out" is "ugly, degrading, obscene—typical of the artist's work, which appeals largely to drooling, lascivious collectors who buy them, and return to their furnished rooms to jerk off"; but it is impossible and morally distasteful to segregate Mapplethorpe's collectors from Ansel Adams's or Henri Cartier-Bresson's—and would the critic prefer if the rooms were unfurnished? Always the worst insult is to call a work masturbatory. It is because Mapplethorpe's images are jerk-off grist that they should be of surpassing interest to serious students of the imagination.

One is grateful that Patricia Morrisroe has gone out and done the research. If the book *Mapplethorpe: A Biography* has a failing, it lies in the biographer's intolerance for her subject's excesses, and her occasional tone deafness to gay liberation's early utopian promise, before AIDS complicated the intuition that at last the sexual body had been released from its manacles. One wishes that she felt more joy at the prospect of sexual multiplicity, more sadness at the closing of the erotic playground. One wishes that she could disconnect the oeuvre from the sensational death, or that she could thrill to the note of the sleazy. Any biographer of Mapplethorpe needs to appreciate porn's cultural and artistic significance, and needs to feel, as Arthur C. Danto observes in his perceptive book, *Playing with the Edge*, that with "AIDS a form of life went dead, a way of thought, a form of imagination and hope."

Danto dignifies Mapplethorpe's enterprise by calling it a search for transcendence, and cites Yeats: "Love has pitched his mansion in the place of excrement." Calling the 1970s aesthetically "the most important decade of the century" (that wasn't my experience), he takes seriously the photographer's claim that "to me sex is one of the highest artistic acts" and with professorial legerdemain flashes Hegel's term *Aufhebung* (from the German verb *aufheben*, meaning "to negate, or to preserve, or to transcend") on Mapplethorpe's images. One senses the heady atmosphere of a classroom in which, like a thunderstorm, acts of intellectual recuperation threaten to break.

To read Danto's book in public is compromising, even though it is published by a university press and mentions Hegel—for the handsome volume reproduces such explicit photographs as a self-portrait of the artist "from behind, in leather chaps and cowboy boots with a bullwhip stuck in his hairy anus and looping out onto the floor like a rat's tail." Riding a train, with this book as my companion, I was seated by good fortune next to an attractive, probably heterosexual stranger who might have been appalled, had he glimpsed—in his peripheral vision—this self-portrait, to which Danto's analysis does entire justice:

> There are plenty of male behinds in the history of art, but there can be relatively few anuses in that history, *roughly* for the same reason that while there are whole battalions of female nudes, there are relatively few displayed vaginas. The vagina does not show itself the way the penis does in the frontally presented nude figure, and can be seen only when the body is specially arranged to show it—only when the woman spreads her legs, as in the famous painting by Courbet rather pompously titled *The Origin of the Universe*. And so it is with the anus: the buttocks must be spread apart.

Italics mine. I enjoy the adverb *roughly*: apt but slippery.

In his preface, Danto recounts seeing the artist's unpublished set of working photographs, stored in a carton labeled SEX, at the Mapplethorpe Foundation: "It was . . . an extremely painful experience to go through the photographs, and I was unable, finally, to look at everything the box contained. I gave up halfway through, and when I got home that evening my wife wanted to know what had happened to me. I looked pale and shaken, and it took a while before the images faded." No doubt this is an accurate recounting of the experience, but as a literary moment it is odd and fabular: acts beyond the pale of wedlock are juxtaposed with the safe haven of "wife," to whom the traumatized anthropologist returns after his day-labor.

Another odd, evocative moment, in which the critic describes the largeness of the penises Mapplethorpe photographed, also takes the form of an autobiographical aside. To put these "well-hung" men in perspective, Danto moves from a literary to a personal anecdote, and then back to literature:

> In a famous episode in *A Moveable Feast*, F. Scott Fitzgerald expresses concern about the size of his penis, Zelda having said it was inadequately small; and Hemingway suggests he compare himself with what is to be found on classical statues, saying that most men would be satisfied with that. In my nearly four years as a soldier, I would have noticed it if anyone was equipped like the Man in the Polyester Suit, or Mark Stevens for that matter. Robert Burns in one of his nastier verses wrote, 'Nine inches doth please a lady'—but something of that dimension would have been negligible in the baths and washrooms of the 1970s if Mapplethorpe's models are typical.

Here, remarkably, a self-identified straight man (note the "wife") discusses penis size, admits to having checked out other men, and acknowledges the pastoral, nontoxic inevitability of men descrying other men's privates under the forgiving dispensations of communal life. Military service provides a pool of evidence, a fount of realism that equips the critic to understand how romantically out of proportion are the artist's dream members. This is a digression, though one not irrelevant to what Mapplethorpe's photographs propose, which is, in sum, that men's bodies ask to be looked at.

(1996)

SMELL OF NIGHT ON HANDKERCHIEF

Ideologies and teleologies hide in a life's thickets, but ultimately an existence doesn't fall prey to reasons; one doesn't survive in order to amass evidence for a cause. Rather, life sputters along, clumsy and driven. Joseph Cornell's life certainly didn't have a linear argument; as it unfolds in *Theater of the Mind*, a selection from his diaries and files, edited by Mary Ann Caws, his career happily refuses to be assimilated to a movement or an idea. No sect—not surrealism, not aestheticism—can explain him. He aimed to prove nothing. Whims assailed him, and it was his lifelong devotional practice to ignore the adamantly legislated difference between reality and imagination.

Even with the diaries here to assist us, we shouldn't think that we understand Cornell. To understand is to pathologize. Let's not place a value, a prescriptive term on him—because it will necessarily be the brand of the eccentric. Let's consider him, instead, a harbinger, a wily assembler whose radicalism we haven't yet caught up to, even if he now seems a domesticated mini-titan of a bygone moment.

"Bulging files," according to Caws, stand behind the Cornell dream boxes. Devotees of his work have long awaited the publication of these files, which mustn't be considered merely the explanatory prolegomenon to the artwork. They have their own integrity: they are prose poems, laid out with the antic scrupulousness of a James Schuyler. Caws has reproduced Cornell's lineation, retained his Dickinsonian dashes, and included the asterisks he used to announce epiphanic instants ("*témoignages*"). He becomes a far more unsettling (and conceptual?) artist if we allow a continuity between private diary and public artifact, between verbal notation and visual object.

Cornell quotes an aphorism: "Life can have significance even if it appears to be a series of failures." Cornell transvalued failure: one of his films was devoted to the actress Rose Hobart, whom Caws described as "rejected from a Los Angeles home for destitute stars as insufficiently famous." So, too, must we transvalue confinement and myopia when considering him. Marianne Moore wrote to him: "Do not make me a criminal"; though not, like Jean Genet, an actual criminal and prisoner, Cornell oscillated between incarcerating, "shut-in" fantasy (at home in Flushing) and liberation (trips to New York City to browse, cruise, loiter, eat, and shop). Like Emily Dickinson, Cornell was an artist of agoraphobia and of the agora: he enjoyed staying beside his kitchen stove ("headquarters"), but he also enjoyed treks in the city streets.

To Cornell, secondhand and variety shops like Woolworth weren't mere dross to be transformed into respectable art; they were already sites of transcendence ("*in the teeth of winter the flowering often of Woolworth local"). Just as we must respect his love for five-and-dime stores, so we must respect the fact that Cornell's most important relations were with his mother and his brother, with whom he lived until their deaths. Cornell didn't couple; like Dickinson, he rejected the repressive fictions of futurity and maturation. He wrote letters to his mother after her death, and bought a Robbe-Grillet paperback for Robert four years after his. There is scant room in contemporary critical schemes for the co-existence of piety and perversion: perhaps the most perverse facts of Cornell's constitution were his love of young girls and his faith in Christian Science, which fed his more conventionally avantgarde engagements, particularly his identification as a fan, a passion as thoroughgoing and intellectually rigorous as Warhol's.

No aspect of Cornell's diaries is more inspiring than the record of his devotion to a range of female cultural figures of varied eras and echelons, including Mylène Demongeot, Susan Sontag, Patty Duke, Hedy Lamarr, Maria Malibran, Barbara Feldon, Eva Marie Saint, and Fanny Cerrito, described by Caws as "Cornell's favorite nineteenth-century dancer, partly because he thought her undervalued." Cornell believed her to be the great-great-grandmother of Jean-Paul Belmondo. Two sample moments of tribute: "in the evening Patty Duke was here via Mahler #3." And "Dear Miss Sontag—After wanderlusting around in 'Interpretation' into the small hours, especially in the Leiris section, I felt that you were the one to have the enclosed, hoping not to presume on your recherché shelves." It makes sense that Cornell appreciated Michel Leiris, for both were engaged in a systematic, archaeological plumbing of obsession, disobeying civilization's punitive command, "Grow up!" Cornell didn't explain or demystify his preoccupations; he pursued them as a spiritual practice. He dived into sentimentality as if into a taboo pond whose mirrored surface enticed him ("transcendental sometimes passed off as overemotional").

Cornell's appetites were irregular, even "decadent." He loved shop girls (the younger the better): he called them *les fées*. Among these was Joyce Hunter, cashier in Ripley's Believe It or Not! in Times Square. He loved shopping: he notes "an urge to splurge— irrational repetitive buying." And he loved starches and sweets: "Shaved and bathed around one—had lunch of donuts, caramel pudding, two cups Dutch process cocoa all milk, wholewheat bread, peanut butter, peach jam (wolfed milky way bar after breakfast). Bought Robert eclair (chocolate) for lunch and baker's assortment Mrs. Wagner's Peach Pie 6 cents, ½ dozen icing cakes Bay West." He valued the sweet and the immediately satisfying over the healthy and the nourishing. Cornell reminds us: pursue desire for its own sake. Need we label desire progressive or hygienic to condone it? Isn't it part of Cornell's radicalism to avoid such categories altogether? No certainties of progress undergird his consumption—only appetite, unbridled and unrationalized.

The appetites Cornell celebrated still occupy a low rung on our ladders of value. His jottings—defenses of solitary (and hence, obscene) pleasure—are profoundly, nourishingly onanistic. Relentless self-examination and self-stimulation are not activities that this culture fully accepts, despite its sometime lip service to sexual diversity. These days, certain homosexualities are considered halfway decent. But what if sex itself isn't decent? What if desire is a destabilizing force? Appetite didn't land Cornell a clear identity, didn't lead him toward maturity, didn't draw him closer to other people. He had more in common with the demonized pedophile than with the heroically lonely artist or the egalitarian sexual radical. Cornell built no communities. Morose hedonist, he cared only for his own titillation, his own melancholy. His aim, in the diaries, isn't to communicate: it's to "get off." That's why they seem so fresh.

In conversation, Cornell could be a bore; his droning monologues sometimes extended for hours. The curator Diane Waldman was so exhausted by his rambling on the telephone that she dropped under her desk during one conversation. The diaries, too, can be trying, even in drastically edited form, and even with Caws's illuminating and amusing notes. His "pennings" grew more and more fragmentary. In 1971, he wrote, "Do not lose the thread of 'elephant' (and girl) TV guide dossiers." In fact, he frequently seems to have lost the thread.

Cornell's body of work, like Gertrude Stein's, exceeds any possible containment within book or museum; the diaries and dossiers will probably never be published in their entirety. Finally, what I admire in them is Cornell's offbeat attention to vicariousness—his awestruck patience with the never-enacted. Cornell copied down a quotation about Dickinson—an observation that her most precious relationships were "so one-sided as to be hallucinatory." The same must have been true of Cornell. His daft aperçus—"Smell of night on handkerchief"—seem acts of conscientious objection to an increasingly dismal world.

(1994)

MY WOMEN OF DADA

hough Dada pretended to be a movement of male origination, it perpetuated an effeminate legacy. In the process, it did what any art movement worth the name accomplished: it blocked clarity.

I am polemical about the worth of effeminacy because if it has the power to unsettle people, it might have medicinal or corrective virtues.

Women are the very stuff of Dada; they are the material hubbub that makes Dada sensational.

I am a woman of Dada because "woman" aspects of my carriage and attitude inherit cheek from that clubby group of gender-obsessed men collaboratively playing around with concocting mannequin women.

Any vision of gender that takes itself too seriously begs Dada to interrupt it.

Emmanuel Radnitzky was a woman of Dada. Why would

anyone get rid of a name like Emmanuel Radnitzky? He changed his name to Man Ray in order to claim universal manhood. "Man Ray" repudiated his original, ethnic identity; he took on manhood as an alias, a con job. His emblem of masculinity was an eggbeater.

Man Ray's 1916 self-portrait has a doorbell on its surface. This doorbell—a petite penis or nipple—suggests that manhood is a protuberance one can push in rather than be pushed around by.

Whenever Duchamp signed a readymade he hollowed out the male signature and mocked the idea of signing as a man.

Rrose Sélavy was a woman of Dada. She made perfume, or was herself an evaporating distillation. Yves Saint-Laurent now owns the pretty bottle of "Belle Haleine, Eau de Voilette." I would like to ask him why he purchased it, what it means to him, and whether a Duchampian spirit underlies twentieth-century (post-Dior) women's fashion. Is Polly Mellen a woman of Dada? Are models in *Vogue*, *Harper's Bazaar*, and *W* women of Dada?

Rrose Sélavy has a strong jaw and an attractive Adam's apple. She should not make you laugh but should produce horny silence. Photos of Rrose Sélavy prod how many viewers into erotic reverie? Odd, that Duchamp *dressed up* while the Baroness Elsa von Freytag-Loringhoven *undressed* in pursuit of self-manufacture and self-evaporation.

Beatrice Wood was a woman of Dada. In her piece entitled *Un Peut D'Eau dans du Savon*, a tiny green scallop-shell of actual soap represents Aphrodite's mound of Venus. To trust Man Ray and Beatrice Wood, genitals are push buttons or soap bumps— detachable protuberances that have comic use-value, dopey (sit-com) functionality: push the button, wash your hands with soap, and produce what aphorism, what punch line, what laugh track, what little pellet of commerce or conclusion, what Necco wafer of closure?

Man Ray's *New York or Export Commodity*, metal ball bearings in a glass olive jar, suggests that New York is a bunch of balls that might sometimes have a use (to ease movement, to lubricate an assembly line) but are now behind glass in a display case, and

therefore Man Ray showcases the city's castration, its metamor-
phosis into a set of beautiful collectibles. He aestheticizes the
city's new identity as eunuch's paradise, a gum machine of penny
masculinities, shined and dispensable.

Paul Strand and Charles Sheeler's film, *Manhatta*, enjoins the
viewer to admire the fantastic, confusing genitalia of the skyline.
Is New York a woman? Did the women of Dada invade New
York, or was the invaded metropolis imagined to be a woman?

The Baroness Elsa von Freytag-Loringhoven was a woman of
Dada, often nude, a fashion radical. Man Ray photographed the
poet Mina Loy wearing von Freytag-Loringhoven earrings: thermometers. Wearing thermometers is art radicalism, which tends
to fade. One role of a museum is to remember lost radicalisms,
some of which happen on the street, in passing, in private. I
haven't been as brave as the baroness: I haven't made art out of
my body. Who has surpassed her unsung role in the Marcel
Duchamp film, *The Baroness Shaves Her Pubic Hair*, or the spec-
tacular mortification of her shellacked, shaven, vermilion-dyed
skull?

Dorothy True was a woman of Dada: Stieglitz photographed
her memorable calf and foot, shod in a high-heeled pump. Who
dominates or owns the photograph—Dorothy True or Alfred
Stieglitz? Does commentary on Stieglitz emphasize women's
shoes? *Stieglitz* and *women's shoes* are probably not cross-listed on
any index or web, so I must create that intersection, that complex
home page.

Mary Garden is a woman of Dada. An issue of the Dada-
infused magazine *Rogue* contained an ad for Mary Garden's
Chocolates, named after the diva because she stooped to praise
them on their lid: she gushed, "Your chocolates are really the
finest I have ever tasted anywhere in the world. Mary Garden."
To praise or endorse is a Dada act. To cross over from opera
singing to candy praising is a Dada journey. Garden also en-
dorsed a perfume, called Gardenia. Elizabeth Taylor followed
Garden's—and Rose Sélavy's—lead, by committing the Dada
crime of perfume endorsement. Women were Dada's advertise-
ments: Dada, the ad campaign for a certain artificial idea of

woman, urgently hawked a product with a more-than-human claim on the senses.

The phrase *the women of Dada* recalls George Cukor's *The Women*, a film in which no men appear. The movie might plausibly have been called *The Men*, so thoroughly is it Cukor's dream of a women's room closed to his participation. Why not call Dada *The Women*? Since Dada has no fixed boundaries, why subordinate women to Dada, and imagine women as the supplement to Dada? Why not replace the word *Dada* with the phrase *the women*? Men filmed it, but it is a woman's picture.

Is the nude descending the staircase a woman or a man? Is the bride consumed by bachelors a woman or a man? In neither case is it possible to verify gender with the eye. And so we have to wing it. Winging it is a pleasure, a flight of conjecture that comes to be known as the art act. Suspending the rules of gravity and the graven image, we ride above authorship, fact, and genitalia.

Look anywhere in literature of the 1920s and you will find the women of Dada. Tiresias is a woman of Dada. At the movement's heyday he guest-starred in a show called *The Waste Land*. Ask Tiresias about Duchamp's *Apolinère Enameled*, a bit of painted tin that tries to cast painting as girl's play; sit on Tiresias's lap, this wintry evening, the water around us green, the cement of Manhattan fading, a bad dream.

In Willa Cather's 1925 novel, *The Professor's House*, the male professor keeps female mannequins—the dress forms of a seamstress—in his study. Similar dress forms appear in several Man Ray paintings, including *La Volière* and *Still Life + Room Interior*. In the following passage from Cather's novel, she describes the dress forms as if they were Dada art objects—say, the Duchamp urinal, which invites yet also repels touch:

> Though this figure looked so ample and billowy (as if you might lay your head upon its deep-breathing softness and rest safe forever), if you touched it you suffered a severe shock, no matter how many times you had touched it before. It presented the most unsympathetic surface imaginable. Its hardness was not that of wood, which responds to concussion with

living vibration and is stimulating to the hand, nor that of felt, which drinks something from the fingers. It was a dead, opaque, lumpy solidity, like chunks of putty, or tightly packed sawdust—very disappointing to the tactile sense, yet somehow always fooling you again. For no matter how often you had bumped up against that torso, you could never believe that contact with it would be as bad as it was.

Facing the Dada object, the viewer may feel her fingers twitch and yearn; and yet the pissoir says "*Noli me tangere*."

God is a woman of Dada, since the Baroness Elsa von Freytag-Loringhoven composed a sculpture, entitled *God*, which is actually a plumbing trap. Note the divinity of sinks and toilets. Duchamp's *Fountain* recalls a font for holy water in a strange church, or a defunct drinking fountain that only a thirsty pervert would bend to use.

Has anyone made definitive inquiries into whether and how often Duchamp and Man Ray slept with men? Both were too louche, odd, and perfumed not once or twice to have taken the plunge. The svelteness of Duchamp's conceptions—the flask of Parisian air—advertises his body, a cuteness across the sea, imported, available only in a limited edition.

Beatrice Wood, in her diary, wrote "Stayed in bed till 12. . . . A fairly happy day at last." Another day, she wrote "Very happy." Another day, "Charming." Isn't that *Mrs. Dalloway* and *To the Lighthouse* in a nutshell? This attitude toward dailiness—the mock-aristocratic apotheosis of "charming"—is a Dada strategy more often seen in the Zen blandness of a woman or a fag who watches the flow of events and responds in an ecstatic or bored syllable: Beatrice Wood's *fairly happy* is ancestor to the slacker's *whatever*, the flower child's *cool*. Beatrice Wood's was a ten-year diary, ten years of January 27ths on the same page, so she could look back upon a cross section of time's passage; her diary is Dada in its laconic attention to what has evaporated.

Marianne Moore was a woman of Dada. Once she lunched with Wallace Stevens and Marcel Duchamp. What was their conversation? In a footnote she described her poem "Marriage" as

"Statements that took my fancy which I tried to arrange plausibly." She *tried* to arrange them plausibly but she didn't break her neck to do so; chucking plausibility for fancy and juxtaposition, Moore practiced Dada, although what encyclopedia of Dada includes this empress of ice cream?

Doris Day as advertising executive in *Lover Come Back* is a woman of Dada, for advertising is Dada's first tongue. Doris Day in *The Man Who Knew Too Much* continues the woman's work of Dada, as do Kim Novak in *Vertigo*, Tippi Hedren in *Marnie* and *The Birds*, and Julie Andrews in *Torn Curtain*—large-souled secretive dress forms with no chance to run away.

If it is useful or incidentally accurate to conceptualize New York City as a woman (as Strand and Sheeler did in the film, *Manhatta*), then the women of Dada are the Flatiron, the Ansonia, the Dakota, the World Trade Center, the Chelsea Hotel, the Empire State, the Chrysler, the Fred French, Radio City Music Hall, Grand Central, and the old Penn Station.

To contemplate the women of Dada is to taste Manhattan's hiss and beatitude of getting and spending, to feel the propinquity of garbage and finery, and to open a magazine without a thought of finding anything of value but opening it anyway because one is a member of a magazine culture once dominated by Dada, a culture whose pulse points were women—a culture that bought the idea of woman and wished to call art a feminine pastime even when men practiced it.

Dwelling among magazines, I become a woman of Dada, a creature of design, juxtaposition, shiny paper, pictures, frivolity, anachronism, pretend modernity, and depletion. Dada lives and dies in magazines—a universe of ads, typography, replicability, and fake choice, a carnival of consumption, akin to department-store window, shopping mall, and arcade. Oscar Wilde, who edited a magazine called *The Woman's World*, is a woman of Dada. Women's fashion magazines are Dada's plush sepulchers.

(1997)

WHAT ALICE KNOWS

What does Alice Neel know? In the 1930s she knows men: cultivated men, rich men in suits, artistic men in turtle-necks, longshoremen loping home from the waterfront, tired laborers cross-legged on the unforgiving chairs of poverty investi-gators, ice-hauling men, men on strike, policemen on horses, sepulchral men shiftless on downtown corners shadowed by El trestles, men flashing cigarettes, men playing guitars, fire-eyed men who might soon become martyrs, slothful men, men with several uncircumcised penises, men who are far from the Semitic but know and husband their distance from it, men on and off their rockers. Alice Neel knows women, too: naked women sit-ting on circus elephants, skull-faced women in calf-length fur-trimmed coats skulking back from shops, sympathetic intelligent women studying the lower classes, poor women with sagging arm flesh, wide women observing revolutionary unrest, women paid to nurse, unremunerated women giving suck regardless, women diapering offspring, women mourning their own babies, women confronting doctors, women with lipsticked ovals flashing geometric teeth, women with Levantine shut eyes, degenerate women, wealthy women, hale women, women with large nipples, women dripping milk, women sitting on gravestones, smiling contemporary women in snoods, women urinating, bold women, women aware of their own vaginas, women asleep, women with surreal unsycophantic sanatorium eyes, women seen from jaundiced angles, women named Ethel. Alice Neel knows the transparency of children and she knows their sometime viscosity: their innocence—a glass of water held up to light—reveals no contaminating tincture, though a dye-drop of corruption lies in wait. No accident that I use the present tense to describe a cognition—Neel's—so entirely contemporary, housed in paintings that continue to emit fireworks; no accident, either, that my tribute to Neel invokes Henry James's *What Maisie Knew*. Like prior, legendary Alices (Alice James, Alice B. Toklas, Lewis Carroll's Alice), Neel avows and disavows in the same breath, sits trapped in the crossfire of superior, mercenary, adult surveillances, and falls down rabbit holes into dreamlands of the bedridden and the unrepresentable. Neel knows the undisplayable vagina of the forthright girl child standing on a striped rug, and she knows the strangled child between the ribs of a bed that should have been ample but proved a grave. She knows the hairless ungendered infant sitting on the degenerate madonna's lap and knows that the kid has perverted the mother: the child gives pleasure but also steals some back, and so the honest artist must depict the infant as a dead doll with an apple hiding its genitals, shamed into pointlessness. Neel knows that the adult man—handsome José playing the guitar—was once a child and may take the liberty of remaining infantile, while the nude Nadya, a placid or troubled woman lying large and naked on rumpled sheets, must forfeit childishness in order to exist among the mature and the portrayed. The artist who mimetically renders a living creature places that body within the cage of portraiture: the artist incarcerates her subject, boxes the sitter inside representational conventions.

If Neel holds her subject captive, however, the motive is kind: she intends release—the spectator's. Looking at a Neel painting, I am condemned to know my parallelism to the portrayed body (I, too, have contemplative hands; I, too, have a high forehead; I, too, close my eyes to symbolize the futility of effort); but after this labor of identification, I am eased from knowledge, granted liberty from strict embodiment.

Alice Neel knows men, women, and children. She also knows that Nazis murder Jews. She displays everything she knows with the same frontality. Her paintings from the 1930s show her clear, early, indignant exercise of social conscience—her awareness of injustice, of difference, of nationalism's turn toward demonism. Neel knows that bodies exist in social webs, subject to strictures of caste. She anatomizes the tenacity with which a person may inhabit a particular identity while also managing to shirk—or ignore—that residence's pitfalls. These paintings say: *I am so entirely embodied—so lodged inside flesh—that sometimes, for sanity, I must forget my body. I must stare right past it, into the safe harbor a canvas offers.* The images in this exhibition are solidly located in the 1930s but they gaze beyond that decade into our time. They speak an epoch's preoccupations and styles—*I come from 1935*— but also shrug off the coils of art-historical periodization, just as their subjects bear the confinement of their bodies only to refuse and transcend that signage. Fanya in 1930 holds a slim hand against her chest and stares at the viewer, as if to say, "Why am I myself? And why do you look at me?" Repose and denial of the sitter: Fanya will next say, "No, you don't mean 'me.' I am not entirely or only myself." And yet notice how regally— with what sublime sufferance—she permits the viewer to doom her to portraiture's apparatus. Though Neel's knowledge is not limited to skin (she knows movie lobbies, cafeterias, and back stoops, too), she specializes in—and thus exalts—acne, bruise, five-o'clock shadow, jowl, love handle, tumescence, baldness, rouge, and flab. For art is not a cheerful practice. Elizabeth Bishop's memorable phrase, "awful but cheerful," comes to mind: Neel's art notices the paradoxical good cheer—a gallows equanimity—of the abject and the outcast. If her subjects can tolerate the rigor of being rendered, then they have reached an armored state of cheerfulness that protects them against the gaze of any dull viewer who might not yet have learned dejection's dependence on its nervy twin, exhilaration.

(1997)

NOTES ON NOT NOW

A style magazine calls me to ask whether any contemporary stars have inherited Jackie's glamour. I mention Jeanne Moreau. Silence on the other end of the line: Moreau is not a contemporary star. Tonight shall I go to the Quad and see her new movie about walking into the sea? (Now the film has fled to another locale.) I suggest to the magazine that I would love to interview Doris Day or Sophia Loren. Silence. I am confused about what's contemporary and what's outdated. I am confused about the spirit of the age.

In dreams I've been trying to teach remedial English. It's not only a class, it's a century: the twentieth. The dream recurs. Last night with a swoon of relief I realized that, though I missed meetings, the students have reading assignments to tide them over until my return: easy books about Bambi. Poor things patiently await

Teacher's reappearance. A friend told me that a teacher can create effects of power by suddenly using difficult language in a seminar, or, better yet, by not showing up. The students will interpret Teacher's absence as a terrifying judgmental presence.

∞

Out of the blue my sixth-grade teacher writes me a letter. Now she is a drug rehabilitation counselor. Does she recall my inability to pay attention?

∞

I lunch with a favorite mentor, and we discuss whether it's possible to lecture objectively about hysteria: can you talk about a subject without enacting it? We converse about coughing and MTV, and we agree, provisionally, that hysteria is a precondition for creativity. I recommend the film *Hysteria* (1964).

∞

At the buffet table, a scholar interested in automatic writing uses the words *iconophilia* and *iconophobia*. Great words. I jot them down. Our age has both syndromes simultaneously: it is enamored of representation but afraid of querying it. Mr. Automatic speculates that Jews have iconophobia, and cites Walter Benjamin, but this seems a case of iconophilia, so we drop the subject.

∞

The day of the O. J. Simpson verdict, an expert appears on a news show to analyze the defendant's body language. Did his gestures broadcast guilt or innocence? I note the presumption that we, as a nation, can't evaluate nuance: why do we need an expert to interpret human gesture? Or, as a teacher once told me, "The reader is not a potato."

∞

At a conference, the scholar Ian Hacking uses the phrase "the wound of the day" to describe the fin de siècle French phenomenon of *les automatismes ambulatoires*, or *vagabondage*: men who, overcome by states of fugue and amnesia, wandered away from family and job. What an attractive disorder! Catherine Deneuve, in *Belle de Jour*, had it. So did the Beats, and Paul Bowles: the compulsion to drift off from identity.

∞

I wander down Twenty-second Street on a hot late September day (global warming) and find Jimmy DeSana's photos at Pat Hearn Gallery. In one, a nude man buries his head in a toilet, suds pouring out the bowl. Good! In another, a high-heeled shoe is crammed inside a pantyhosed crotch. Satisfaction! Jimmy DeSana died in 1990, and these photos document what one calls, knowingly, "another era." I am interested in our era only to the extent that it is also not ours, not here, not now: an era of replacement.

∞

Eighth Avenue: in the crosswalk a young man and I talk about aesthetics. His neck looks like food.

∞

From obituaries I glean the spirit of the age. Ida Lupino died this year. She was only seventy-seven. I should have written her a letter. "Her leisure pursuits included skin diving, writing short stories and children's books and composing music. One work, 'Aladdin Suite,' was performed by the Los Angeles Philharmonic Orchestra." If I can locate her vehicle, *Ladies in Retirement*, the story of "a stolid housekeeper who kills her overbearing employer so she may use the house as a sanctuary for her two insane sisters," then I can deduce whether the sisters are really insane, and I can define *sanctuary*.

∞

Eva Gabor died this year. From her obituary, this snippet of an interview: "Because of my allergies I like to buy very cheap makeup with no perfume. I buy things on sale. The prices today are shocking." She ran a multimillion-dollar wig company. To discern what's "now," I follow wigs. Eva Gabor's sister starred in *Queen of Outer Space* (1958), which reshuffles a half century's card deck of catastrophes and insurrections: Hiroshima, lesbian utopias, Orientalism, Eastern European nationalisms and revolutions, the beautiful fictitiousness of heterosexuality. . . .

∞

Red Gucci bags. Red Patrick Cox Wannabes. Some men's shiny shoes now recall 1959 women's pocketbooks. *Unzipped,* the documentary about Isaac Mizrahi, proves that fashion ideas come from fags watching revivals and paying acute attention to fugue and fatigue. I want to file *fag* in a clean manilla envelope named *fugue*, and to store *men's shoes* in a conceptual box called *les automatismes ambulatoires.*

∞

At a Whitney Museum symposium on Florine Stettheimer, cultural historian Steven Watson plays a tape of the voice of old Virgil Thomson saying "Gertrude loved nuns" and asserting that high camp is the only technique that can represent religious experience. How weirdly modern Virgil Thomson sounds, and how happy we are to have him back. After the symposium I shake the hand of Joseph Solomon, who once held the shoe box containing Florine's ashes. I muse on his virile handshake, a dream of historical continuity.

∞

In a conversation I use the word *surreal,* twice, and an art historian says I am overusing the word, so, a little drunk, I defend my penchant for *surreal.* I say, "In search of the zeitgeist, I'm reading surrealist manifestos! I'm committed to fugue states, trances, derangement!" Later I call the body a temple, not to be profaned, and a neuropsychologist tells me that brains require interaction in order to evolve. I ask him whether my brain is dying or whether it is generating new files.

∞

A sociologist tells me that the notion of a zeitgeist is a "crock of shit." Then we talk about the teacher-student fornication in *To Die For* and I offer him a splash of CK One unisex cologne.

∞

Was Florine Stettheimer a political artist? Can a merely "decorative" artist be considered political? An artist removed from the spirit of her age but also profoundly at its helm, she participated in a public discourse while seeming merely to be painting pretty, private, salon art. If her work is exhibited in full only now, can her paintings address today's circumstances, or must we understand her art only within the context of her own time?

∞

A friend has compiled an anthology of contemporary world poetry. On the train, he shows me the table of contents. I am afraid I will get my doughnut glaze on it, but magically the manuscript escapes ruin. I'm unfamiliar with most of the writers he's included. My ignorance appalls, hyperstimulates: new poets to discover, many of them alive, composing the age. In today's mail, PEN's newsletter arrives, suggesting that members send holiday greetings to incarcerated writers—Pramoedya Ananta Toer, under town arrest in Utan Kayu, Jakarta.

∞

Much as I distrust anthologies, I compulsively page through *Poems for the Millennium*, edited by Jerome Rothenberg and Pierre Joris: it advocates futurisms galore, and includes artifacts that don't usually travel under the name *poem*. In an entrancing excerpt from Mallarmé's *Le Livre* (he died in 1898 but I have yet to take his measure), the poet has crossed words out: lines through *end, conscience, And sorrows, street, childhood, double, their, crowd, crime, sewer*. The editors quote Maurice Blanchot on Mallarmé: "At times his work solidifies into an immobile white virtuality, at times—and this is what matters most—it becomes animated by an extreme temporal discontinuity, given over to changes in time and to accelerations and decelerations, to fragmentary stoppages, the sign of a wholly new essence of mobility in which another [sense of] time seems to be announcing itself, as foreign to eternal permanence as to quotidian duration: [in Mallarmé's words] 'here moving ahead, there remembering, in the future, in the past, *under a false appearance of the present.*' " The anthologists mention Paul Valéry's *Carnets*: "For the rest of his life his main labor consisted in rising daily at five A.M. to write down his thoughts & meditations in his *Carnets*, the notebooks that eventually numbered two hundred fifty. The study of consciousness as such was to be the fulcrum of his notebook writing, & there, however unable or unwilling he was to integrate them into his poetics, he could not escape the essentially fragmentary possibilities of his century. . . ." To do: read Valéry's *Carnets*.

Emily Dickinson understood the fragmentary possibilities of her century. In a letter, published in an Amherst College newspaper, *The Indicator*, February 1850, she suggests revolutionary displacements: "we'll pull society up to the roots, and plant it in a different place." Also: "That's what they call a metaphor in our country. Don't be afraid of it, sir, it won't bite." But what if metaphors *do* bite? Fragments of an agoraphobe's poetry touch—maul—the outside world.

Poetry makes nothing happen, and yet Adrienne Rich has published a new volume, *Dark Fields of the Republic*, from which I quote these rhetorically compelling lines:

> But the great dark birds of history screamed and plunged
> into our personal weather
> They were headed somewhere else but their beaks and
>   pinions drove
> along the shore, through the rags of fog
> where we stood, saying *I*

(I love "rags of fog": musical.) Rich falsely polarizes "birds of history" and "personal weather." Birds and weather are figures of speech. To diagnose a national malaise is to employ metaphors.

∞

Revivals and republications trumpet the indescribable reveille of this instant. Johns Hopkins University Press has republished Gertrude Stein's *The Geographical History of America*, originally published by Random House in 1936. She writes: "How many animals birds and wild flowers are there in the United States and is it splendid of it to have any." From her private vantage, Gertrude Stein unsentimentally fingered public textures, historical birds; her every sentence constitutes a republication.

∞

A recitation that Stein might have enjoyed, John Keene's *Annotations*, appears from New Directions. Its first sentence: "Such as it began in the Jewish Hospital of St. Louis, on Fathers' Day, you not some babbling prophet but another Negro child, whose parents' random choices of signs would disorient you for years." More and more I choose a voice that disorients. The last sentence: "And so, patient reader, these remarks should be duly noted as a series of mere life-notes aspiring to the condition of annotations." On the book's cover, an untitled painting by Glenn Ligon, from which I can make out only a few words: *BUT THIS, DISGUISE, EXPECTED, MYSELF, SEE MYSELF.* The autobiographical project: to discover, through close attention to the texture of the speaking, self-revealing voice, what body is being obliquely annotated.

∞

Also from *Annotations*: "Missouri, being an amalgam of nearly every American region, presents the poet with a particularly useful analogue for an articulation of the 'American,' though close inspection shows a sum less metaphorically potent than its metonymically dissoluble parts. Show me." I want to write more about the beauties of "show me" but it is time to go to a lecture.

∞

On the way to the lecture, my friend and I meet Renaud Camus, author of *Tricks* (1979), reissued this year by High Risk Books. My friend, once cutely sedate, now has five piercings. I go to his hotel, where the hormonally imbalanced woman who used to work at the dry cleaners is now running the reception desk. She wears heavy pancake makeup, compensatory. She winks at me. She knows I recognize her from the dry cleaners. Then Leo Bersani, at his lecture, proposes that we redo the "relational" by paying attention not only to micropolitics but to desire's structure. We can destroy "regimes of the normal" by stepping outside psychological law (in the manner of Caravaggio or Genet). Bersani pronounces *homosexual* the way Julie Andrews did in the original *Victor/Victoria*: Homo Secks Ewe Ull. Perhaps this pronunciation demonstrates a stance toward sibilance.

∞

Movies recirculate. Without their recirculation, the imagination would lose ghostlimbs to gangrene. *Queen of Outer Space,* in CinemaScope, starring Zsa Zsa Gabor, reappears at a nearby theater, and then, miraculously, Joan Crawford's last film, *Trog* (1970), rises to sight—so ignored, at its origin and its return, that it has liberty to sing of the future. If I were to begin to explain the significance of *Trog*, I'd keep you here all night: wigs, microphones, caves, voice-box transplants, boy nudity, unloved daughters, slimy drunk men who disrupt Joan's quest for scientific progress. . . . In the last moment of the film and the last frames of her career, she strides offscreen, refusing to comment on the slaughter of Trog (protégé, monster, double)—emblem of the pathologized has-been's oracular voice. Outdated images still detonate. Trog (diminutive for troglodyte, cave dweller, hasbeen) still demands reading, still demands that—in its presence—we not be potatoes but that we listen to instructions.

∞

A year before *Trog*'s first release, the painter Marilyn Minter took photographs of her mother, a series finally exhibited this year under the title "Coral Ridge Towers." Looking at Minter's mother, I succumb to iconophilia: this lost woman, smoking, mirror-obsessed, seems glamorously agoraphobic, and I revel in her avoidance of crowds. Fear of the marketplace can engender the backwards, smashed glamour of the shut-in. Bury Trog for twenty years, or "twenty centuries of stony sleep," and then the ignored, abject object will come slouching toward you, its mouth full of fragmentary possibilities.

∽

The circuit of one's own preoccupations leads to agoraphobia (I don't want to leave my apartment, I want to stay here in bed and smoke and put on makeup and stare at the mirror and the dust bunnies) or to wanderlust (I want to travel outside the "Coral Ridge Tower" of my personality in order to rediscover lost coordinates). When I lie alone in bed, am I Trog? Am I a dark bird of history when I cruise the streets, looking for a good movie or a metaphor?

∽

Emily Dickinson, in 1842, is away at school. Soon she will commit forever to her father's house. She writes, in a letter, "this Afternoon is Wednesday and so of course there was Speaking and Composition – there was one young man who read a Composition the Subject was think twice before you speak. . . ." And from a later letter (1851): "I dont think deaths or murders can ever come amiss in a young woman's journal – the country's *still* just now, and the severities alluded to will have a salutary influence in waking the people up." The country is motionless. Meanwhile I contemplate the underground rapport between the words *Subject*, *twice*, and *speaks*. The Subject speaks twice. No one hears the Subject the first time, so the Subject speaks again. The Subject doesn't exist until the second coming.

∽

To do:

1. Wake the people up.
2. Think twice before I speak.
3. Write down all the recent deaths and scrutinize them—including the death of Larry, who lent me a bootleg Ida Lupino video, and rode a taxi once with Anita O'Day (she reappeared this year at the Rainbow and Stars).
4. Remember to show up for the class called The Twentieth Century and assign a book other than *Bambi*.
5. Ransack heaven and earth to find *Ladies in Retirement*.
6. Try to meet Marilyn Minter to ask if her mother was agoraphobic.
7. Piece together the rest of the words in Glenn Ligon's *Untitled*.
8. Examine Florine Stettheimer's decorative politics.
9. Discover *Trog*'s relevance to the future.
10. See *Master Class*, *Victor/Victoria*, and *Company*, even if I end up hating all three.
11. Flip a coin to divine whether, as *Penthouse* suggests, the penis can save Broadway. (It can't.)
12. Stop writing sonnets.
13. Find Valéry's *Carnets*.
14. Figure out whether metaphors bite.

(1995)

VI

READING

LOGORRHEA

*U*sually, in judgments about language and literature, we appraise the meaning, the quality of an utterance. Rarely do we confess attitudes toward quantity.

When we do comment on quantity, we disparage it. And the old-fashioned term of contempt is *logorrhea*: malaise of the writer who writes too much, the speaker who speaks too much; malaise of excess language, of words luxuriating in their own profusion.

Men talking too much equals patriarchy. Then what exceptional state of male verbosity is *logorrhea*? When does male power, embodied in language, turn, through a failure to regulate, into pathology? If, as Avital Ronell has suggested, male autism is our era's preeminent political malaise, then logorrhea is autism's nightside, when male inexpressivity and inarticulateness collapse under a torrent of words—a torrent that symbolizes, paradoxically, a loss.

The term *logorrhea* seems intrinsically misogynist, as well as anti-effeminate: for it casts flow as a failure to be masculine.

Writing about logorrhea, one wishes to avoid extremes. One wishes simply to list those who have suffered from it, and to note the paradoxes and peculiarities of the affliction.

Men who had it: Proust, James, Freud. Whitman had it. Melville had it. So did Coleridge. Trollope had it, feared it, controlled it. Conrad had it; so did Wagner, and Nietzsche. (You begin to see that logorrhea is indistinguishable from genius, creativity, linguistic abundance.) Spenser, Milton, and Wordsworth had it: *The Faerie Queene*, *Paradise Lost*, and *The Prelude* are three masterpieces of male flow. Maybe punning Shakespeare had logorrhea—for the pun, according to Max Nordau, is a prime symptom of graphomania: graphomanes have an "irresistible propensity to play on words."

It is difficult to distinguish graphomania (defined by Nordau as the condition of "semi-insane persons who feel a strong impulse to write") from logorrhea (defined by the OED as "prolixity," or "excessive volubility accompanying some forms of mental illness"). Of the two terms, *graphomania* and *logorrhea*, *logorrhea* is the most resonant, for it reflects revulsion at flow, and revulsion at the speaking mouth. Displace the horror onto the hand, and then we are in the territory of *graphomania*.

Mass culture flows, propulsive as Niagara. Appropriately, Warhol had logorrhea, and popularized it. Garrulously, with little affect, he dictated diaries, and called his tape recorder his wife. Logorrhea—addiction to talk—is inevitably a matter of solitary binge, of isolation. The malaise is never interpersonal, never dialogic (though Warhol placed a gab mate, a "B," at the other end of his patter, a "B" to receive his flow: "B is anybody who helps me kill time"). Logorrhea is not social speech. Logorrhea is the hallmark of contemporary discourse: to be contemporary it must be boundless, it must be fatiguing, it must be manically self-perpetuating.

An eminently modern writer who doesn't have logorrhea, however, is Dennis Cooper, who writes in his story "Epilogue": "All that remains is this cold black rectangle of words I've been picking at." He picks at his words, and so avoids logorrhea, the affliction of those whose desires and whose sentences are old-fashioned, purple, tumescent, waiting to be evacuated; not Cooper's cool, hard, gaunt trade. Logorrhea is contrary to the quickie. Logorrhea is language of the bloated, reactionary, nostalgic liaison, not the cyborg fuck.

To believe in logorrhea you must believe in sexual desire's glamour, and in the possibility of desire turning into death and loathing. To believe in logorrhea you must believe in sex: must fear it, worship it, wish to exorcise it. You must believe in the possibility of overexcitation, promiscuity, loss of control, loss of the self's borderlines.

Logorrhea is writing haunted by asymptote: writes Nordau, "No linguistic form which the mystically degenerate subject can give to his thought-phantoms satisfies him; he is always conscious that the phrases he is writing do not express the mazy processes of his brain; and as he is forced to abandon the attempt to embody these in words, he seeks, by means of notes of exclamation, dashes, dots, and blanks, to impart to his writings more of mystery than the words themselves can express."

Logorrhea is writing *against* the aphorism. Writers who mince words, writers of few words, are not troubled by logorrhea. Logorrhea is not conducive to deceit, for if you flow, you inevitably stumble on the truth. *Be brief:* this injunction staves off logorrhea. *Get to the point. Summarize.* The one with logorrhea dreads these commands, or is deaf to them, and abstains from epigram.

Narcissism: the sentence that regards and desires itself is afflicted with logorrhea. Barthes, in *S/Z*, describes logorrhea as "piling up words for mere verbal pleasure." No other account of the condition mentions that *pleasure* is logorrhea's result or goal: that one speaks too much, writes too much, because the mere piling up of words—apart from their meaning—brings relief or delight.

Logorrhea is a term that emerges, like so many categories and critiques, from male paranoia: one man desires another man's speech, and doesn't know where one man's mouth ends and the other's begins; one man kisses a mirror; one man spits in a mirror; one man speaks into a mirror and calls the cloud of steam on the mirror an abomination.

Gertrude Stein had logorrhea: but the boxy structures of epigram, sentence, and truism broke up her otherwise stopless rush, and partway concealed it. Note, in this fragment from *Tender Buttons*, how flow is counteracted by hesitation: "Book was there, it was there. Book was there. Stop it, stop it, it was a cleaner, a wet cleaner and it was not where it was wet, it was not high, it was directly placed back, not back again, back it was returned, it was needless, it put a bank, a bank when, a bank care."

Three famous flows: fluvial, menstrual, anal. But semen does not flow. One cannot say that semen flows. It jets, spurts, leaks. Hence logorrhea, as a term used to condemn language, implies a divergence from common masculine climactic practice. Logorrhea means waste, worthless flow, flow without destination or remuneration. It describes a mess, a divulgence and evacuation no one believes is monitored, sanitary, or justified.

Logorrhea is Emily Dickinson's "Infection in the sentence": the sentence that carnally knows itself, that breeds and germinates. The sentence breaks open, and more words, more sentences, crawl out. Call it cloning, or festering, or spontaneous generation, or infection, or panic, or incest: it is the structure of autobiography. (For the space of this essay I am avoiding autobiography, even avoiding the first-person pronoun, as if autobiography were equal to logorrhea, and as if succumbing to autobiography, or to the first-person, would inevitably entail surrendering to logorrhea.)

Words breed words; language's awareness of itself breeds more language. These conditions of the mouth's or the hand's fructifying self-regard reach their literary apotheosis in Proust and Leiris. Proust staves off the malodorous aura of logorrhea through his elegant symphonic paragraphing: each paragraph, a sculpted, boundaried organism, develops a theme, a scene, a figure, and thus, though it is fueled by logorrhea, and is buoyed by an informing logorrheic tide, avoids the appearance of lost control, lost will. Leiris, on the other hand, lets the anxiety of logorrhea, of run-on speech, become the informing instinct of his autobiographical recitals. In *Scratches*, Leiris writes, "All these things I rearrange, all these ideas I hook onto one another, relying on my words to make them follow from one another, as though I had nothing left in my heart or head but a certain specious capacity to talk—in the end, I'm not sure they aren't the products of a most useless literary artifice even more than of a kind of logorrhea." Lydia Davis, Leiris's translator, doesn't herself suffer from logorrhea: witness her first book of spare, unsparing stories, *Break It Down*, some a paragraph long, of which the following sentence is exemplary: "X is with Y, but living on money from Z."

The preeminent poetic testament to logorrhea of our fin de siècle seems to be John Ashbery's *Flow Chart*: "And the river threaded its way as best it could through sharp obstacles and was sometimes not there/and was triumphal for a few moments at the end." Once, long ago (the nineteenth century?), literary production was modeled, with far less shame than now obtains, after torrential movements.

Logorrhea seems potentially an anti-Semitic slur. Aren't Jews stereotypically talkative, and isn't our received, pejorative sense of how Jews talk an enactment of a cozy, infectious logorrhea?

Is logorrhea a class affliction, a mark of aristocracy gone to seed? Eliza Doolittle thought so. "Words, words, words, I'm so sick of words," she sings, after her stay in the rich bachelor household of word-mad, woman-hating Henry Higgins. Does the proletariat have the luxury to succumb to logorrhea?

Logorrhea is a trait of memory writing, sometimes called stream of consciousness. Modern novels that employ a style of artful logorrhea are Oscar Hijuelos's *The Mambo Kings Play Songs of Love* and Manuel Puig's *Betrayed by Rita Hayworth* and *Kiss of the Spider Woman*. In these novels, nostalgia takes the form of linguistic excess and spill, imitating the loop of memory, and the distance of voice from the beloved objects it strives to recapture. And in these novels the circling, ceaseless voice is (in the case of Puig) gay, or (in the case of Hijuelos) the voice of a

Cuban-American man mourning his dead father and a vanished cultural identity, however illusory, however dependent on mechanical reproduction (the phonograph, the stereotype).

We need logorrhea to catch up to the past.

Coloratura, logorrhea: coloratura interrupts the aria, perpetuates the aria, as logorrhea interrupts language's work of meaning. One fears the quintessentially operatic, irrepressibly ornamenting voice for the same reason one fears logorrhea: both practices (coloratura and logorrhea) showcase the mouth threatening to go out of control, the mouth flowering as an independent organ of pleasure.

Calling language *logorrhea*, we deny its depth, its codes. We deny that it is always a meaningful system, that it has the power to express, through artifice, an interiority. *Logorrhea*—the term— denies the ubiquity of subtexts, secrets: denies that everywhere, in every sentence, however loose, a message lies hiding, waiting to be interpreted. Saying *logorrhea*, we momentarily refuse language's invitation; we stop listening. We insist that the flowing sentences form a poisoned, infectious surface; that the sentences must be stopped. *Logorrhea*—the word—expresses a murderous distaste for human speech, human productivity, human flaw and flow.

(1992)

THE POETICS OF INDIFFERENCE

1.

Here is an unfinished essay about difficulty, recalcitrance, bad temper, sloth, and writing. Its argument: the refusal to explain—even the near-refusal to write—is a valid kind of writing; composition's nature includes the avoidance of writing; a negative bliss exists when hand or voice goes lax and unsupple and fails to say what it means.

Difficult, to write about the poetics of indifference. One wishes to be passionate; to contemplate "indifference" is to begin to feel engulfed by silence.

So I return to my formulation, my philosophical benchmark: however exultant a work's texture may be, terror and wandering laziness shaped it.

Of late I am pursuing spartan language that refuses to make

an effort—too fatigued to lift itself out of primordial sludge. Such utterance seems indolent but secretly runs a fever.

Infatuated with the beauty of stingy speech, I turn to Jean Rhys.

2.

I prepared to write this essay by not writing it. On a dark blizzardy January day, I transcribed with fountain pen onto a cheap legal tablet some drab passages from Rhys, whose mute, bleak, parsimonious gestures seemed the opposite of my former love, opera.

At the start of her novel *After Leaving Mr. Mackenzie,* a brief paragraph begins the conventional task of description and then gives up. What interests me is the moment of renunciation:

> The landlady was a thin, fair woman with red eyelids. She had a low, whispering voice and a hesitating manner, so that you thought: 'She can't possibly be a Frenchwoman.' Not that you lost yourself in conjectures as to what she was because you didn't care a damn anyway.

Because this is a novel, Rhys must describe the landlady. So she tries. "The landlady was a *thin, fair* woman with red eyelids. She had a *low, whispering* voice. . . ." Pairs of adjectives sound the alarum of a job—description—perhaps not worth doing. Then, in a spasm of freethinking, she stops: "you didn't care a damn anyway." This salty, idiomatic outburst—this cranky refusal to describe the landlady—doesn't impede writing; rather, it provides our novelist her first opportunity to exert her personality.

Deflection pushes the work forward; shirking a task, she secretly performs it.

Maybe one cares deeply about the landlady. Maybe one is far from indifferent toward her.

3.

Jean Rhys's unfinished, dry husk of an autobiography, *Smile Please*, defied being written. Note, in the following passage, the slide toward the unemotional vanishing point:

> My mother was more silent but not so serene. Auntie B never lost her temper, my mother often did. My mother sewed beautifully but she could not cut out a dress. Slash, slash went Auntie B's scissors with a certainty and out of the material would appear a dress that fitted.
> My mother could make pastry light as a feather.
> Auntie B mixed famous punch.
>
> Gradually I came to wonder about my mother less and less until at last she was almost a stranger and I stopped imagining what she felt or what she thought.

I know the slash, slash of Auntie B's scissors: the slash, slash of revision, of cut-and-paste (Rhys's method)—a cruel technique, involving material loss. Slash, slash is violence in the name of a suitable dress, a fitting story.

Auntie B's famous punch is a beverage, but it is also a blow. The word *punch* stops Rhys's narrative. *Punch,* a stiff drink, causes oblivion and indifference; a slug, it knocks out the sometime contender. With the blow, the prose-flow subsides. The novelist skips a space. The mother fades.

I wish Rhys had pushed herself to imagine more fully. I wish she hadn't forgotten her mother. I wish Auntie B's famous punch hadn't knocked the writer unconscious. But I also acknowledge that she can best evoke a memory by permitting its obliteration.

4.

Jean Rhys's mean letters give enormous pleasure but mostly concern abstinence and hardship, balanced by occasional debauchery and longing.

Here is a letter she wrote in 1963:

Oh God how I hate penny in the slot thoughts and actions, and oh God what terrible harm they cause. If I live I will call my next and last book *There is no penny and no slot* and if you pinch that title or variations I'll climb up to your window and give you nightmares. (This is a joke.)

Anyway there is *no* penny for the slots. Not for writing or the black versus white question—the *lies* that are told—or for anything at all that matters. Only for lies. Yet everybody believes in the non existent penny and the invisible slot. So what to do?

For your coin at a pay phone, you receive a few minutes of conversation; or you can gamble a penny in a slot machine and hope to hit the jackpot. But big problems (racial oppression) or small (writing block) won't budge.

There Is No Penny and No Slot, a book that Rhys never wrote, is the severe, inaudible New Testament of the punished aesthetic I am pursuing.

Wrongly, we often imagine that, as exercise burns off calories, industrious habits can force writing into existence. (Put a penny in the slot, produce a sentence.) The practice of poet Louise Glück contradicts this foolhardiness; in her collection of essays, *Proofs & Theories*, she insists that "the fundamental experience of the writer is helplessness" and that "writing is not decanting of personality." Her austere poems give evidence of a sensibility as stringent as Rhys's.

Amnesia and muteness approximate real writing—far better than a hunt for slots.

No writer transcribes thoughts and plots that already exist, complete in embryo; rather, he or she confronts blankness, repression, fatigue, and collapse—enervations of the will to complete the sentence, let alone the paragraph, or the chapter.

If Rhys is as good as her word, she will climb to my window and give me nightmares.

5.

Rhys wrote the letter about "no penny and no slot" while struggling to finish her most celebrated novel, *Wide Sargasso Sea*. She couldn't type, and, living in a drearily isolated part of England, she apparently couldn't find a typist. She'd been absent so long from any public scene that many of her fans assumed she had died. The manuscript appeared on some days lucid and near completion, and, on other days, incoherent.

The penny and the slot recur in a later letter, in which she complains about a friend who thinks that writing depends on willpower:

> Also she thinks that writing is easy. I have told her that it is hard. Very hard. I have told her that it isn't a penny in the slot and I don't think she believes me.
> There is no penny, no slot. Not thousands of pounds could work that slot if it existed. There is only trying to make something out of nothing, or what seems to be nothing. (Except of course disbelief in oneself and failure and emptiness. And above all waiting for the time when all that does not count).
> (I did not tell her this rubbish of course.)

She dismisses her own fervent claims as rubbish. Negatives, pessimisms—these are the materials from which writing (the fitted dress) is stitched. In her drafty, ratty house in Cheriton Fitz Paine the wind blows fiercely; she is cold and impecunious, has writing block, needs to earn bread. She wants money, and she hopes that prose will save her, but Grub Street, new or old, holds no place for Jean.

The finished piece of writing may resemble a "production" (critics sometimes refer to writing as "cultural production"), but writing is not a product, and I make this assertion not because I believe that writing is ethereal and lofty, or that it need evade social analysis, but because my own experience as writer and reader has never been one of mastery, but rather of an indolence and an absence of goal that sometimes feels seductive but often feels like death. And therefore I oppose any notion that writing produces results, whether feelings, or money, or social amelioration. (Sometimes, sentences can catalyze all three.)

I have a minor point to make and I will try it again. I am in the business, as teacher, of proselytizing that if you work on your writing, you'll get better at it; my profession depends on the conviction that one can evaluate an essay as a finished entity. Against these dogmas of my job I know that writing drifts away from productivity, that it resembles destruction, or a steady, antisocial erosion of the evident. It appears that I'm writing, but actually I'm tunneling away from "writing." Every sentence I now write escapes from the essay I am in the process of composing, and this has always been my experience. I am not probing some concrete thought, emotion, or scene that self-sufficiently exists, prior to my depicting it; rather, I am succumbing to inertia, and the paragraph, when I have finished it, will represent unfixed, mixed emotions. I move in a visceral, unwilled relation to stupor; composing sentences is not a reprieve from the hour of lead, but a return to it.

I have in mind an essay I read several years ago—Joyce Carol Oates's "Notes on Failure." Something she said in a *Paris Review* interview, too, about the soul being flat as a playing card, and the connection between writing and spiritual numbness, stays with me. Writing lifts its practitioner from enervation? But also the writer *must* be enervated.

6.

In her essays, Louise Glück speaks firmly against the sentimental myth that poems cozily gestate while a writer endures inactivity or block: "over a period of more than thirty years, I have had to get through extended silences. By silences I mean periods, sometimes two years in duration, during which I have written nothing. Not written badly, written nothing. Nor do such periods feel like fruitful dormancy." Hear the vigor of the *not* and the *nothing*. Describing inactivity, Glück assumes a fastidious, somber attitude I love, a tone much like the sternness of Rhys's *no* ("no penny, no slot") or like the firmness of Elizabeth Bishop admitting to Robert Lowell, in a letter, "I've always felt that I've written poetry more by *not* writing it than writing it. . . ." Glück: "most writers spend much of their time in various kinds of torment: wanting to write, being unable to write; wanting to write differently, being unable to write differently." This sense of being dominated by silence does not end when the act of writing begins. Composing, one succumbs to indifference; by surrendering to fatigue (by agreeing that the true thoughts will never be put into words), one produces a changeling text, a compromise, a replacement for the real infant. Toward this imposter one feels indifferent. Or at least I do. The babies have been switched. Here I am, stuck with the false child, and though I must raise it, I can't love it as if it were genuine. So I will put the sentences into some kind of decent shape—I will clothe and feed the rascals—but I can't really do much more for them. Real text has been replaced in the middle of the night by fake text that nonetheless will have to pass, in the world, as veracious. Bishop says, in another letter to Lowell, "Oh heavens, when does one begin to write the *real* poems?" By the time of this letter she had already published two sublime books, some of the finest poetry of this century. And yet she felt—without false humility—that she hadn't commenced the real poems.

At what a sodden remove the poet always lives from the true poems, momentarily near to hand, then vanished.

7.

The writer fully aware of the act's hampering dimensions will feel the strangeness of sitting down to write, and will scarely believe in its necessity. So Keats said, in a letter: "The first time I sat down to write, I co[ul]d scarely believe in the necessity of so doing. It struck me as a great oddity—[.]" The poet feels that the "production" currently taking place is false. In a letter that is a poem without being one exactly, Keats exulted, "After all there is certainly something real in the World—Moore's present to Hazlitt is real—I like that Moore, and am glad I saw him at the Theatre just before I left Town. Tom has spit a leetle blood this afternoon, and that is rather a damper—but I know—the truth is there is something real in the World[.]" Tom's blood is real; sentences rarely are. Or their reality eludes the torpid soul in the midst of writing them.

The mood I am trying to describe is not the indifference I promised you in my title, but a bittersweet aphasia: basic, useful, natural, and part of my body. And so I wish to celebrate it. Or acknowledge its existence, and its remoteness from utilitarian, penny-slot thoughts and actions.

8.

To my ear, "penny in the slot" has the ring of prostitution, and thus recalls Renaud Camus's *Tricks*, in which the narrator recounts a series of erotic escapades with strangers. His explicit prose will strike some readers as pedestrian and others as aphrodisiac. A typical passage (translated by Richard Howard):

> We kissed each other, licked each other, hugged and rubbed against each other. We sucked each other's cocks, took each other's balls between our teeth. We were soaked with sweat and at the height of enthusiasm.
> He came in my mouth, I swallowed his sperm. I came in his, he swallowed mine.

Elizabeth Hardwick once wrote, "Mrs. Trollope's *Domestic Manners* may be said to have squeezed the American lemon very profitably"; Renaud Camus may be said to have done the same for the homoerotic lemon. And yet he shows no profit, no trace of the penny-slot mentality. Some skeptics saw gay male sexual license, at its peak in the 1970s, as a mimicry of Western capitalism; others, more utopian, saw erotic serendipity and ever-availability as exempt from the punishing logic of the factory and the market. In his introduction to *Tricks*, Roland Barthes praises the novel's economy of unsentimental (unkind?) accuracy; I'd like to send his description (again, translated by Howard) as a posthumous valentine to Jean Rhys, for it obliquely describes her own prose's wondrous banality, the jaded aesthetic of "you didn't care a damn anyway":

> Sexual practices are banal, impoverished, doomed to repetition, and this impoverishment is disproportionate to the wonder of the pleasure they afford. Now, since this wonder cannot be said (being of an ecstatic order), all that remains for language to do is to figure, or better still, to cipher, as economically as possible, a series of actions which, in any case, elude it. Erotic scenes must be described sparingly. The economy here is that of the sentence. The good writer is the one who utilizes the syntax so as to link several actions within the briefest linguistic space . . .; the sentence's function is somehow to scour the carnal operation of its tediums and its efforts, of its noises and its adventitious thoughts.

While Barthes separates himself from the bedroom and the hard trick, he cleverly acknowledges the sexiness of the undescribed, the scoured, and the brief.

Camus ends his novel with customary, workaday drabness: "Terence kissed me several times. He seemed very moved." Jean Rhys could have written those lines. How similar the two writers are, in their desire to move on, to get past the hurdle of this trick, this sentence—and their confessed inability to do so.

One is trying to overcome the obstacle of this sentence, this theme. If I can just make it past this paragraph. . . . Then the *real* paragraphs will begin! But art's clock does not progress, even if the pulse of the writer always urges the heart to move on. In a letter describing a typical night and dawn, Rhys indirectly depicts writing's unbaptised nonmovement toward nowhere:

> Such a funny existence here. I go to bed at *eight* P.M. Can you imagine it? But by that time it's been dark for *hours*. So I take a shot of whisky (which is too expensive really) and pretend it's bedtime. Then at three or four A.M. I'm broad awake. So I toss and turn a bit, then get up, still in the dark, and go into the kitchen for tea. It is, funnily enough, the best part of the day. I

drink cup after cup, and smoke one cigarette after another, and watch the light, if any, appear at last.

The light, if any: I love her dour disbelief.

After the theme is written, it ceases to matter. Time to move on to the next trick. Rhys, in a letter: "I've had no training as a journalist dear, I mean *dear* Selma, I cannot work to rule or to order. Not *won't—can't*, and any criticism or worry *before it's done* freezes me up and I'm unable to work at all. Afterwards—couldn't care less!"

9.

Here, in summary, are the phrases that matter to me, and that crystallize a chill, unprofitable, ghostly aesthetic, the poetics of indifference, which I have begun, slowly, to pursue, though I know it will always elude me:

Couldn't care less. You didn't care a damn anyway. Gradually I came to wonder about my mother less and less. I stopped imagining. There is no penny, no slot. The light, if any, appears. He seemed very moved. I've always felt that I've written more by not *writing than writing.*

10.

In a crowded, dusty room across the hall from the poetics of indifference, the climax of act two of Puccini's opera, *La Rondine*, libretto by Giuseppe Adami, overpowers me. The heroine Magda, courtesan, who resembles a character from a Rhys novel, sings a pining phrase that embodies the opposite of everything I have been saying here. *Rondine* has some sweet numbers but lacks intensity—until suddenly the soprano, who has been singing unemphatically, switches into dramatic mode. Pushing toward what a musicologist might call her "pitch ceiling," edging upward, a half step at a time, to a high B-flat ("Ah!"), which meets the exquisitely dissonant resistance of the orchestra's B-natural, Magda tells her banker boyfriend that she has found love in another's arms, and that she must be allowed to follow her destiny. The rush toward the climactic dissonance, and the hurried words en route to it, intertwine with my subject here—indifference—but I can't formulate how or why: perhaps because this passage hits, at a taboo angle, on the closed question of what I find sexually thrilling and what leaves me indifferent? The English translation of the passage:

> But don't you know
> what it is to be thirsty for love
> and to find love,
> to want to live
> and to find life?
> Ah! let me follow my destiny!
> Leave me! It's finished!

How can I explain the distance between these words, even in Italian—

> *Ma voi non lo sapete*
> *cosa sia aver sete d'amore*
> *e trovar l'amore*
> *aver voglia di viver*
> *e trovar la vita?*
> *Ah! lasciatemi seguire il mio destino!*
> *Lasciatemi! È finita!*

—and the impossibly sentimental emotions roused in me by this music and by the erotic situations it represents? I have lived for a decade off the marrow of this *Rondine* phrase (as performed by Anna Moffo on a 1967 RCA recording)—enough time, you'd think, to find words for its effect! Don't you know what it is to be thirsty for a phrase and to find it and then not be able to remember it?

The passage is so quick, it's over before I can wake myself from congenital stupor and say, "Now it's time to understand the exciting phrase!"

I am exhibiting a hectic, touristy relation to my own passions, perhaps because the essay is almost over, and I still haven't described excitements that may die if I don't give them a proper polish.

Penny-slot protocol insists that I should explain why the Puccini phrase excites me. But I can't.

It either represents the anomie summarized by Jean Rhys saying "Not that you lost yourself in conjectures as to what she was because you didn't care a damn anyway." Or it represents the antidote.

11.

For a decade I've felt this phrase's presence. Why mention it now?

I am in a rented car, driving away from San Francisco, listening to *La Rondine* on a cassette. I miss the freeway exit, and end up driving back toward the home I grew up in. (This is a dream.) It is my brother's wedding. He is marrying a boy. By accident I drape my plaid, summer-weight blazer over my mother's face (she sits in the row in front of me). I order a strange cocktail and charge it to the bridal party. I lose my jacket on the way back from the ceremony. I walk down the avenue past familiar apartment buildings that have the authority of pornographic ads in the *San Francisco Chronicle*, or the transmitting apparatus of a classical music station, KKHI, which I remember passing on the way to San Francisco, near a drive-in that once showed the erotic film *Helga*.

This is not a dream, this is an essay, and we haven't arrived in the city yet. We are still in the car, and will always be on the way to the fabulous, improbable destination, my father hammering Toscanini beats on the steering wheel with his blunt fingertips, sometimes picking dirt from under his nails with the black teeth of a plastic comb he keeps in his shirt pocket.

(1996)

A BRIEF DEFENSE OF
PRIVATE POETRY

1.

Let me begin, as I will end, with Emily Dickinson, whom I take
to be a prototype of the private artist—remote from marketplace,
readership, society. She lived in Amherst during the Civil War
but on the surface didn't seem to write about it; she wouldn't
leave her father's house, and refused to publish her poems, even
when asked. And yet I want to hold her up as a democratic artist,
whose work spoke democracy long before readers discovered and
canonized it, whose work has political vitality because of its disre-
gard for audience.

If we want to bridge the snaky, rickety ampersand between
art & democracy, we must not limit ourselves to widely circulated art. We must value private utterance—obsessive, meticulous,
ecstatic—that may never, in its writer's lifetime, be consumed by

readers. We must value arts that exempt themselves from commercial exchange.

My question is: how does a private citizen playing with language advance democracy?

I'm paying compulsive, mannered attention to the rhythms of my sentences: a fussiness inseparable from my subject.

2.

Poetry isn't real. For its falseness, it has often been condemned. Although Shelley called poets the "unacknowledged legislators of the world," Plato disparaged poets for their divergence from truth, and wished to ban them from his Republic: "hymns to the gods and praises of famous men are the only poetry which ought to be admitted into our State. For if you go beyond this and allow the honeyed muse to enter, either in epic or lyric verse, not law and the reason of mankind . . . but pleasure and pain will be the rulers in our State."

From Plato onward, iconophobia—a fear of representations, a prejudice against graven images—has governed the reception of art. Contemporary American iconophobia centers not on poetry, with its ornate trickster behaviors, but on pornography: recent controversy over the arts has pinpointed visual representations of homoerotic acts, or acts deemed sadomasochistic, or pedophilic, or sacrilegious. To begin to discuss or critique homoeroticism, sadomasochism, pedophilia, or sacrilege, we'd need to start reading poetry, or writing it.

The images currently provoking outrage are rarely abstract. On the contrary, they are literal: photographs that aspire to the condition of evidence. And yet reactionaries, who fear the mimetic arts, paradoxically rely on hard copy to advance antidemocratic agendas. For example, after so-called partial-birth abortion was banned by the House of Representatives, a *New York Times* editorial remarked on the critical role that pictures played in the decision: antiabortion groups "circulated graphic drawings in their inflammatory campaign to impose a ban." In this case, pictures, posing as evidence of the real, led to a crucial liberty's curtailment.

Much social legislation, much domestic and foreign policy (even the notion of what is domestic, what is foreign), leans on visual images and on language that pretends to be as transparently representational as a photograph.

If we want to escape propaganda's sway, we must learn to mistrust a photograph's ability to capture reality; and we must grow to mistrust the sentence's rapport with the actual. Sentences aren't copies of truth. Sentences are duplicitous. They say two (or more) things at the same time.

3.

Poetry is the most figurative, the least literal or least imitative, of the arts. It is therefore the least marketable, the least useful to capitalism. Poetry runs interference: ideally, poetry confounds the law.

Just as the most intelligent visual art of our day tampers with how we interpret what we see, so the most necessary poetry of our day upsets how we are accustomed to seeing sentences, phrases, and narratives behave. I don't mean to suggest that all advanced or progressive art must be formally innovative. But I do believe that poetic as opposed to prosaic utterance must take a stand against received ideas; poetry exists to unseat truths that have grown too self-evident.

Language, as a living tissue of strictures and possibilities, is shared by millions. Poetry, however, is individual: poetry bursts forth when someone, in private, tampers with words—takes them apart, destroys them, makes them fester and multiply. Poetry seems antidemocratic (or anticollective) because it concerns one solitary woman's, one solitary man's, manipulation of the linguistic apparatus—a selfish act of "hogging" (or privatizing) a public resource. And yet poetry has value only if it bears the imprint of individual will—a will that sometimes represents larger communities, but only indirectly. And the poetic gesture will always fail at representing any one idea or any one community; *community* is exactly the sort of word, like *art*, or *democracy*, that poetry is adept at questioning.

4.

Poetry knows itself to be a liar. A sentence aware that it is a sentence is free to think about democracy. Language wise enough to look in the mirror is unafraid to endure moral self-examination. To justify poetry's intrinsic place in a democracy, we must not expect it to behave in public ways; in fact, we must respect its privacy, its self-recycling, its narcissism. Narcissism saves the sentence from the deeper vanity of the demagogue.

Keats said, in a private letter, "We hate poetry that has a palpable design upon us. . . ." Demogogues have a palpable design upon us. So do journalists; the media want us to believe they convey the truth. Watching the latest installment of the O. J. Simpson debacle on the news, I marveled at TV's self-congratulation—how brave and quick the journalists were saying they'd been, to capture the scene as it was happening. How much more noble, I thought, if the cameras had stayed away, if the story had arrived late, if, somehow, the journalists had all flubbed, failed to report the story, acknowledged that they'd mistranslated it. . . .

Not journalism, but the most irrelevantly artistic poem in the world, is democracy's best friend—because a poem will admit to being a miscommunication, a mistake.

I distrust all language that isn't snaky, and I think it is healthy for a democracy to make room for devilish arts that disobey the straightforward—arts that acquaint us with the church's former adversary, the erroneous.

5.

Poetry substitutes new names for the old.

Dickinson wrote, in a letter, "Your beautiful Hymn, was it not prophetic? It has assisted that Pause of Space which I call 'Father.'" Coyly she renames the "Father"—an insubordinate act. She retitles him a "Pause of Space"—because he is dead, and because she may trip, confuse, or alter "Father," place marker of power, by accusing Him of being just a pause, a caesura. Ideally, this is what a poem does: it replaces Father with a pause. It replaces tyranny with a question mark. It replaces lumpish assumption with absence. And these replacements take musical or rhythmic form. Every time Dickinson breaks a line or breaks up a thought, she is uttering "Father," or uttering "Pause." "Father" is the gasp or rip in sequence, where sense stops.

Consider, for a moment, punctuation. To punctuate is to insert points, indicating vowels, in the Hebrew psalms. To avoid punctuating, or to reinvent punctuation, or to grow self-conscious about punctuation, as poems make us do, is to reconsider the blank places in the psalm where the name Father might be but where maybe there is no Father. What are the ramifications, for democracy, of Dickinson's adventures with punctuation and pause? This: to pause is to abolish doctrinal solidity; poetry should puncture our life with pauses from which questions, uncertainties, and disavowals might flower.

Consider: that Pause of Space which I call the United States; that Pause of Space which I call place; that Pause of Space which I call race; that Pause of Space which I call identity; where there was once security and sound, replace it with Pause of Space, when Space, as if it were Time, holds its breath.

Poetry incorporates seizure, silence, return, and recoil; it notes the pauses, doesn't dismiss them.

To listen attentively to the pauses of space inside the words passed around in the House of Representatives: that is poetry.

Is the representativeness of a congressmember the same as a poem's or a photograph's representativeness? Consider. Senators represent citizens. Poems represent experiences. Photographs represent objects. These three kinds of representation are not the same. Elected officials use photographs to advance malign legislation. Let us, in private, practice poetry in order to unrepresent and complicate our sense of who represents us, and how this process of representation—of similitude, of likeness—operates.

The United States of America is a representation: actual, yes, but also imaginary. Its figurative aspects may be among its most lethal. A democracy needs the listening, self-scrutiny, and restlessness that poetry promotes. Poetry unravels the sentence. Poetry punctures certainty with a big hole, so it doesn't know any longer where it stands. Poetry makes it difficult to know when the speaking voice is solitary and when it is communal. Poetry uncovers the imaginary dimensions of that Pause of Space we call the social contract. Once we realize that a contract is imaginary—pause—we can begin to rewrite it.

(1995)

STEIN IS NICE

1.

Reading Gertrude Stein takes enormous patience. The skeptical reader might wonder: what if Stein is not worth this level of attentiveness? What if her writing doesn't reward close scrutiny?

Ask of your own life the same hard question: what if you stare fervently into your own mind and discover nothing there?

Stein insists that we enlarge our capacities—*even if the enterprise turns out to be bankrupt.* Reading Stein, we imagine a cognition of inordinate latitude and longitude; we hypothesize a literature as vast and self-sufficient as she imagined hers to be. Whether or not Stein achieved it, by reading her we are postulating the existence of a spacious poetics; we are bringing such a poetics into being, even if it exists only in the form of the ambitions we attribute to Stein, the fealty that she requires of us, the expectations that she arouses and then excuses. Reading Stein is a process of having desire excited and then forgiven: she says, *you wanted a literature as huge and undetermined as the one I am offering you. I forgive you for the hedonism and the hubris of that wish.*

Be nice to Stein; you will thereby learn to be tolerant of your own Steinian voracity—a hunger for sentences, a dissatisfaction with every extant sentence except those that you invented, an intolerance for any sentence that you are not in the midst of writing.

2.

Much of Stein's work remains unread, classified as unreadable. Three recent offerings begin to change this picture: Ulla E. Dydo's masterful compilation of largely forgotten Stein pieces, *A Stein Reader*, in a handsome purple-covered paperback from Northwestern University Press, complete with detailed headnotes but, mercifully, no footnotes; Sun & Moon's pristine ivory-covered reissue of *Stanzas in Meditation*; and Dalkey Archive Press's reissue of *A Novel of Thank You*, with an illuminating introduction by critic Steven Meyer. Dydo has criticized Sun & Moon for reprinting what she calls, with reason, a "corrupt" text of the *Stanzas*—a revised version, in which, at the insistence of Alice B. Toklas, Stein removed and disguised the many occurrences of the word *may*, which apparently were oblique references to Stein's former lover May Bookstaver. Though I look forward to an edition of the "original" *Stanzas*, with all the *May*s intact, I am nonetheless grateful to have this reprint of the 1956 Yale University Press edition, which John Ashbery, among others, read, and which therefore has a certain literary-historical importance, whatever its textual inconsistencies.

The reappearance of these major Stein works means that the odd Stein, not the Stein of the *Autobiography of Alice B. Toklas*, but the defiant Baby Woojums of *Stanzas in Meditation*, has become part of our contemporary literary landscape. And yet some of the pleasure of Stein—whether in print or out of print—remains the difficulty of access to her texts and her meanings, and the privacy that this difficulty affords her reader. Because academics have largely left Stein uncolonized, she is still free to function, in our reading and writing lives, apart from fossilized rules of what matters and why it matters. Because her reputation combines the offbeat and the central (a wonderful paradox, the major minor writer, or the minor major), we are free to make of her what we wish, and to read her more obscure texts in a state of liberated remoteness from dogma, protocol, and usefulness. There have been convincing feminist and lesbian reappraisals of Stein's work, including such studies as Harriet Scott Chessman's *The Public Is Invited to Dance*, and Language poets have laid claim to the antireferential Stein; but despite these moves to make Stein useful, she remains underread, and therefore neutral. Her texts can be marshaled, coherently and legitimately, to bolster a thousand different arguments, but there will always be a Stein text—say, *A Long Gay Book*—that no one will have bothered to explain and that no one is reading; therefore, if you choose to read it, you will be more or less alone with it, alone with Stein, and at liberty to use it or not use it as you see fit, without having to explain her meanings or nonmeanings to any authorities, without having to summarize or redact, without even having to remember it, after you've put it down. Because you won't ever have time to read all of Stein (there will always be more manuscripts), she will forever exceed your grasp, resist enclosure, and permit you, therefore, to reverse and foil your own readerly gestures. Reading Stein is always reading in a void, reading the void, reading to avoid—to avoid plot, significance, work, pain, and the past.

Stein is not *about* anything. She will not force anything on you, except her own dreams of magnificence, and her certainty that her magnificence is your property, too; because she's void, it doesn't matter who owns her sentences. They're not worth anything; but because they evade accounting, and because they do not circulate with any regularity, it is your right to determine their worth. And it will not be a tragedy if you decide that they are worthless. Even if they're radically devalued, they won't vanish: there are too many. Even if each sentence is worth only a penny, pennies add up.

I am at liberty, reading Stein, to interpret or not interpret her as I see fit—because she occupies a netherworld (the territory of the majestic has-been) where magnification and diminution occur at a startling frequency, without warning; and where the perversity and eccentricity of individual taste still hold sway.

3.

Stein writes against maturity, against development. Her writing is "a rested development." She rests—naps, dreams—by enjoying the arrested state of going nowhere.

Stein's paradigm of the writer was the baby: the author as infant. Toklas and Carl Van Vechten referred to her as Baby Woojums. But in Stein's terms, to be a baby is not to be asexual. In fact, Stein's babyishness, her immaturity, is a profoundly sexual condition. From "Mildred's Thoughts" (reprinted in *A Stein Reader*):

> Baby I am happily married Baby. To whom am I happily married.
>
> Baby I am happily married to my husband. Baby. And to whom is my husband married. Baby. My husband is married to me. Baby. And to whom is my husband happily married. Baby. My husband is happily married to me.
>
> Baby. When was I married.
>
> Baby. I was married like a queen before I was seen.
>
> Baby. And how was I seen.
>
> Baby. As a baby queen. Baby. And so I was married as a baby it would seem.

To be a baby is a condition of supreme mastery: like Dickinson, Stein constructed a literary system in which she was undisputed potentate—a Baby Queen, enjoying full sexual privileges. We need to approach Baby's throne if we want to understand the system; but Baby is too busy with her pleasures to answer our petty queries.

4.

In Stein, the central amusement or beauty is often the name, the proper noun that arrives unexplained, uncontextualized. Jane Bowles and John Ashbery give this pleasure, too (they might have learned it from Stein): a character in Bowles's fragment, "Friday," announces, "My name is Agnes Leather," and we are free, as readers, to meditate on Leather and Agnes, their interpenetration, without the narrator moderating the debate. In Stein, the proper name offers respite from dry diction and nonreferentiality; the proper name seems to refer to someone—seems to bring with it a plot (this person was born, desired, died)—but the context never appears, and the name sits solitary on our plate. In *Stanzas*, Stein writes:

> I think very well of Susan but I do not know her name
> I think very well of Ellen but which is not the same
> I think very well of Paul I tell him not to do so
> I think very well of Francis Charles but do I do so
> I think very well of Thomas but I do not not do so
> I think very well of not very well of William

Knowledge and ignorance coexist; I think very well of Susan but I do not know her name, even if I can say "Susan." The name is the tip of gossip's iceberg; each name implies a verdict, a titter, a possible condemnation. Has the person behaved appropriately? Or has Susan disobeyed? Is Susan a saint? In Stein, names canonize; just to be named is to become part of a Parnassian dramatis personae.

My favorite name in all of Stein is Kitty Buss. The name is amusing because each word—*Kitty, Buss*—has a secondary connotation. *Kitty* is a diminutive for *kitten*; *buss* is slang for *to kiss*. This is the Agnes Leather effect: to the reader, *Agnes Leather* is a marriage of lamb and leather, not a person. Similarly, Stein writes, in "Pink Melon Joy," "James Death is a nice name." The last name is death, but it is also just his name. Therefore the phrase "James Death" goes somewhere—toward meaning, toward "death"—but also sits plumply motionless on the page, just a name of someone we'll never know, James Death (inevitably I misread it as James *Dean*).

Stein understood that names are comic, accurate, and eerie. They signify our social and psychological identities but they also allegorize us—turn us into death, into kitty, into leather. The buzz of names in Stein's work, like entering a party and hearing the pleasant roar of conversation and laughter, reminds us that people are everywhere, that society (Stein's work reflects and rewrites society) is full of overdetermined relationships and kinship structures, most of which we won't be able to figure out or master. In "Saints and Singing" (from *The Stein Reader*), she writes, "Constance and Elisabeth have not the same name. One is Constance Street and the other is Elisabeth Elkus." Constance and Elisabeth stop at their names: *street* and *elkus* prematurely arrest the process of identification even while seeming to justify the arrest by saying, "Now we know who you are: you are street, you are elkus."

5.

Constance Street is not my business. Most of human history is not my business. Despite Stein's ample desire to include everything in her work—in *The Making of Americans* she attempted a history of every kind of human being who had ever lived—she also relentlessly specialized, deciding what mattered to her, and dispensing with all dross. In *Lectures in America* she wrote, "It is awfully important to know what is and what is not your business. I know that one of the most profoundly exciting moments of my life was when at about sixteen I suddenly concluded that I would not make all knowledge my province." Desire's specialization: Stein chose language, and Alice. I choose Stein, and language: I choose Stein as a way of choosing language. Stein's private life was not our business: and so she omitted it (except as it appears in code) from her texts. To choose Stein is to refuse every other writer.

Your only business, when reading Stein, is the sentence before your eyes. Not the sentence you've just finished, or the sentence you're about to begin. Just the sentence unfolding right now. To attempt to synthesize Stein's attributes or stories is an infringement on her privacy; what Stein meant, or how the sentences fit together, is not the reader's business. The reader's business is the sentence as it stands. And to have one's responsibilities limited, in this fashion, is a tremendous relief; Stein allows one the peacefulness of staring into space—*her* space.

6.

The story in a Stein text—even those, like "Miss Furr and Miss Skeene," that purport to have a sort of plot—is the way a word, or a set of words, permutates, the way a word, like a reuseable train ticket, is used (or stamped, or perforated) by the various sentences and fragments it passes through. What the word means is none of your business, but it is indubitably your business where the word travels. So in "Miss Furr and Miss Skeene" your business is the travel of *quite*, of *voice*, of *regular*, of *cultivating*, of *living*, of *then*, of *not*, of *sat*, of *stayed*, of *little things*, and of *gay*. What *gay* means will not be decided; but you can follow where *gay* goes, how *gay* moves, impatient and ambulatory, through sentences—so that *gay* begins to seem a drive or a propulsive force more than a stable attribute or personality characteristic. Similarly, reading "A Book Concluding With As A Wife Has A Cow A Love Story," your business is *cow*, *wife*, *as*, *love story*, *day*, *prepare*, *happening*, *expect*, *now*, *just*, *feel*, *six*, and *and*. These are the significant players, whose movements the reader must monitor. Or simply observe their progress, lazily noting their recurrence. Be surprised by their absence and then relieved by their sudden reappearance.

7.

The world of Stein may be divided into two categories: luxuries and banalities. The principal luxuries in Stein's work are profusion, repetition, and magnaminity. The principal banality lies in the flat language—plain, straight, uninflected. But this banality is extremely comforting. No synthesis, no summary, will demand your attention; you may wander safely, without guidepost, in an unremarkable countryside of adverbs, nouns, conjunctions, and simple verbs. Plainness allows sensuality: note, in the following passage from *A Long Gay Book* (reprinted in its entirety in *A Stein Reader*), how she first asserts the importance of being plain—almost as if plainness were an ethical imperative—and then how this assertion of plainness permits her the sudden delectation of "blue houses and blue horizon" (the strange introduction of the sensual and the visible into a cerebral framework); and then, note how plainness permits privacy, and, in turn, permits singing (i.e., writing):

> To begin to be plain. To begin to be plain is a plain duty. The right to be plain is a plain right. The resumption of being plain is the resuming being plain. There is a conviction and a satisfaction and a resemblance between blue houses and blue horizon.
>
> A private life is the long thick tree and the private life is the life for me. A tree which is thick is a tree which is thick. A life which is private is not what there is. All the times that come are the times I sing, all the singing I sing are the tunes I sing. I sing and I sing and the tunes I sing are what are tunes if they come and I sing. I sing I sing.

We want Stein to sing; and we want, ourselves, to have the liberty of singing. To reach the land of singing one must travel through banality and plainness. It is difficult to achieve plainness—to renounce embroidery and narrative, to refuse community and location. Stein's plainness and her privacy are equivalent, hard-won possessions: through them, she may begin to sing.

What is ugly in Stein's writing—or plain—is therefore potentially beautiful, if you see it as the necessary penance that earns privacy, and therefore earns sensuality, vision (blue houses, blue horizon), and song.

8.

I don't know how frequently Stein bathed, or washed her hands; but I do know that an essential ingredient in this private world that Stein's plain language champions (and encourages us to claim for ourselves) is soap, that hard and soft, vanishing and permanent household object that Francis Ponge celebrated in his prose poem, *Le Savon*, whose title implies a missing *nous: nous le savon[s]*. We know it. What do we know? Not much: after all, as Stein instructed, we've decided not to make all knowledge our province. The little we know we're also happy to rinse off. It's possible to think of Stein's work as one long rinsing or cleansing operation: the sentences that remain are the suds, or the dirt that gathers in the sink basin, traces of a past ablution. To wash is to spend: just as Stein's sentences don't assemble or accrete into hard currency, but resemble a miser's hoardings (or a spendthrift's trail of bounced checks), so her sentences might be considered a gleefully repeated act of masturbation as well as its Lady Macbeth self-regulating corrective, handwashing. The dialectic of progress/stasis that informs all of Stein's compositions (we're getting somewhere, we're getting nowhere) obeys soap's law: soap serves its function only in the process of disappearing; you must rub and unmake soap in order to enjoy its cleansing properties; using soap corrects and repeats the autoerotic act.

Stein on soap, from *A Long Gay Book*: "This is the time to say that a bath is not so clean when there is no soap to be seen. A bath is clean when the bather has the wish to state and is fulfilling everything." Imagine Stein's entire collected opus as a single painting—a representation of a woman engaged in an absorbing, uncompleted action. Would you call the painting *La Lectrice* (the reader) or would you call it *La Baigneuse* (the bather)? In either case this painting—Stein's work—exposes a solitary ritual, and is informed by a queer amalgam of intentness (goal-oriented action) and futility (self-indulgent idleness).

9.

The best single adjective to describe Stein's sensibility and style is *queer*, not simply because of the word's association with sex-and-gender ambiguity, but because of the word's evocation of what is simultaneously *uncanny* and *pleasure-giving* in a phenomenon's or a person's refusal to match a predetermined grid. Again and again, the word turns up in Stein, usually to signify a moment of stubbornness, refusal, displeasure, fear—combined with the exhilaration that comes from defiant inexplicability. An example, again from *A Long Gay Book*: "It is a queer thing that singing is a common thing." Is singing queer? Or is it queer that singing, a sign of divine election, should also, paradoxically, be common, dispersed among all of a democracy's members? Here, in a passage from *The Making of Americans*, *queer* signifies the ability of words to flee their meanings: "Categories that once to some one had real meaning can later to that same one be all empty. It is queer that words that meant something in our thinking and our feeling can later come to have in them in us not at all any meaning." Words experience the gravitational pull of nonmeaning, or of fluctuating significance: this, Stein suggests, is a queer tug. A word or a category is queered when it slips away from what it has been. For Stein's purposes, and, momentarily, mine, it doesn't matter what category the word or the person had been inhabiting; what counts is the experience of slipping away from past definitional fixity. It should come as no surprise to any serious reader of poetry that not just Stein's but *everybody's* language, particularly in dense or highly coded literary artifacts, experiences a similar epistemological slippage. Stein's contribution to the literature of slippage is that she gave a *personality* to this tropic pull exerted on language; she made the queerness of words seem her own personal queerness, or made language's slipperiness seem a reflection of her own psychological and stylistic eccentricity.

For Stein, the process of writing was itself marked by this queerness, an uncertainty of position inspired not only by language's eerie liquidity, but by the social ostracism that comes from a lifelong practice of odd utterance. Dydo, in her preface to

A Stein Reader, quotes Stein on the difficulty of extreme writing: "You know you will be laughed at or pitied by every one and you have a queer feeling and you are not certain and you go on writing." Stein's charm: she stubbornly *goes on*, despite or because of the queer feelings, despite or because of being thought queer. Again, from *The Making of Americans*: "It is a queer feeling that one has in them and perhaps it is, that they have something queer in them something that gives to one a strange uncertain feeling with them for their heads are on them as puling babies heads are always on them and it gives to one a queer uncertain feeling to see heads on big women that look loose and wobbly on them." Queerness consists in big women having the looseness—the lability?—of babies. Or else queerness, in another passage from *The Making*, consists in alien truculence, a refusal to be assimilated to genteel ways: "Mrs. Hersland never liked to have queer people near her she wanted her servants to be of the same kind of nature that was natural to her in the living at Bridgepoint the good living that was natural to her, she needed a servant around her that she Mrs. Hersland in her feeling could be of her and above her, she never wanted any servant to have servant queerness in her."

By invoking queerness I do not mean to imply that Stein's texts may be "solved" by finding the key to her codes, particularly the sexual ones. Stein's writing is at once luminously clear about lesbian sexual pleasure, and bafflingly nonspecific. She opens her erotic "A Book Concluding With As A Wife Has A Cow A Love Story" with an invocation to a closet, and to a possible key, but any simple inside/outside formulation immediately dissipates, and even if we've been presented with a phantom "key," we don't in the least believe that it has the power to unlock anything.

KEY TO CLOSET.
There is a key.
There is a key to a closet that opens the drawer. And she keeps both so that neither money nor candy will go suddenly, Fancy, baby, new year. She keeps both so that neither money nor candy will go suddenly, Fancy baby New Year, fancy baby mine, fancy.

Closets and keys, and certainties of locking and unlocking meaning, disappear, as the repetitive litany of baby pleasures and luxuries resumes, with its notes of fanciness, of beginning (New Year), and of quick exchanges and pleasures (money, candy). No key will unlock Baby's heart; or, Baby is already unlocked, and it is not Baby's concern to spoon-feed comprehension to us.

Despite the freedom with which Gertrude, in her texts (which may be interpreted, all of them, as a continuous love letter to Alice, the primary audience and amanuensis), displays a lesbian sexuality which it doesn't take a highly schooled set of linguistic keys to decode (part of the pleasure of Stein, in fact, is the ease of interpreting almost any of her texts from an erotic vantage point), in "real" life she seems to have been rather reticent about revealing her lesbianism, even to friends. According to Samuel ("Sammy") M. Steward, in his memoir of Stein, she spoke to him openly about lesbianism only once, when she said, "I like all people who produce and Alice does too and what they do in bed is their own business, and what we do is not theirs." And she said, "most of our really good friends don't care and they know all about everything. But perhaps considering Saint Paul it would be better not to talk about it, say for twenty years after I die, unless it's found out sooner or times change. But if you are alive and writing then you can go ahead and tell it, I would rather it came from a friend than an enemy or a stranger." Certainly much of the work that appears in *A Stein Reader*, including such libertine texts as "Pink Melon Joy," is wildly candid about incoherent, unclassified, and socially unsanctioned sexuality. Therefore it's poignant to know that Stein in person (at least with her dear Sammy) could not speak as openly, as libidinously, as she could in her difficult literary texts—or that she was not entirely aware of how nakedly her texts revealed erotic agendas.

10.

I am haunted by the title of Jane Bowles's short-story collection, *Everything Is Nice*. Of course Bowles thought that *nothing* was nice. The phrase "everything is nice"—perfectly bland—comes from a sensibility so wounded, so consumed by its consciousness of the world's flaws, that the mind has energy to formulate only the most attenuated generalization. Similarly, Stein is so assured of her genius, and so assured of the world's ability to remain itself without being imitated—why bother with mimesis?—that she can rest content with platitudes, with vague phrases that point to objects but don't plumb or describe them. Such as, in *A Long Gay Book*, "This is cute." What is cute? It doesn't matter. Everything is cute. She need not flatter the world by reproducing it; in her sentences she pats reality on the head, saying "Nice dog"—a technique of shelving and pushing aside the patted object. Stein is, like most babies, cute; I note her cuteness. I don't want to describe, paraphrase, or reproduce her. In this critical assessment, I don't want to aim toward mimesis. Instead, I want to act toward Stein as she acted, in her sentences, toward the material and affective world: I want to say, "Nice! Cute!" In "Geography," reprinted in *A Stein Reader*, she writes, "Geography as nice. Comes next geography. Geography as nice comes next geography comes geography." Stein is nice. I want to go no farther than this: nice Stein, cute Stein.

Stein was also not nice, and not cute. Hence *nice* and *cute*, and other platitudes, point away from bad temper and discontent, distracting us with a veneer of good mood. Stein's work enrages, expresses rage; but it also writes the flat, non-undulating geography of contentment.

11.

Next to *nice* and *cute* sits *fat*. Stein's public persona was fat and her writing, too, sold its own solidity and pulchritude—fat with densely typeset pages; fat with meaning, fat with the refusal of meaning; fat with privilege; fat with isolation, the tinned meat (confit, foie gras) of exile. When *fat*—the word, the concept—appears in Stein, it signifies complacency, freedom, prosodic waywardness. To be fat is to be nice, cute, safe, and exempt. In

"Pink Melon Joy," Stein writes, in a passage subtitled "Fourteen days":

> I meant to be closeted.
> I should have been thin.
> I was aching.

Should Stein—her body, her text—have been thin? Certainly not, the devoted reader answers. In "Doctor Faustus Lights the Lights" (reprinted in *A Stein Reader*), Stein wonders

> What does a fatty do
> She does not pay for it.
> No she does not
> Does not pay for it.

That is the joy and importance of the fatty: not paying for it. Babies at their best are fat; a writing life that enjoys its own pleasures and obscene fluidities is a fat life. As Eve Kosofsky Sedgwick suggests in the provocative title of her collection of poems, *Fat Art, Thin Art:* do we want a fat art or a thin art? Do we want an art of penury or of expansion? Is it possible to have one without the other? Is prose fat, and is poetry thin? Was Stein's art, despite its obvious fatness, also thin—avoiding the solidity of faithful representation? Avoiding the meat and potatoes of real American life?

To pursue a fat art is to pay attention to the food in front of you on the table. As Alice B. Toklas—and the meals she made—always underwrites Stein's production, so all of Stein's formulations (not only works, like *Tender Buttons*, that self-consciously refer to food) can be reduced to nutriment. To write a swelling prose poetry like Stein's is to confess that nourishment has been had. She writes in *A Long Gay Book*, "When the twin is not one and there has been a fat one the thin one is not losing delicate existing. Singing is everything." If singing—or writing—is everything, must not we give the fatty every inch of privilege and room that she needs? Stein's demand for space and more space includes an insistence that her body, the body of her work, not be starved by the usual decorums, and that her oeuvre, fat and maybe bad for you (think of all the butter and cream that Toklas's recipes require), be allowed its extralarge seat.

Stein refused conventional referentiality; and yet her difficult work always returns to two comforting materialities—the sexual body, and the food that nourishes it. From *A Long Gay Book*: "If the potatoe was there and the light were bright then it would be sweet to be clean and to have the same seat. It is always necessary to carry the same piece of bread and butter. It is nicely brown and yellow and prettily sticking together that with what it is when it is where it is and it is where it is as it is only where it is. It is the particular attraction by which it is the piece that is eating and being eaten. It is mentionable. It is not deceptive. It is the practice of everything. It is what is necessary." Stein relates to language as a cook (or a hungry eater) relates to staples: her interest is not in the elite concoction, but in the ordinary ingredient, the *it* and *and*, the slice of nicely buttered bread. From "Bon Marche Weather" (in *The Stein Reader*):

> Very nice eating everybody is having. Very nice eating I am having. Very nice eating they are having. Very nice eating you are having.
> Very comfortable travelling they are having.

12.

Travel is nice, especially if you suspend belief in destination.

Where are one's thoughts directed at any moment? Impossible to fix them. Stein's writing celebrates and enacts cognition's travel. Emily Dickinson wrote, in a letter, "To shut our eyes is Travel." Stein put this aphorism into practice: she shut her eyes—turned her back to the landscape—and then traveled where her sentences led her, and didn't describe the destination but rendered instead the systematic movement of sentences toward the unspecified. Although her writing is often nonreferential, it always refers to the migration of thought, the free-floating movement of a mind at peace with its own fatness. From "Mildred's

Thoughts": "Mildred's thoughts are where. There with pear, with the pears and the stairs Mildred's thoughts are there with the pear with the stairs and the pears. Mildred be satisfied with tomatoes, apples, apricots, plums, and peaches, beets and ever greens, peas and potatoes." Where are Mildred's—or Gertrude's—or the reader's—thoughts? In the pantry. The mind follows the stomach. The sentence digests the anticipated repast.

As Stein's sentences enjoy and preach the freedom of the wandering mind, so all of Stein, taken together, reads like a travel brochure for an island—a place of difference, of separation from the mainstream and the mainland. Reading Stein, I want to travel to the position of umpire privilege (she who calls the shots) from which she seemed to write and reign. From "Mildred's Thoughts": "I have decided that in any case I will love islands. Islands are to the main land what poetry is to plays." Stein is literature's island of exemption—freedom from any rule that might interfere with the exercise of high caprice.

This land where Stein may write as and when and if and how she pleases—this island, far from the mainland, is also far from capital (cultural, economic, national): she writes, in "Capital Capitals" (reprinted in *A Stein Reader*), "Capitals are the places where every one exactly deprecates the necessity of going away, where every one deprecates the necessity there is to stay where every one utters a welcome that is sufficiently stirring and where every one does know what makes them so, so what so very nearly wider." Do we want to know what makes us so? Or do we say *so what?* All Stein wants is respite from the deprecation that her extravagant eccentricity will continue to incite. Stein's oeuvre is a place where the reader may experience a misbehavior that provokes insult, and an elaborate brochure for a journey away from insult, away from punishment, away from any rituals but one's own bodily and mental processes.

13.

Stein pleases herself; she leads the willing reader to imagine a regime of self-pleasure. From "Capital Capitals": "I know why I say what I do say. I say it because I feel a great deal of pleasure of satisfaction of repetition"—and why not continue, thinks Stein, since I am having so much fun?—"of indication of separation of direction of preparation of declaration of stability of precaution of accentuation and of attraction." Stein is attracted, here, to *-tion* words, to nouns that describe her own virtues of settledness, of stubborn repose. Why write, Stein suggests, except to please yourself?

Self-pleased writing is not simply arrogant; rather, it earns a reader's trust by sufficing, without supplement. You are permitted to forget a Stein sentence the moment you finish reading it. Her writing perpetually toys with its own erasure: thus it always promises the reader relief from having to memorize, to learn, to sift. As she refused to believe in the unconscious, so she disavowed subtext, despite her plethora of double entendres and puns: the writing is exactly what it seems on the surface. It has no hidden depths. In "Identity A Poem" (from *A Stein Reader*) she observes, "It is extraordinary that when you are acquainted with a whole family you can forget about them." Likewise, it is extraordinary that once you finish a Stein text you can forget it; it bears you no grudge if you dismiss it forever from consciousness.

The condition advocated by Stein's texts is sitting. In *The Autobiography of Alice B. Toklas*, Stein suggests that Toklas might have called her memoir "Wives of Geniuses I Have Sat With." What does sitting mean? Alice sat with the wives: to sit, in this case, means to wait patiently, to occupy a subordinate position. A model sits for a painter, as Stein sat for Picasso. Stein herself wrote many word portraits—including the *Autobiography*, in which Alice sits, as subject, for Stein. Alice also baby-sat Stein: she minded Baby Woojums. To sit is to be patient, to be represented, but also to be lazy or immobile—to refuse to stand up, to refuse direction. Said "Alice" in the *Autobiography*, about Stein's sitting practice, "Mademoiselle Stein has no patience she will not go into offices and wait and interview people and explain, so I do it for her while she sits in the automobile." This is the conceptual posture in which Stein's work takes place: sitting.

Above all Stein did not want to be bored. From the *Autobiography*:

"Gertrude Stein desperately unhappy said to me, where is Louvain. Don't you know, I said. No, she said, nor do I care, but where is it." Above all one must remember this about Stein: *she did not care.* And yet she asked "where is Louvain"; she tolerated the civilized insistence that names refer to places, even though location for her was malleable and relative. From the *Autobiography*: "You should I think suggest to the french government that they give us Pondichéry. After lunch Gertrude Stein said to me under her breath, where the hell is Pondichéry." Where the hell is anywhere. Stein, as dandy, understood that refusing boredom is one's first obligation: "Her very close friend Marion Walker pleaded with her, she said, but Gertrude Gertrude remember the cause of women, and Gertrude Stein said, you don't know what it is to be bored." Early in life Stein discovered the horror of boredom, and although she went on to write in a style that would bore most of her readers, she seemed to believe—and I think she was justified in this belief—that she had coined a literary mode that combated boredom by embracing it. She knew how to mind her own business ("Not, as Gertrude Stein explained to Marion Walker, that she at all minds the cause of women or any other cause but it does not happen to be her business") and to keep busy doing exactly what she wanted, which was to make sentences, boring sentences some of them, but others sheer perfection: "I am so sorry, answered Gertrude Stein, but Miss Toklas has a bad tooth and beside we are busy picking wild flowers." When any task (such as communication or obedience) interfered with sentence-making, Stein seems to have said *I am busy picking wild flowers.*

Another activity that Stein refused was backing up. In the automobile as in the sentence, she would only move forward. From the *Autobiography* comes this marvelous description of Stein's progressive writing practice: "Wrong or right, said Gertrude Stein, we are going on. She could not back the car very successfully and indeed I may say even to this day when she can drive any kind of a car anywhere she still does not back a car very well. She goes forward admirably, she does not go backwards successfully. The only violent discussions that we have had in connection with her driving a car have been on the subject of backing." Alice backed Stein; but Stein's sentences appear to have no "backing" (no unconscious, ideology, or thematics undergirding them). She backed Picasso, but who backed Stein? No recognizable clique. Her avoidance of retrospection, of anteriority and interiority, corresponds to her preference for forward motion, right or wrong, usually wrong, and if wrong, somehow right, anyway, because doing the wrong thing prevented Stein from being bored, and allowed her to stay seated, facing the sun.

In *The Making of Americans*, she says, "I write for myself and strangers," but mostly she writes for "myself," who sometimes coincides with the reader's "myself." Certainly when I read the following passage from *Making*, I become Stein's "myself," and experience her love of writing and telling: "I love it and I tell it. I love it and now I will write it. This is now a history of my love of it. I hear it and I love it and I write it. . . . I love it and now and always I will write it. . . . This is now a history of the way I love it."

Because Stein never backs up, this love of writing and telling is not regressive, even though it is gloriously infantile. Stein never moves backwards. She moves forward into the future of literature. But here, in the future, does she have readers? And does it entirely matter if she succeeds in finding them? She wrote without an audience, and she wrote against the idea of an audience. From "Identity A Poem": "I am I because my little dog knows me even if the little dog is a big one and yet a little dog knowing me does not really make me be I no not really because after all being I I am I has really nothing to do with the little dog knowing me, he is my audience, but an audience never does prove to you that you are you." Stein's ideal audience is a dog, mute and loyal.

14.

Stein's quest was the redefinition of beauty. Although her work seems to repudiate conventional aesthetic beauty, she subtly claimed it. In "Composition as Explanation," she observed, "If every one were not so indolent they would realise that beauty is beauty even when it is irritating and stimulating not only when it is accepted and classic." Stein's irritating surface is nonetheless beautiful, in its occasional straightforwardness as well as in its perpetual flight from directness; the beauty lies in her attention to objects, names, pleasures, commonplaces, banalities, indulgences, impieties, as well as in her unceasing campaign for the preservation of the syllable, the exact sound of one syllable landing next to another. In this attentiveness she is one of our purest poets. Amid the din of her often unmeaningful sentences, the clang of the syllable is always audible. And so I turn to Stein because I want intimacy with language at its most atomistic; I want truck with the grubby particles of English, and with the narcissism of the American voice declaiming the pleasure that may be taken in speech's ordinariness. From *A Long Gay Book*: "Pale pet, red pet, pink pet, blue pet, white pet, dark pet, real pet, fresh pet. . . ." It is pleasant to greet, as if for the first time, the word *pet*, to hear *pet* next to *white* and *dark*, to think about petting and about Stein's relation to companions (animal and human), and to consider questions of family, camaraderie, and solitude within the bracing framework of a syllable-by-syllable list, each word ringing out with brass banality—*pale pet, red pet, pink pet, blue pet, white pet, dark pet, real pet, fresh pet. . . .*

Is this poetry or prose? One needn't decide. *Stanzas in Meditation* declares itself poetry, and is divided into verse lines. But much of the work collected in *A Stein Reader* also falls into lines. Do we consider the following passage from "A Circular Play" to be a poem, dialogue from a play, or a series of ultrabrief prose paragraphs?

Sing circles.

Can you believe that Mary Ethel has plans.
Indeed I do and I respect her husband.
Do you dislike her children.
I have not always had a prejudice against twins.
To be catholic to be african to be Eastern.

Have you always had a prejudice against twins.
Tomorrow we go.
If you say so.

               Circular watches.

Methods.
How do you recognise hats.
How do you marry.

Are these fragments of dialogue, each separate line to be uttered by a different character? Or are these lines of a poem, spoken by one haphazard yet subtly unified authorial voice? Or are these minute paragraphs of a prose work broken up into titled fragments ("Sing circles," "Circular watches")? One reads Stein as if it were poetry not simply because it is dense and highly patterned, but because of its arrangement on the page. Indeed, the passage quoted above is not particularly dense. Each line, interpreted separately, is an ordinary idiomatic statement, located in an implied social milieu. What makes the passage "poetic" is not only the disjunction between the separate lines, and the absence of overall narrative, but the erasure of *paragraph*: the paragraph—a prose unit that Stein said was "emotional," as opposed to sentences—has been eliminated, or converted into a poetic line. Indeed, Stein's paragraphs satisfy because they are radically abbreviated, often as short as "Methods," or "How do you marry," or "If you say so." Stack together fourteen paragraphs as short as "Tomorrow we go," and you have a sonnet.

Here, for example, is a short poem by Stein, from *Stanzas in Meditation*, notable for the directness of its praise of the landscape that she often refused to describe but always seemed to be staring at ("I can look at a landscape without describing it"):

I could not be in doubt
About.
The beauty of San Remy.
That is to say

The hills small hills
Beside or rather really all behind.
Where the Roman arches stay
One of the Roman arches
Is not an arch
But a monument
To which they mean
Yes I mean I mean.
Not only when but before.
I can often remember to be surprised
By what I see and saw.
It is not only wonderfully
But like before.

Stein refused to submit to the tyranny of writing referentially *about* a subject. She can say *about* because she rhymes it with *doubt* (she doubts that language can be "about" anything), and because she puts a period after the *about*, interrupting the movement toward the direct object, *The beauty of San Remy*, which becomes its own sentence.

I said that Stein's principal purpose was redefining beauty; what this project means, in the context of the above stanza, is that sometimes Stein lets herself be surprised by what she sees and what she saw, but usually she will seesaw, and because of her oscillation between tenses and between sight and blindness, the arch will not long remain an arch, the cited object will not long remain cited. Even within the seesawing—the process of a paragraph's or sentence's decomposition—she remains solidly a lover of beauty in Alice and beauty in landscape, beauty in exile and beauty in home. It is dizzying to watch Stein move so confidently across the prose/poetry divide, without embarrassment, and to see her end the long *Stanzas* with the unemphatic "These stanzas are done," as if saying, *Time to move on to other stanzas,* or *I told you I could write a long poem.*

Is *Stanzas* a poem? Is *A Novel of Thank You* a novel? Probably *A Novel of Thank You* is a poem, too. Or else it doesn't matter. Stein impersonating Toklas in the *Autobiography* says, "I always say that you cannot tell what a picture really is or what an object really is until you dust it every day and you cannot tell what a book is until you type it or proof-read it." *A Novel of Thank You* is a fake novel; *Stanzas in Meditation* is a fake poem. They are novel or poem only because they chose the appellation, somewhat arbitrarily. Novels are nice; poems are nice. Stein knew the novel's niceness, wanted to inhabit that niceness, and so often called her works novels. The designation "poem" must have seemed less nice, because she less frequently chose it. Even when she did opt for it, as in "Identity A Poem," she dared us to *identify* her text as a poem or to distinguish a poem's quiddity. Stein's *Stanzas* suggest the roominess she still believed could travel under the name "poem," as her *Novel* suggests the size and permission she believed that "novel" could still, this late, afford. Each book wants to meet its genre head-on: wants to be a novel, wants to be a poem. The intensity of this wish equals our readerly desire to feel contained by genre, to believe that "novel" or "stanzas" can promise a unique brand of aesthetic sensation. The title's *Thank You* is Stein's statement of wishing the genre well ("thank you for being a novel" or "thank you, novel, for remaining alive"), as *In Meditation* is her salute to the stanza, her sanguine promise that stanzas abet meditation rather than impede it.

Stein's method: call it a novel, or a poem, and put in it everything you want. Everything is nice, and so use everything: in "Composition as Explanation" she described her method as "using everything." The appeal of "poem" or "novel," as genres, today, consists in their promise of having enough room to hold everything and everybody.

15.

As a consequence of Stein's immunity to any critical vocabulary that might contain her, when I read *A Novel of Thank You* I didn't underline passages. I knew that I would not be able to generalize about Stein, or adequately explicate her, and so I left the text unmarked—except for three ordinary sentences. The first: "Zucheville Dupoint Gavotte, a cheese." Why did I underline it? Because

I was grateful that Stein referred to cheese, even a fictional or nonce cheese, whose name sounded like a dance ("gavotte") as well as the sort of ne'er-do-well with whom Becky Sharp, in the later years of her exiled life, might have whiled away an evening at cards, at some watering hole along the Riviera. The second line I marked: "To-day is most of the time." The sentence reminded me of James Schuyler (I seek his shade in the writers who indirectly influenced him); I was reading *A Novel of Thank You* in order to explore more deeply the present time of writing (what Stein in "Composition as Explanation" calls a "continuous present") and in order to explore the principle of "using everything," including banality. Also, I wanted to avoid writing, and, while doing so, wanted to contemplate the fierce, engaged poetics that emerges from *not writing*—the kinds of prose and poetry that states of so-called writing block can empower. I remain convinced that the work of literature's legendary underproducers (such as Jane Bowles) has much in common with work of logorrheic overproducers (Stein, Trollope); Stein through her continuous present, and Bowles through her unyielding self-scrutiny and self-punishment, found a certain mean spareness—a withering conviction that *nothing is nice* and yet writing may *use everything*, including the not nice, the dull, the ugly, and the pedestrian. Reading *A Novel of Thank You*, I wanted to understand how to-day could be most of the time, and to find a writing mode that included today and most of the time, a lyric or expository voice that might resemble silence, mumbling, droning—that might need, in fact, to include silence, or exist in dialogue with silence. Stein's writing makes most sense if it is read aloud; and yet hers is the most silent voice I know—silent because, under the guise of including everything in the world, it includes remarkably little.

The third line I marked in *A Novel of Thank You*: "Any one can use a chapter and never recall it at all." Use everything, Stein counsels; use everything, including boredom, and the dread of boredom. The value of her work is the use we make of it as we read it, and the uses we contrive, after the fact of reading, even after the memory of her work's detail vanishes. I don't remember anything about *A Novel of Thank You*, except that it fed my conviction that writing and reading are vehicles for exploring the vastness that lies outside a civilization's regular patterns of commerce and conversation. The book also convinced me that many things in the world are nice, and that writing, even *not nice* writing, has the power to point out this astonishing fact.

(1995)

WHY I READ

Some of the first books I remember reading: a biography of Harriet Tubman; Signet witchcraft paperbacks (how-to manuals); *Tituba of Salem Village*; encyclopedia entries about the movies. I spent recesses, in elementary school, at the library, reading *World Book* and *Collier* encyclopedia capsule histories of cinema, which always included references to *Nanook of the North*, which I've still never seen. I read a book by Lita Grey, Chaplin's child bride, about her scandalous relationship with Charlie (the star corrupted her by exposing her to such erotica as *Fanny Hill*). I read guides to childbirth: this was in the days of *Childbirth without Fear*. I also read novels, and boy-child crap like *Encyclopedia Brown*, and *Black and Blue Magic*, and the classic *Half Magic* (by Edward Eager): I'd go for anything about magic. Mostly, I read for illicit information: I sought arcane knowledge about how to mesmerize enemies and friends (a favorite spell concerned burying a mirror at the crossroads, and so I puzzled about how to bury a mirror beneath a paved sidewalk), how to give birth, how to have sex, how to make movies. . . . I was fond of books about amateur photography, even though I wasn't particularly interested in cameras.

I started reading poems in junior high: my eighth-grade teacher, a world traveler named Mrs. Clarke, made us read Emily Dickinson, go out to the field and eat daisies, and then write a poem about the experience. (I may be conflating recollections.) Another assignment was to memorize one hundred lines of poetry. For no good reason I chose "The Raven," in which my favorite phrase was, indubitably, "balm in Gilead," because I didn't know what it meant. I memorized a lovely Sara Teasdale poem in my mother's copy of an Oscar Williams anthology—a poem about loss, September, and trees in a park? Also I memorized Richard Wilbur's poem about the dead dog, Robert Frost's "Mending Wall," and an Elizabeth Barrett Browning sonnet. I thought of poems as elaborate, beautiful, spidery homework, but not part of the reading enterprise, which meant the pursuit of forbidden knowledge, mostly about magic and sex and movies.

Then I fell into a reading coma: books went underground, became unconscious. I read for thrills, at this point, but didn't call it reading; I'd look for dirty passages in great books. My favorites were *Myra Breckinridge*, *Our Lady of the Flowers*, *Lady Chatterley's Lover*. I never read them cover to cover; I sought the sexual bits. Myra's rape of Rusty! I read *Valley of the Dolls* in a hotel room in Mexico City. My glasses were broken, and I couldn't see the tourist sights.

This isn't very highbrow!

The first book of poetry I bought and tried to read on my own was by Hermann Hesse, whom I considered a European eminence, a great thinker, right up there with Freud and Jung. The poems were terrible but I loved the novels: I read *Steppenwolf* and thought it was like a Fellini film, though I'd never seen one.

I read *Gone with the Wind* in fifth grade; I wanted to read it in fourth grade, but my mother told me it was trash, and wouldn't let me check it out from the library. A year later she changed her mind about its merits, and I bought a blue paperback copy at

Macy's. I identified with Wade, Scarlett O'Hara's son, whose re-
frain was "Wade hungwy." In sixth grade I wanted to give a book
report on *Gone with the Wind*, but my teacher had a rule: we
couldn't report on a book if we'd seen the movie version. I was
crushed. I remember telling my father that my life was over, because the one book with which I'd formed a passionate attach-
ment was forbidden as subject for a book report: supreme genre
of vindication, the chance to prove and demonstrate a plot to a
captive audience of schoolchild peers. He recommended, as com-
pensation, *Crime and Punishment*. I didn't take him up on the
offer.

I also remember a formative encounter with *Doctor Zhivago*,
which I wanted to read because I loved the ads for the movie. I
went to the public library to check out the book, and looked under *Doctor* in the card catalogue. A librarian came up to me and
asked if she could help. I said I was looking for books about doctors, and I had one in mind especially—*Doctor Zhivago*. She said,
"That's in the adult section," and guided me instead to medical
books in the juvenile area. On a different day, when another librarian was on duty, I returned and checked out the oddly numi-
nous *Zhivago*.

I loved Andrew Lang fairy tale books. They came in colors:
yellow, blue, red. I also loved Grimm's fairy tales: I remember one
story about a simpleton chasing a wheel of cheese that rolls down
a hill. I can still picture that wandering, out-of-control cheese
rolling through village after village.

I forgot to mention the all-important autobiography of Helen
Keller, the biography of Annie Sullivan, and a children's novel
about a boy blinded by a firecracker.

Then came adulthood, and I read T. S. Eliot's essay about dis-
sociation of sensibility. He thought that a poet was a type of soul
for whom the smell of cooking and the philosophy of Spinoza
were united—ideas felt on the pulses. Wanting to overcome self-
division, I fell in love with poems: O'Hara, Rich, Sexton among
contemporaries, and Yeats, Pound, Keats, Wordsworth among the
oldsters. In college, a dear friend read "Tintern Abbey" to me on
the lawn. Already I felt quite ancient.

In high school I loved inspirational autobiographies of musicians and performers—Wanda Landowska, Pablo Casals. (Many mornings I remind myself that Casals began every day by playing a Bach Prelude and Fugue.) I read Elie Wiesel's *Night*. And *Marjorie Morningstar*. And Mel Tormé's *The Other Side of the Rainbow*.

My parents subscribed to *Newsweek*, *Time*, and *The New Yorker*. From these magazines, I clipped movie reviews and saved them in a file. I knew that history was happening: the debut of Barbra Streisand. For my collection I cut out a cover story about her rise to fame. This, too, was reading.

On Friday evenings—right after supper—our family went to the public library. I was in love with the corridor where the film books were shelved: *The Face on the Cutting Room Floor*, a history of screen censorship. . . . In the fairy tale region, the books leaned against each other, because there weren't enough to fill out the shelf. One summer I joined a library club and read twenty books to earn a certificate on which fake pearls (one per book?) were pasted. I lived for certificates.

I spent a long time exploring my parents' ample shelves, without reading the books—just sounding them out. Certain volumes seemed premonitory beacons: I was fascinated by Sartre's *Saint Genet* because it was fat, its cover beige and bland; and by Simone de Beauvoir's *The Second Sex*—a cheesy paperback edition with a nude woman (soft-focus) on the cover. These two were on my father's shelves. From my mother's shelves I recall the especial luminousness of a paperback *From Here to Eternity* (it was a reversible book: you could turn it upside down and a second novel—a bargain!—was nestled, a twin, beside it); an early Joyce Carol Oates novel, *With Shuddering Fall* (I loved the word *shuddering*), and the photo of Oates on the back cover of *them*; Nabokov's *Ada* (nice fat book with a short title, written by a man but named after a woman); and *The Duino Elegies* (the weird nonword *Duino*). I admired the paperback Modern Library editions of Victorian novels, leftovers from my mother's college years, with maternal handwritten marginalia: a new idea to me, that one could write comments in a book. The books that excited me the most were those she had signed with her maiden name: they seemed glamorously bygone.

To this day, I associate books with boxiness, squareness, and size. Chunkily a book—deckle edges soiled—can close on its secrets.

(1995)

About the Author

WAYNE KOESTENBAUM, poet and critic, is the author of *The Queen's Throat: Opera, Homosexuality, and the Mystery of Desire* (nominated for a National Book Critics Circle Award) and *Jackie Under My Skin: Interpreting an Icon*, as well as three books of poetry, *Ode to Anna Moffo and Other Poems*, *Rhapsodies of a Repeat Offender*, and *The Milk of Inquiry*. He has written a libretto for an opera, *Jackie O* (music by Michael Daugherty), has taught at Yale, and has won a Whiting Writer's Award. He is currently a professor of English at the City University of New York's Graduate School, and lives in New York City.

© Timothy Greenfield-Sanders